A HISTORY OF

MARK HALL MANOR

THE SITE OF

THE MUSEUM OF HARLOW

by the Friends of Harlow Museum

Edited by Hazel Lake

2010

For Jean   March 2010

From Hazel Lake.

Published by Hazel Lake

February 2010

© The Friends of Harlow Museum

Contact hazellake007@btinternet.com

ISBN 978-0-9527599-2-8

Cover and family trees designed by Robert Tovey

CONTENTS

1086

2010

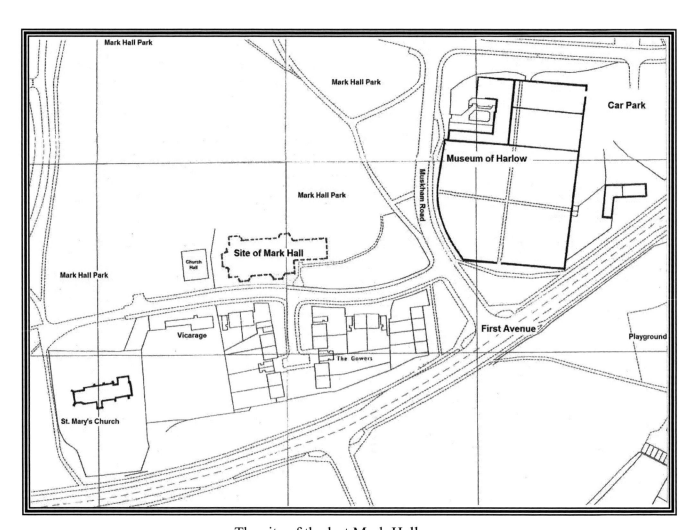

The site of the last Mark Hall manor
house

iv

Introduction

Today there is no manor house called Mark Hall. The lawns and grounds that once surrounded the mansion still retain the name, which has also been given to a school, but nothing remains of the buildings above ground except the walled gardens and the stables, now the Museum of Harlow.

Fire consumed the eighteenth century house in 1947 but the history of Mark Hall manor, which stretches back before Domesday, can still be traced in the landscape, the church of St Mary-at-Latton, the buried cellars and in the Museum itself. This book is an attempt to summarise and illustrate that long history, showing the relationship of changes in one small parish to national and international events.

Though the first named owner of the manor that became Mark Hall was Ernulf, a Saxon free man, in 1066, there is archaeological evidence that some of the land was already occupied long before Ernulf's ancestors arrived in the fifth century AD. The Romans had come and gone leaving clear traces, and, though the evidence is fragmentary and controversial, it seems certain that there had been small settlements here for centuries before the legions arrived. This early period is briefly summarised in the Chronology but, as accounts of pre-Roman times are still largely guesswork, our story begins with the groups of dwellings that were to become Harlow and Latton as they might have appeared soon after Aulus Plautius landed on the coast of Kent in AD 43.

The story of Mark Hall manor is impossible to separate from Latton Hall and Latton Priory. Between 1066 and 1950 the names of seventeen families connected with Mark Hall, either as owners or occupiers, are known and several of these also owned Latton Hall. The names of five other Latton Hall families are also recorded. Some remain little more than names but many have surprisingly interesting connections. This account consists of a series of chapters describing each family, and ends with a brief history of Latton Priory, which was linked with both Halls at different times. For quick reference, each topic after 1086 begins with a short list of relevant dates, names and events.

Lying within easy riding distance of London, Mark Hall has frequently been owned by wealthy merchants and statesmen who also held property in the City and elsewhere. Some owners may never have visited the manor but their success or failure in business or at Court would have directly affected their tenants in Latton.

The Chronology, a list of national and international events, is intended to provide a context for the events occurring in one small parish. Because of the central part played by belief systems in the evolution of our society, significant dates concerning religious matters have a separate column beside the list of important secular events that would have affected the whole country including Latton.

The family trees in chapters 7 to 17 are designed to show both the direct descendants of the lords of the manor and the interrelationship of many families that resulted from the second, third and even fourth marriages of both widowers and widows. Sources often disagree about names and dates and spelling often varies, even within one document. Further information will be welcomed.

The recent history of Mark Hall, which is also the story of the creation of the Museum of Harlow, is dealt with in chapter 19.

Acknowledgements

This book has been produced by the combined efforts of Friends of Harlow Museum with the co-operation of the staff and volunteers of the Museum of Harlow. Among the Friends, John Collier and Brenda Miller have been responsible for the chapters on coins and on the Altham family, and Joyce Jones has contributed architectural information and drawings. Ann Pegrum's knowledge of early medieval history and her skill at deciphering old documents have been invaluable. Other Friends who have helped in a variety of ways include Robin Harcourt, Ron Bill, Stan Newens, Graham and Mary Pitt, Shiela Herbert, Cherith Lowry and Terry Sothcott.

Without the painstaking research undertaken by Jenny Handley and by Jean Wright online and in libraries, in the City of London and in record offices, the project would have been impossible.

We have also been generously assisted by a variety of experts including Jennifer C.Ward on medieval Latton, Dr Herbert Eiden on Harlow's involvement in the 'Peasants' Revolt', Professor Short on the writings of Walter Bibbesworth, and Georgina Green on Humphrey Repton's visit to Mark Hall. Brenda Miller's work on the Altham family has been enriched by Dr James Altham of

Gonville and Caius College, Cambridge, his sister Jane Lagesse, Ralph Hawtrey and Robert Gray, House Manager of Kingston Lacy. Thanks to Stan Newens, who brought the 1616 estate map back to Harlow, we have been able to study Sir Edward Altham's property in detail. Wally Wright, once curator of the Bishop's Stortford Local History Museum, has provided information on the Leventhorpe and Gilbey families.

The last Mark Hall has been described to us by the late Mr Simon Gilbey and Nancy, Lady Agnew, grandchildren of Newman and Victorina Gilbey who took on the tenancy in 1894. We are also indebted to Mr Ralph Gilbey, another grandson, and to the Rt. Rev. Thomas McMahon, Bishop of Brentwood, for invaluable suggestions and permission to include photographs by Frank Osborne and others.

For the history of Latton in the early twentieth century we have been helped by several local people whose families lived in or near Harlow long before 1947. These include Ann Pegrum, Jean Hudspeth, Betty Wiltshire, Jack and Evelyn Baker, Keith and Heather Taylor and Malcolm Bradford.

For details of the last days of Mark Hall before the fire, and of the period when the remaining wing was used as a school, we are very grateful to those members of the Women's Land Army and to all the old scholars who shared their memories with us.

We would also like to thank Ray Hooper and Alan Whittingdon of A.D. Architects who designed the conversion of the stables into the Cycle Museum and have most generously contributed first-hand recollections as well as detailed photographs.

Katina and Rachel Lake and Tony Maher have provided essential help as well as constant encouragement.

Glossary

acre – unlike the modern acre the medieval acre could be a measure of length (66 ft.) as well as area.
advowson – the right, often possessed by the lord of the manor, to choose the priest or vicar.
apostolate – mission of an apostle – going forth to preach the gospel.
baronet – (from 1600s) one who holds a heritable minor title 'Sir.'
baron – military leader with major peerage title, holding estate from king.
bordar – a peasant of lower economic status than a villein.
cartulary – collection of charters, title deeds etc.
chantry – chapel endowed for a priest to sing masses for the founder's soul.
cooper – a maker of barrels or a dealer in wine.
demesne – land whose produce is devoted to the lord rather than his tenants.
escheator – officer appointed to look after land forfeited to the overlord for misdemeanour, lack of heirs or lack of a will.
feofees – trustees.
franc pledge/tithing – subdivision of a hundred – a system in which ten men were responsible for the appearance of each other in court if summoned.
free man – a non-noble landholder. Sometimes used as equivalent of thegn.
hide – the amount of land that would support a household, divided into four virgates. The standard unit for tax assessment.
hundred – an administrative subdivision of a shire. Number and size varied from shire to shire, sometimes a hundred hides.
inquisition – judicial or official enquiry.
knight – a military retainer, subordinate of a baron, holding non-heritable title 'Sir.'
knight's fee – payment owed by a knight to his lord, in military service or in money, for tenancy of a manor.
lordship – territory or personnel under the direct authority of a lord.
manor – an estate administered as a unit, usually including a manor house, the home of the owner.
mercer – merchant dealing in fabrics, usually silk.
messuage – a dwelling house together with outbuildings and land assigned to its use.
penny, pence – d. = denarius. In the eleventh century 240 d. were struck from one pound of silver.
piscina – perforated stone basin in church for carrying away water used in cleaning chalice etc.
quitclaim – a quitclaim deed is a document in which a person disclaims any interest he/she may have in a piece of property and passes that claim to another person
reeve – a king or a lord's agent in charge of estates or a village representative in charge of manorial dues.
receiver – person appointed by a court of equity to hold disputed property in trust.
recovery – sale complicated by a legal fiction of prior ownership.
steward – lord of the manor's man of business, in charge of rolls (documents).
thegn – usually a man of noble status as opposed to a peasant.
toft – homestead.
verderer – judicial officer of a royal forest.
villan/villein – a peasant of higher status than a bordar, living in a village. Top ranking serf.
virgate – land measure, usually quarter of a hide. Approximately thirty acres.

1
The Romans Arrive

See Chronology pages 140-41

Soon after the Emperor Claudius had accepted the capitulation of more than a dozen minor British kings at Colchester in 43 AD, sections of the enormous Roman army must have explored their newly conquered territory north of the Thames in order to assess its produce and eliminate any remaining opposition.

If one squadron had approached the Harlow area from the direction of Colchester, the men would have emerged from dense woodland into a large clearing filled with round thatched huts at the base of a small hill, surrounded by a river and marshland. Information concerning an ancient centre of worship on this hill would certainly have reached the centurion from local contacts before his men set out and they were probably accompanied by conscripted interpreters who knew the district well. Warning of the soldiers' approach would have reached the village well in advance and, on this first occasion, most of the able-bodied slaves and peasants had probably disappeared into the forest, carrying as much food and as many valuables as they could by the time the Roman troops arrived.

Leaving some men to set up camp and start collecting supplies, a chosen officer might have led a small squad across the track over the swamp and up the hill to the old shrine in order to report on the attitude of the priest in charge. A suitably deferential reception might have encouraged the soldiers to leave a few coins as votive offerings to ensure themselves a safe journey back.

Roman soldier in Colchester

Thanks to the existence of their holy hill, later known as Stanegrove, the families who lived near its base would have been used to visitors from neighbouring kingdoms. Trade both within Britain and with Gaul had greatly increased in recent years and the Stanegrove settlement probably included several prosperous households. The security of the lives and property of the community could have been bought from the Roman officer at a price by negotiation with a local merchant or priest. The aim of the Roman conquerors was to control the land and to make use of its wealth, not to destroy it. Met with hostility, the legions wiped out their adversaries with great efficiency, but peaceful domination was the preferred policy.

Peaceful negotiation was not, however, the natural British response to invasion and humiliation. Revolts frequently broke out and after Governor Aulus Plautius returned to Rome the behaviour of one group of Roman officers, led by Procurator Catus Decianus, provoked a widespread and devastating rebellion in the south east while the Governor, Suetonius Paulinus, was dealing with the Druids in Anglesey.

According to Tacitus, son-in-law of Agricola, a later governor, this rising was caused by the treatment meted out to Boudicca, widow of the king of the Iceni people in Norfolk. Misjudging the power of this warrior queen, the Romans seized her land, flogged her, raped her daughters and then allowed her to escape. Faced with a common enemy, the British tribes of neighbouring kingdoms united as they had never done before. Colchester, St Albans and London went up in flames and it has been estimated that over 150,000 soldiers and civilians died before the revolt was suppressed.

The settlement around Stanegrove Hill cannot have been isolated from these events. Any cordiality that might have developed between the community and visiting soldiers would have been replaced by suspicion and terror during the savage retribution that followed the uprising.

Several English towns claim a connection with 'Boadicea' – the red-haired British heroine famously depicted standing in her war chariot. A local legend maintains that she fought and lies buried somewhere in the region of Upshire, having killed herself with poison obtained from a local herb, and she is also claimed by Coventry, Lichfield and Mancetter, a village near Nuneaton. The details of her campaign are uncertain but one definite result of her defeat was the weakening of the power of the Druids in the west, the most obstinate opponents of the Romans, both in Gaul and Britain.

Boudicca's death marked the end of native uprisings in the south and the Romans resumed their well ordered plan of ensuring control by building a network of roads converging on London, erecting forts and establishing prosperous towns with fine temples dedicated to a variety of gods.

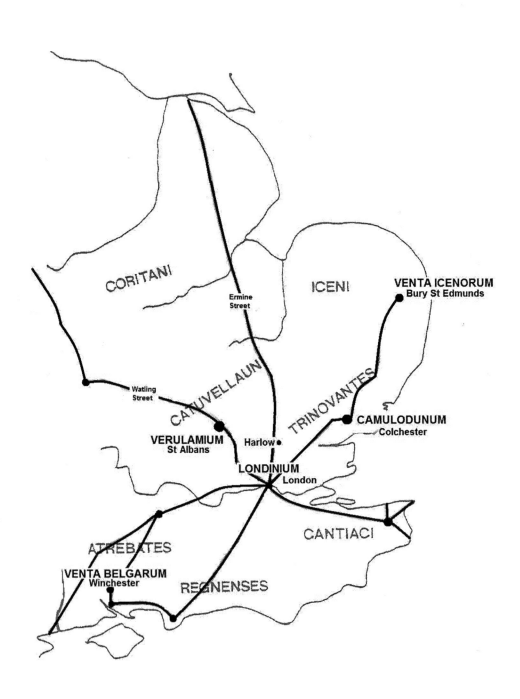

Early Roman Britain

The shrine on Stanegrove Hill probably remained undisturbed for another twenty years while the village grew and the wealthier citizens began to imitate Roman customs. A few retired legionaries may have taken advantage of grants of money and land to build villas in the area and the neighbouring British nobility gradually became used to new ideas of architecture, plumbing, dress and education.

Then, possibly in response to orders from Agricola, an enlightened Governor who was mainly responsible for improving the relationship between Britons and Romans, a temple dedicated to Minerva was erected on Stanegrove Hill, burying the last traces of the old shrine. Coins reveal that soldiers continued to visit the area and as the years passed these men would no longer have been regarded with hostility. The legions based in Britain were increasingly recruited from western Europe and from Britain itself and probably came to be accepted by many citizens as indispensable defenders of civilisation against attack by ferocious barbarians.

For the slaves and peasants little changed. Shallow ploughs were still used to produce the corn that was stored in pits near the dwellings and ground into flour between querns – small circular stones rotated by hand. Native slaves in the Roman households became aware of books and the art of writing but the labourers remained an underclass, even more distant from their masters than in earlier times.

For three hundred years after the death of Boudicca, the Empire retained its power. While the reinforced legions continued to repel attacks from the distant north, the prosperous classes in the south began to take peace and luxury for granted. Britons and foreigners inter-married, the new cities became entirely dependent on imported supplies and trade flourished. Roman emperors were accepted in the pantheon of the gods and the Stanegrove temple, like many others, was improved and extended.

At varying intervals, rumours were whispered of a strange new sect that believed in a single god but it was safer to ignore such talk until the extraordinary news arrived that the great Emperor Constantine himself had accepted the new religion. In the last days of the Empire, Christianity was proclaimed the official religion and orders arrived to destroy the temples.

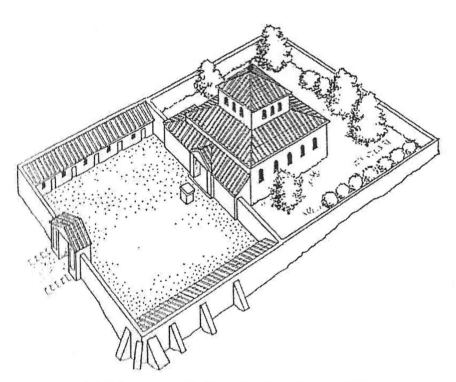

Artist's impression of the Roman temple on Stanegrove Hill

Ancient coins found in Harlow
John Collier

The north-east corner of what is now Harlow New Town, bordered on the north by the river Stort and the east by the road to Cambridge, has produced the majority of ancient coins from the Harlow area. The two principal archaeological sites are the Romano-British Temple at Stanegrove Hill and nearby 'Holbrooks' – named after the engineering works that used to occupy the site in more recent times.

The coins range from the late Iron Age through to the end of the Roman occupation of Britain – approximately 50 BC to 400 AD.

The most prolific area for both Iron Age and Roman coins is Stanegrove Hill, which is thought to have been a sacred site to Iron Age and then Roman peoples throughout this period.

Nearly one thousand gold, silver and bronze Iron Age coins have been excavated in Harlow, making this one of the largest collections of its type from the whole of Britain.

The kingdom of the Catuvellauni comprised North Thames, Hertfordshire and Bedfordshire, with their capital at Verlamio, near the later Roman city of Verulamium. The kingdom of the Trinovantes included Essex and counties to the west, with their capital at Camulodunum (see page 4). As Harlow was located on the border between the Catuvellauni and the Trinovantes it is hardly surprising that most of the Iron Age coins are from these tribes.

Coins of Tasciovanus and his son Cunobelinus (Shakespeare's 'Cymbeline'), chiefs of the Catuvellauni, predominate but various other tribes and rulers are also represented together with some Gallo-Belgic issues from the Continent.

Actual Iron Age coins from Harlow Temple

Gold Quarter Stater   Bronze Coin Unit

Compared with the complex issues of the late Iron Age, Roman coins are relatively easy to classify as they have been subjected to much study and are well documented.

The Temple coins provide an almost perfect record of the Roman coinage in Britain, reflecting the ebb and flow of supplies of new coins and the periods when locally made copies had to fill the gaps left by the lack of official issues.

The earliest Roman coin from the Temple site is a silver Denarius struck by Marc Antony prior to the battle of Actium in 31 BC. These coins were produced to pay the legions loyal to him but were never popular as they contained less silver than the official issues of the time and thus largely avoided the regular recall of old coins for melting down. These coins are usually found in a very worn state but our example is still easily identifiable.

Below is a similar coin to the one from the Temple but this commemorates the XXII Legion rather than the XXIII of the Harlow coin.

'Legionary' Denarius of Marc Antony

The most interesting of the 'Contemporary' copies, referred to above, are the 'Minerva' Asses of Claudius. These were produced in the early years after the invasion when lack of coins from Rome meant that the Army could not be paid. The most popular coin of the time for everyday use was a copper 'As' of Claudius showing Minerva holding a spear and shield on the reverse. This is very appropriate as it is thought that the Temple was dedicated to the worship of the goddess Minerva. The copies are usually smaller and of cruder style than the official type and were almost certainly either struck by the Army or at least had official approval. The most likely source of these coins is Colchester (Camulodunum) where large quantities have been found. Forty-six examples have been found at the Temple making it, by far, the most common first century coin type from the site. The presence of these coins in quantity usually indicates a military camp or fort but as no such structure has been found in the Harlow area so far, it is most likely that soldiers stopped at the Temple to make an offering on their way to Camulodunum or Verulamium.

Official and unofficial versions of coins

Official issue copper As of Claudius
showing Minerva with shield and javelin

Typical contemporary copy of a
Minerva As of Claudius

The latest coins are probably those of the Emperor Arcadius, who ruled until 408 AD but they may be slightly earlier than this as supplies of new coins to Britain had ceased by about 395 AD.

Small bronze coin of Arcadius
Late Roman small change

It should be noted that almost all the coins from the Temple site, Iron Age and Roman, were deposited there deliberately as votive offerings.

Although the Iron Age coins are sometimes gold and silver issues, hardly any Roman coins of precious metal have been discovered. This may of course be because, during the Roman period, the Temple would most likely have had a permanent 'priest' who could take the best offerings as payment for his services. Alternatively, this may just reflect the relative poverty of the average Roman soldier or other visitors to the Temple. Votive offerings were considered to be only 'tokens' and were often deliberately damaged to prevent reuse, so the actual value of the item may not have been important.

2
The Saxons in Latton

See Chronology pages 141-44

The story of the transition from Roman Britain to the Anglo-Saxon kingdoms that replaced it is so controversial and uncertain that it is impossible to summarise accurately. Some dates are generally accepted and numerous chronicles and other documents seem to shed light on events but new archaeological finds often contradict previous assumptions.

In the Harlow area we know for certain that there were Romanised British settlements here before the Saxons arrived but there is no evidence to suggest precisely when or how these were replaced by the pagan newcomers who established their villages along the Stort. Were the natives wiped out by raiding parties or did they integrate, possibly as slaves, with the newcomers? Legends maintain that resistance to the Germanic invaders persisted for years in many areas, including Epping Forest, and it is certainly true that Romanised urban life still existed in some places late in the fifth century. Apart from two brooches, a coin dating from after 757, a few pieces of broken pottery and post holes on Stanegrove Hill that might indicate some kind of Saxon building, no evidence has yet appeared locally to suggest when Ernulf's predecessor first established his family on the farm that was to become Mark Hall manor. This absence of early Saxon artefacts is typical of most of Essex and Hertfordshire.

Whatever the exact dates of their arrival in different areas, there is no doubt that it is to the descendants of these invaders that we owe the roots of our language, the boundaries of our parishes and shires and the basic laws and customs which still underlie our way of life.

Among the essential farm equipment used by the newcomers, heavy ploughs and large millwheels rotated by water power were of most importance because they determined the position of the new settlements and their minimum size. Each extended family needed access to a river or stream to provide power for a water mill and nearby clearings large enough for up to eight oxen to pull a heavy plough. Land already cleared and ready for ploughing would obviously have been preferable to virgin forest but timber for building and for fuel also had to be easily obtainable. These considerations provide a probable explanation for the position and strange elongated shape of the Saxon settlements which, at some unknown date, probably before 600 AD, became the villages of Harlow, Latton, Netteswell (first mentioned in 1195) and Parndon. Of these Harlow was much the most populous and important as it contained the moot or meeting place and gave its name to the area later described as Harlow Half Hundred. [1]

Embroidery of Saxon peasants ploughing with oxen

[1] One explanation of the term 'half-hundred' is that some hundreds, originally in Essex, were divided and their other halves are now in Hertfordshire.

The later Saxon period saw three major developments, each of which directly affected the people of Latton.

First came the return of two versions of Christianity in the seventh century, spread originally by missionaries from Lindisfarne and from Rome. Monks carried on the work of preaching, baptism and burial and eventually almost every Saxon village had its own little wooden church with a priest and a defined parish boundary.

Secondly, by the end of the ninth century, Wessex had become dominant over the warring Anglo-Saxon kingdoms. Only increasingly successful invasions from Denmark and Norway limited the area controlled by the three last kings of Wessex: Alfred, his son Edward and grandson Athelstan. England became a prosperous land dotted with fortified towns where high standards of coinage and trading regulations were enforced. Efficiency in battle coupled with a love of learning and order characterised Alfred and his descendants and by the mid tenth century Athelstan ruled over a land renowned in Western Europe for *'peace and abundance of all things'*.[1]

Thirdly, at the same time as the Danelaw was being contested in England and Danish kings were seizing the English throne, Viking adventurers gained control of Normandy. The Danelaw, which was established in part of north and east England from before 886, had little effect in the Harlow area, but the creation of the new aggressive Norman-French nation across the Channel was to have a profound effect on every English manor less than two centuries later.

By 1066 England was a productive country ruled by a single king – Edward the Confessor, half-brother of the last Danish king. Compared with Normandy, recently settled by the Vikings, it was a rich land of established families whose ancestors had occupied the same estates for several centuries. Since Edward's accession to the throne in 1042 there had been increased Norman influence in the higher reaches of the aristocracy and in the Church but the great majority of English thegns, free men and peasants remained unaffected either by Danish or by Norman customs or language.

Ironically, the only detailed description that exists of the farms and the inhabitants of late Saxon England was compiled for the Conqueror, William of Normandy. Although the great survey nicknamed 'the Domesday Book' was not completed until after 1086, William's greed for money led him to demand information about the produce, population and taxable value of each manor before the Conquest, as well as twenty years later. A group of commissioners appointed by the King visited each county town where they were supplied with information by the priest, the reeve and four men from each village and small town. Historians of Essex, Suffolk and Norfolk are fortunate as their counties were included in 'Little Domesday Book,' a later and more detailed survey than 'Great Domesday'.

An indication of the importance of the Church to both the old and the new regime is shown by the fact that, in almost every shire, the first landowners listed after the King are archbishops, bishops, abbots or other church dignitaries. Even the most powerful members of the Norman nobility appear in third place. In Essex at least ten religious institutions existed before the Conquest, of which the most important to Harlow and the surrounding parishes was King Harold's college of secular canons at Waltham Holy Cross. St Edmund's Abbey near Bury St Edmunds in Suffolk had held the lordship of Harlowbury since 1045.

At some stage six water mills were constructed along the river banks from Roydon to Harlow though only three are mentioned in Domesday – Harlow, Little Parndon and Roydon. The Abbot's Mill, later known as Burnt Mill, does not appear because the parish of Netteswell was omitted from the great survey. The reason for this omission is not documented but it is usually associated with the fact that Netteswell had belonged to Earl Harold's college of secular canons at Waltham Cross and had not been reallotted by 1086 when the Bishop of Durham was given Waltham. The fact that Netteswell may have been directly owned by William I in 1086 does not really explain its absence from the Survey as many of the Conqueror's lands are listed there. The explanation may be that land once included in Netteswell was listed with adjoining parishes in 1086. Waltham Abbey regained it in 1177.

Latton apparently had no mill in 1066 or 1086 which suggests that its little farms were dependent on the mill in Harlow – a bigger and more prosperous parish. Latton mill is first recorded in 1449 but was probably constructed earlier by the first Norman owners or tenants of Mark Hall.

---

[1] Quoted by Michael Wood from *'an English writer of the 980s'* p.139 *In Search of the Dark Ages* 1981.

Latton parish in 1066 as listed in Domesday Book: two manors and another larger estate.

1) later Mark Hall	2) later Latton Hall	3) later possibly split up
Owner-Ernulf, a free man	Owner – a free man	Owner – Thurgot, a free man
1½ hides + 30 acres 2 ploughs 1 villan 2 bordars 4 slaves woodland for 300 pigs 35 acres of meadow a church a priest with ½ a hide manor worth 50s.	2½ hides + 30 acre 2 ploughs 1 villan 4 bordars 4 slaves woodland for 350 pigs 35 acres of meadow a priest manor worth 60s.	4½ hides (3½ in some editions) 2 ploughs in demesne the men had 1 plough 4 villans 4 bordars 4 slaves woodland for 200 pigs 35 acres of meadow 4 head of cattle 50 pigs 30 sheep 25 goats manor worth £6

Saxon landowners in the five parishes before 1066

as listed in the Domesday book

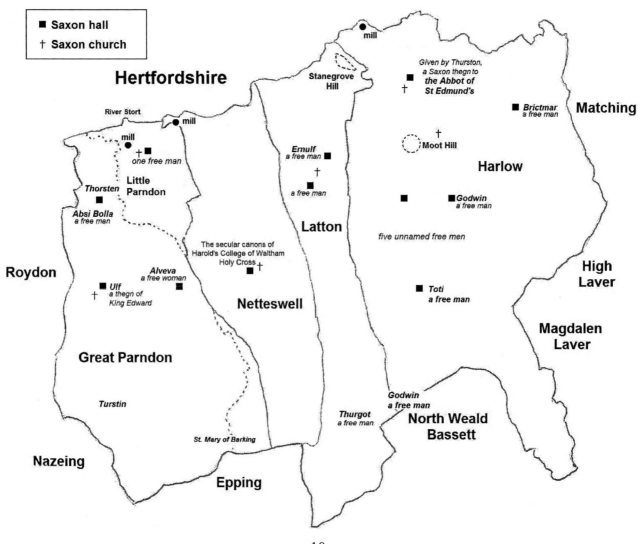

3
The Coming of the Normans

See Chronology page 144-150

The first years after the Conquest were occupied by William I in asserting his power. This often involved mustering his forces to suppress frequent rebellions among his new subjects. His knights were very frequently summoned to earn more of his gratitude, repaid in English manors, by returning to his side on the battlefield.

It has been estimated that two thirds of the Saxon nobility had disappeared by 1086. The majority had probably been killed but some could have fled to Ireland.

Next to fighting to secure his property and raising taxes to pay for his wars, the new king's main obsession was hunting. The Harlow area was included in the King's forest and for many English peasants the loss of freedom to make use of the woodlands was more devastating than losing their Saxon lords.

The Church as an institution did very well by the Conquest, though most of the important English churchmen were replaced by Normans. Chief among these beneficiaries was Odo, the Bishop of Bayeux, the

The White Tower, built by William I

King's half-brother, who was granted manors in twenty shires. Some of the old churches and abbeys, including St Edmund's, gained land and the bishops and abbots of seven new Norman foundations were allotted manors in Essex taken from Saxon free men and women. The Bishop of Bayeux acquired most of his Essex land in the Chelmsford Hundred.

In 1086 a total of 1027 rural priests are listed in Domesday. Latton was unusual in having two.

Latton parish in 1086

1) Mark Hall	2) Latton Hall	3) undefined area
Overlord – Count Eustace de Boulogne	Overlord – Peter de Valognes	Overlord – St Edmund's Abbey
Tenant Adelolf de Merk	Tenant – Turgis	No tenant named
1½ hides + 30 acres	2½ hides + 30 acres	4½ hides (3½ in some editions)
1 plough in demesne	1 plough in demesne	2 ploughs in demesne
1 villan	the men have ½ a plough	the men had 1 plough
2 bordars	1 villan	4 villans
2 slaves	4 bordars	5 bordars
woodland for 300 pigs	no slaves	4 slaves
35 acres of meadow	woodland for 350 pigs	woodland for 200 pigs
a church with ½ a hide	35 acres of meadow	35 acres of meadow
a priest	a priest	4 head of cattle
manor worth 60s.	manor worth 60s.	50 pigs
		30 sheep
		25 goats
		manor worth £6

The Family of Eustace II Count of Boulogne.
Overlords of Mark Hall manor from 1086

Eustace Count of Boulogne (c.1015-1093) had connections through his first marriage (1050-1055) with Saxon England. His first wife was Godgifu, daughter of Ethelred the Unready and sister of Edward the Confessor. They had no children.

After divorcing a second wife, Eustace married Ida de Basse Lorraine, the daughter of Godfrey III Duke of Lorraine. The date of this marriage to Ida was probably 1057. Their son, Eustace III, Count of Boulogne c.1058-1125 married Mary, the daughter of Malcolm III of Scotland. Two younger sons, Godfrey and Baldwin, became leaders in the First Crusade. Baldwin succeeded Godfrey as King of Jerusalem in 1100 and died in 1118.

Eustace II was a proud and ambitious man whose career both before and after the Conquest was marked by a series of rebellions against those in authority. In 1051, on a visit to England, he fell out with Godwin, the powerful Earl of Wessex, father of Harold and father-in-law of Edward the Confessor's daughter Alice. Earl Godwin was the first Warden of Dover where Eustace landed and caused an affray with the townspeople who were extremely loyal to their Saxon Warden. Although Eustace was allotted extensive lands in England after the Conquest – he was granted manors in ten other counties as well as those in Essex – his relationship with William of Normandy was erratic.

Imaginative historians have linked Eustace's name with subtle messages in the Bayeux tapestry suggesting that it was he, rather than William I, who was the hero of the battle of Hastings and would perhaps have been more acceptable as king.

William of Normandy and Eustace de Boulogne

This embroidery, based on a battle scene in the Bayeux tapestry, shows Eustace riding beside William and pointing at him as the Duke reveals his face by raising his helmet. Apparently a rumour claiming that their leader was dead had disheartened the Norman knights and Eustace is helping his friend to disprove the lie. Besides proving Eustace's loyalty and gallantry, the scene also emphasises his importance. No other knight in the battle is shown carrying his own standard. He certainly earned William's gratitude at Hastings but in the year after the Conquest Eustace joined in an unsuccessful attack on Dover Castle, led by the men of Kent. As punishment, his newly acquired lands were forfeited but it seems that, as most of the manors were soon returned to him, the Conqueror must either have felt he still owed Eustace a debt for his help in defeating Harold or was forced to bribe him to ensure his continued support.

Facts and dates are few and unreliable. Eustace and his descendants were certainly closely linked with several reigning monarchs and he may well have felt capable of exercising power more efficiently than they. Some of the earliest wooden motte and bailey castles were erected by him including one near Dover and one in Chipping Ongar. Nothing remains of the buildings today but the great mounds on which some stood can still be seen.

It is very unlikely that Eustace himself ever visited Latton. He owned vast territories in both France and England and soon returned to the Continent. His link with his tenant Adelolf de Merk has not yet been investigated. Eustace was also granted the manor of Kitchen Hall where his tenant was Geoffrey de Mandeville. The boundaries of neither manor are clearly defined but Mark Hall manor included woods on Rye Hill and some woodland that had belonged to the Abbot of Waltham.

Eustace was succeeded by his son, Eustace III and his granddaughter Matilda who was to marry Stephen, king of England 1135-1154.

The significance of the title of 'overlord' faded through the centuries. By making sure that his great knights never received their English manors in one concentrated area but scattered over several counties, William I reduced the likelihood of successful rebellions. He also weakened the barons' power by insisting that, in any conflict of interests, sub-tenants and all those beneath them owed their first allegiance to the king, not to their overlord.

Norman overlords and tenants in the five parishes after 1086

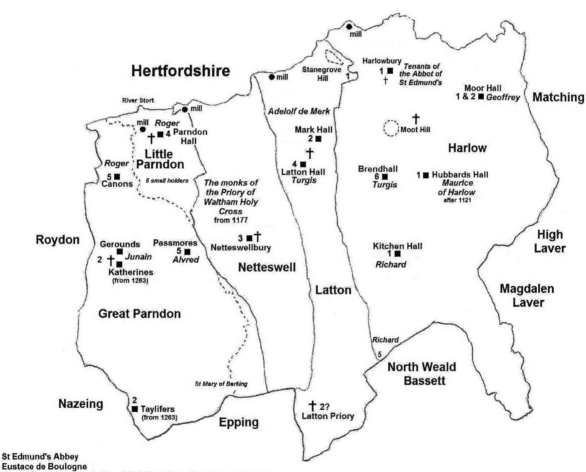

1 St Edmund's Abbey
2 Eustace de Boulogne
3 The Bishop of Durham? After 1177 The Priory of Waltham Holy Cross
4 Peter de Valognes
5 Ranulf, brother of Ilger
6 Eudo the Steward
7 Richard, son of Count Gilbert

The de Merk Family. Tenants of Mark Hall manor 1086-1317

By 1086 Count Eustace de Boulogne has granted Adelolf de Merk tenancies in Essex Hundreds and Half Hundreds including:

Dunmow: manors in Great and Little Dunmow

Hinckford: manors in Shortgrove, Steeple Bumpstead and Weston.

Chelmsford: a manor in Runwell.

Thurstable: manors in Tolleshunt and Goldhanger.

Tendring: manors in Great and Little Holland and Lawford.

Freshwell Half Hundred: manors in Great and Little Bardfield.

Harlow Half Hundred: Mark Hall manor.

1200 Eutropius de Merk inherits Mark Hall manor. Peter de Merk succeeds his father Eutropius.

1210 Henry de Merk is named as 'demesne tenant' of Mark Hall. He marries Rose.

1234 Henry de Merk dies. Rose, his widow, disputes the tenancy with their son Ralph.

1240 Mark Hall is conveyed to Henry de Merk, Ralph's brother.

1258 Henry de Merk dies leaving an infant son Henry who marries Juliana. No children.

1270 Henry de Merk dies. Juliana marries 2) John de Charteney 3) Elias, son of John of Colchester.

Niece Aubrey Dynant inherits Mark Hall.

1276 Aubrey Dynant dies. Great uncle Andrew de Merk inherits.

Andrew de Merk's son Thomas inherits Mark Hall. The claim is disputed by Juliana's third husband Elias of Colchester.

1309 The property is divided and sold. Henry de Seagrave buys Thomas de Merk's portion.

By 1317 Thomas de Merk has died. Augustine and Maud le Waleys buy the entire estate.

Much remains to be discovered about the first family that became the 'sub-tenants' of Mark Hall manor (under Eustace de Boulogne and the King) after the Conquest. What we do know is that they built the first Norman manor house, gave the place their name and remained the virtual owners until 1317. In early documents the manor is often described as Latton Merk.

The spelling of their name presents the first problem. In different documents it appears as Merc, Merk, Merck, Mark and Marck. The genealogist of the Marsh family thinks there may be a link between the names Mark and Marisco. Adelolf varies from Adelulf to Adelwulf. 'De Merk' is used here while the family still held Mark Hall.

The usual theory suggests that Adelolf came from Marck near Calais where there was once a castle of that name, but it seems that his first name is Anglo-Saxon. The Revd Shilleto, writing in 1865, suggested that he was a Saxon merchant and that he used the name Merk, meaning merchant, to suggest Norman connections, but this provides no explanation for Eustace de Boulognes' generosity towards him. J. Horace Round maintains that the Marks became lords of Ardres, a small town that lay within the Boulonnais, an area controlled by Eustace. Adelolf belonged to a younger branch of the Mark family, trained as a knight and, probably accompanied by brothers or cousins, followed his lord to war across the Channel. J.H. Round declares that their descendants 'increased and multiplied' and that members of the family still held land on the Boulogne fief in the days of King John.[1]

There seems to be general agreement that Adelolf fought at the battle of Hastings and was rewarded with at least ten manors in Essex, including Great and Little Dunmow, as well as one small manor in Latton. Whether any of his descendants decided to make their home in Latton is not known. A Eustace de Merk is recorded as the second husband of Adeliza le Fleming, born c.1074 in Yorkshire. This could be a son of Adelolf, and Henry de Merk, described as the father of another Eustace, born 1172 could be a grandson, but no reliable family tree exists. The history of Bobbingworth includes a John de Merk as patron of the living and Ralph de Merk, probably his son, who disposed of the advowson to a John de Lovetot in 1280.

It is possible that Ernulf, the Saxon free man in 1066, was left in charge to run the farm while Adelolf rode around the country checking on each of his estates but Ernulf's status would have declined from master to bailiff and rent collector. By 1086 Mark Hall manor was not suffering quite as much as its neighbour Latton Hall from shortage of men and equipment but it was rated at ten shillings more than before 1066 with two fewer slaves and one plough in place of two to produce the extra output demanded.

---

[1] See Victoria County History, Vol 1 p. 344

In his account of the manor of Royston in the *History of Hertfordshire* J.J. Cussans quotes: *'About the year 1180, Eustace de Merc founded in this place a Priory of Black Canons. Shortly afterwards his nephews William and Ralph made further grants of land in the parish of Parkway...'* This information is interesting because it adds weight to the assumption that the de Merk family were deeply interested in the Church and especially in Augustinian establishments. Twenty years later Eutropius de Merk, then the tenant of Mark Hall, demonstrated his own reverence for representatives of the Church by giving *'that acre over which Ailmar the bishop passed'* to the Preceptory of the Knights Hospitallers at Little Maplestead. Ailmar had been appointed bishop of the South Saxons two centuries earlier.

As both Mark Hall and Latton Hall are credited with employing a priest before 1066 it is probable that Ernulf had cooperated with his Saxon neighbour at Latton Hall, an unnamed free man, in

preserving their old wooden church and supporting the religious observances of their farm workers. Two priests were still in residence twenty years later so it seems that the de Merks were sympathetic with their work and were responsible for ordering the replacement of the old church with a stone and flint building, perhaps as early as 1200.

Though much has changed, St Mary-at-Latton retains many elements of its original Norman structure but today it is glowing with light and embellished with decorations. In the adjoining parish, Harlowbury Chapel with its rounded Norman entrance and simple dark interior would probably have been more

Harlowbury Chapel

familiar to Eutropius and Peter de Merk. Even so, attendance at church must have provided a valued break from heavy farm work for the villeins, bordars and slaves on the estate.

Life had always been hard for the labourers but the Normans imported a more systematic regime of forced labour in exchange for the right to farm a plot of land on the lord's estate. In his translation of the Cartulary of Harlow, Canon Fisher gives a detailed description of the labour expected in 1287 from the holder of a virgate (about thirty acres), a half virgate or an even smaller plot of land belonging to the Abbot of St Edmunds in Harlow. Conditions were probably very similar on de Merk's manor, if rather less generous.

'A virgater was expected to work on the demesne, (the lord's land) four days a week, viz. Monday, Tuesday, Wednesday and Friday, feast days excepted, from Michaelmas to August 1st. The daily tasks, consisting of ploughing, sowing, harrowing, etc., were not severe. Five weeks were holidays, viz. Christmas-week, Easter-week, Whit-week, and the first fortnight of August. Between August 15th and Michaelmas the work was much more strenuous: while the day-work for the rest of the year was only valued at 6s, the harvest work was stated to be worth 5s. 4d. Mowing in the lord's mead

Saxon dwellings based on the Bayeux Tapestry

was a boon-work, and from this no tenants were exempted, but food was provided twice a day, viz. soup, bacon, cheese, and ale at noon, and wheaten bread, two dishes of stewed meat and ale in the evening. Every other week, if required, the tenant had to carry as far as Stapleford (another manor of the abbot) or to Stortford, Ongar, or Waltham for one work, or else to London, or anywhere up to twenty miles, for two works. Other works which might be required of him were thatching, ditching, and the scouring or embanking of water-courses. The virgater could not give his daughter, nor marry, nor sell oxen or horses born to him, without the lord's license'.

Only after completing work for his lord was the peasant free to cultivate his own plot if there was still daylight before sleep on his straw mattress. The labourers' homes were little more than huts.

The few representations of peasants' dwellings in the Bayeux Tapestry show windowless rectangular buildings, usually constructed of slats of wood with arched doorways. The roofs are either tiled or thatched. The pictures of the homes of wealthier townspeople suggest that the living quarters were on the first floor.

The first Norman manor houses in Latton, Mark Hall and Latton Hall, were probably built a few years before the new church.

Secular medieval buildings in Essex were invariably timber-built and rendered externally with coarse lime plaster. Stone had to be imported from other counties and was reserved for churches, where it was used for strengthening angles, providing buttresses and dressings for door and window openings, while the rubble walls were built with flints gathered from the fields. Thick Roman tiles from the ruined Temple can still be seen in the walls of several Harlow churches.

The standard manor house plan evolved from a general living space with a central hearth around which most of the activities of the lord of the manor and his household took place. As time passed a number of features were introduced to increase their comfort and convenience, resulting in a basic arrangement which remained consistent over several centuries. The central hearth was soon replaced by a brick-built recess in an outer wall with a flue and chimney, while a porch protected the entrance from the elements. The two ends of the hall developed distinct functions; at the entrance end a passage, separated from the body of the hall by screens, had doors leading to service rooms, pantry, buttery and kitchen, which was often separated from the main building for safety. The lord and his family dined at the far end of the hall, sometimes on a raised dais. This end was often lit by a larger window set in a projecting bay or oriel.

As families required greater privacy, separate rooms were added at the dais end, sometimes on two floors. Early furniture was portable: trestles and loose boards were used for sitting, eating, sleeping and storing food and utensils, but permanent 'joined' furniture was developed for use in the private quarters.

After 1270, when the last Henry de Merk died without an heir, his widow Juliana married again. Henry's mother retained the house and died six years later. The manor should then have passed to Henry's uncle Andrew de Merk and his son Thomas but a dispute occurred. By this time, Juliana had married yet again and her third husband, Elias of Colchester, claimed part of her property in Marks Tey and Latton. Elias Fitz John was a prominent citizen of Colchester, sixteen times an MP and warden of the ancient leper hospital which had been founded by Eudo the Steward. His claim to some of his wife's property succeeded and Thomas de Merk received only part of Mark Hall which he sold in 1309.

The beginning of the fourteenth century was marked by cold temperatures and a series of bad harvests that brought widespread ruin and starvation to a country almost entirely dependent on agriculture. Even wealthy Abbeys fell into debt and were forced to sell off some of their land for cash or payment in kind when their tenants could no longer provide enough food and wool to support the establishment.

The purchaser of Thomas de Merk's part of Mark Hall manor was the third son of a man who had the means to profit from the new availability of land. Nicholas de Seagrave, the first Lord Seagrave, who married Matilda de Lucy in 1255, was born into a wealthy and well-connected family

based in Seagrave in Leicestershire. As well as serving the king in various capacities, Nicholas ran a very profitable business that included selling fine Irish wool to Italian merchants. During the depression he increased his land-holdings by striking bargains with landowners who had received advance payments for goods they could not provide.

Nicholas Seagrave and Matilda had five sons and at least one daughter. His Seagrave eldest son, another Nicholas, was appointed custodian of Northampton Castle and Marshal of England by the new king Edward II in 1308, the year before his younger brother Henry (1260-1318) bought Thomas de Merk's section of Mark Hall. By this time the Seagraves held land in at least five counties. The outlay on Mark Hall would have been a very minor item among the Seagrave family's investments.

In 1317, when Thomas de Merk died and Augustine le Waleys bought both parts of Mark Hall manor from Juliana and Elias of Colchester and from Henry de Seagrave, the manor's connection with the de Merk family finally ended.

Peter de Valognes & Descendants. Overlords of Latton Hall 1086-c.1280

By 1086 Overlord – Peter de Valognes. Tenant of Latton Hall manor – Turgis. Peter de Valognes' manors in Essex include Sheering, Latton, Great and Little Parndon, North Weald Bassett, Leyton, Higham, Loughton, Billington, Binsley and Theydon. c.1100 Roger de Valognes, Peter's son, is the next named overlord of Latton Hall.	c.1200 Gunnora de Valognes, great granddaughter of Peter de Valognes, marries Robert Fitzwalter of Roydon. 1235 The overlordship of Latton Hall falls to Isabel de Valognes, wife of David Comyn. 1277 Isabel Comyn's son William, Lord of Kilbride & Lanark, holds the overlordship of Latton Hall. 1283 William Comyn dies.

Valognes

Before the Conquest the Valognes family held land in the Cherbourg peninsular. The little market town of Valognes, once known as the Versailles of Normandy, was virtually destroyed during the Normandy landings in June 1944.

Peter de Valognes married Albreda, sister of Eudo Dapifer, sometimes called Eudo FitzHubert, a powerful knight whose main castle was at Preaux near Valognes. Eudo held the post of Steward to William I, William Rufus and Henry I and was responsible for the building of Colchester Castle on the site of the great Roman Temple. In 1086 he was awarded land in five English counties including a very small manor in the part of Harlow parish later known as Brent or Burnt Hall and now New Hall.

Eudo the Steward

Soon after the Conquest, Peter de Valognes took possession of Benington Lordship[1] in Hertfordshire which had doubled in value by 1086 (£6 to £12). This eventually became the family home and their most important property. It is about seven miles north of Hertford Castle where Peter was appointed as the first Governor. William I also awarded him seventeen other manors in Hertfordshire, eleven in Essex, several in Norfolk, one in Cambridgeshire, and one in Lincolnshire.

In the Domesday Book Peter de Valognes is described as

The moat at Benington Lordship

Sheriff of Essex and of Hertfordshire. In the list of Sheriffs[2] his name appears in the reign of Henry I (1100-1135) after Geoffrey de Mandeville. This proves that, unlike Eustace de Boulogne, he remained in England and took an interest in his property here. He may even have visited Latton and stayed a day or two with his tenant, Turgis. Kings, overlords and tenants who held more than one manor spent their lives riding with their attendants from one property to another, consuming the rent from their farms which was usually paid in kind. It was not until the seventeenth century that most great landowners began to limit their homes to one country mansion, one town house and a few shooting lodges.

After the death of Henry I in 1135, Peter's son Roger de Valognes sided with Stephen in the long struggle to determine the Succession. He enlarged and fortified his castle at Benington but when Henry II finally claimed the throne in 1154 he had Benington castle demolished *'with 100 picks'*.

Roger had six sons and one daughter and his descendants intermarried with other powerful

---

[1] The ruins of Benington Castle still exist in Benington Lordship gardens (four miles east of Stevenage) and are sometimes open to the public.
[2] Compiled c.1850 by Sherwood, Gilbert and Piper.

Norman families and held high positions both in England and in Scotland.

Early in the thirteenth century the Valognes family was again involved in confrontation with a king. Roger's granddaughter Gunnera's second husband was Robert Fitzwalter of Roydon and Little Dunmow. When King John appointed Richard de Mountfitchet as Governor of Hertford Castle, Fitzwalter claimed that the position of governor was his by right of heredity through his wife and seized the castle by force. The king's troops drove him out but, having asserted his authority, King John then appointed Fitzwalter as Warden. Their relationship deteriorated again and in 1213 Fitzwalter fled to France while John had Benington Castle demolished for the second time in its history. Two years later Robert Fitzwalter led the barons who forced John to sign Magna Carta.

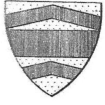

Fitzwalter

By the end of the thirteenth century the concept of the tenants of Latton Hall owing service to overlords had almost disappeared and the Bibbesworth family became the virtual owners.

Hertford Castle

18

Turgis and the de Taney family. Tenants of Latton Hall 1086- c.1280

Overlord – Peter de Valognes. 1086 Tenant – Turgis. 1184 Ralph de Latton is first mentioned as 'tenant in demesne of Latton Hall holding a knight's fee'. 1236 Latton Hall is tenanted by William Fitz-Richard. 1246 Latton Hall is inherited by William's daughter Margaret, married to Sir Richard de Taney.	1250 Richard, Peter & Walter de Taney witness a deed from Richard Gernon concerning Latton Priory. 1253 Richard de Taney is licensed to cut timber in his own woods. 1270 Richard de Taney dies. Son Richard succeeds at Latton Hall. c.1280 The de Taney estates are all sold to Hugh de Bibbesworth.

Turgis, the tenant of Latton Hall manor appointed by Peter de Valognes, was also chosen by Eudo the Steward, Peter's brother-in-law, to manage his small manor in the parish of Harlow. Probably the area now known as New Hall, this estate seems to have lost five of its seven labourers and two of its three ploughs in the years after the Conquest and could not have been farmed on its own. Latton Hall manor had also lost four of its nine farm workers but the 'worth' of both manors, the basis of their taxable value, was left unchanged at forty shillings and sixty shillings.

Tomb of Sir Richard de Taney 1270
St Botolph's Church, Eastwick

Turgis may well have been the great grandfather of 'Ralph of Latton' who was 'holding a knight's fee' for Latton Hall a century later in 1184. Ralph's successors had become the effective owners of the Hall by 1246 when it passed, after the death of 'William' (no surname), to his daughter Margaret, the wife of Sir Richard de Taney.

The de Taney or Thaney family came into possession of Eastwick and other Essex properties soon after the Conquest and held them for more than two hundred years.

Sir Richard was the son of Sir Peter de Taney who had been Sheriff of Essex and Hertfordshire and Governor of Hertford Castle from 1235 until 1241. Twenty years later Sir Richard became Sheriff after Richard Gernon (later Mountfitchet) and they both joined the Barons' Revolt led by Simon de Montfort. Their lands were forfeited to Henry III but soon restored and shortly before his death Sir Richard de Taney was made Governor of Hadley Castle. Further proof of royal favour enjoyed by his son, another Richard, was provided when his claim to free warren and the right to run an annual three day fair in Hertford was accepted.

The exact date when Richard de Taney sold Latton Hall to Walter Bibbesworth is not known but by 1280 it was not Walter but Hugh Bibbesworth, probably a nephew, who completed the purchase.

The de Taney family ceased to be lords of the manor of Eastwick after 1330.

4
The Bibbesworth Family of Latton Hall c.1277- c.1488

c.1277 Latton Hall passes from Richard de Taney to Sir Walter Bibbesworth, favourite of Denise de Munchensi.	1449 John de Bibbesworth of Latton Hall dies leaving son Thomas aged three.
c.1280 Walter Bibbesworth dies. The de Taney estates all pass to Hugh de Bibbesworth.	Inquisition at Ware into the Bibbesworth inheritance led by John Skrene.
1346 John de Bibbesworth is at Latton Hall.	1466 Goditha Bibbesworth dies.
1361 John de Bibbesworth dies at Latton Hall. Succeeded by his son Hugh.	By 1485 Latton Hall is in a ruinous state.
1402 Edmund and Goditha de Bibbesworth are probably living at Latton Hall.	1485 Thomas Bibbesworth dies with no direct heirs.
John Bibbesworth, son of Edmund and Goditha, marries Joan.	1486 Latton Hall is conveyed to Richard Harper.

See Chronology pages 150-54

Bibbesworth

Described in the Dictionary of National Biography as an Anglo-Norman poet, Walter Bibbesworth was a knight from the small manor of Bibbesworth in Kimpton or Kempton, Hertfordshire. The family also owned South House in Great Waltham near Chelmsford. Walter seems to have acquired Latton Hall from the de Taney family by 1277.

Born some time before 1219 Walter won royal favour at a time when relations between Henry III and his barons were becoming increasingly strained. In the company of Nicholas de Moles, a knight of the royal household, he served with the king's forces in Gascony which Henry was defending against attacks by Alfonso of Castile. In 1235 Walter was acting as attorney for the Earl of Hereford and in 1248 he received his knighthood. In that same year his name appears as a member of the jury in two grand assize courts.

In 1254, having antagonised the English barons by repudiating Magna Carta and reafforesting large areas of land formerly exempted from the forestry laws, Henry III found himself desperately short of the means to carry on his wars on the Continent. In order to levy more funds and men willing to bear arms he demanded that the leading clergy and all the sheriffs should organise the election of representatives from every county to attend a parliament, bringing detailed information of the contribution their county could raise. In spite of the king's promise to comply with the provisions of Magna Carta in return for support, there was no enthusiasm to be among the elected few. Sir Walter Bibbesworth was chosen but was exempted and the sheriff of Essex was directed to choose another knight since Bibbesworth was *'keeping the King's forest in his county'*. In 1253 Walter had been permitted to hunt foxes and cats in the forest of Essex and was exempted from holding any of the major offices, including that of sheriff.

If Walter Bibbesworth had merely been a loyal servant of an unpopular king his name would have been completely forgotten. It is as a prolific poet and author, some of whose work has survived, that he is remembered. One poem, dedicated to his friend Henry de Lacy, Earl of Lincoln (1249-1312), is concerned with the Eighth Crusade which Bibbesworth may have joined in 1270. In his book *'Chasing the Sun'*, concerned with the evolution of dictionaries, Jonathon Green writes. *'De Lacy was poised to depart on a Crusade, but was torn between his religious duties and his affections for a certain lady. So great were the latter that he was loath to depart for the Holy Land. Bibbesworth, pressing the moral strictures of one whose own emotions were not at stake, urges him to go.'*

Perhaps Bibbesworth's best known work is the *'Tretiz'*, thought to have been written in the 1240s. This work was dedicated to Dionysia or Denise or Joanna de Munchensi (c.1230 - after 1307), the daughter and sole heir of Nicholas of Anstey in Hertfordshire. Her second husband was Warin de Munchensi, the Earl of Pembroke, who died in 1255 leaving Denise with considerable wealth, several step-children and two children of her own. In 1260 she married yet again. Her third husband was Robert or Richard Butyller who died in 1272.

The *Tretiz* takes the form of rhyming couplets and triplets in Norman French describing domestic and farming activities, with English words in the margin. Apparently this was designed to help the children of noblemen, including the offspring of 'his mistress' Denise de Munchensi, to become familiar with rural vocabulary in both languages. The entire work that survives in sixteen manuscripts consists of '1134 rhyming octosyllables'. One section concerns the sounds made by a variety of birds and animals as represented in Norman French and Middle English:

Norman French	Middle English	Modern translation
Columbe gerist e coke chaunte	*croukes*	*Dove coos and cock crows,*
Vache mugist, gruue groule	*cow lowes crane crekez*	*Cow lows, crane cries,*
Leoun rougist, coudre croule	*romies hasil quakez*	*Lion roars, the hazel-tree quakes,*
Chivaule henist, alouwe chaunte	*neyez larke*	*Horse neighs, lark sings,*
Chate mimoune, cerpent cifle	*mewith cisses*	*Cat miaows, snake hisses,*
Asne rezane, cine recifle	*roreth suan cisses*	*Donkey brays, swan whistles,*
Louwe oule, chein baie	*wolfe yollez berkes*	*Wolf howls, dog barks*
E home e beste sovent afraye	*fereth*	*And often frightens man and beast*

Thirteenth century scribe

Walter Bibbesworth would have been nearly sixty when he bought or rented Latton Hall, and it is probable that he died before 1280, passing the Hall on to Hugh Bibbesworth, possibly a nephew. The place of Walter Bibbesworth's death is uncertain but he is thought to have been buried at Little Dunmow.

Information is also scanty concerning the eight generations of the Bibbesworth family who apparently owned Latton Hall through the fourteenth and fifteenth centuries. By 1303 the Latton Hall manor had been divided between Latton Priory and Hugh Bibbesworth, who is recorded as paying 'half a knight's fee' for his portion. In 1346 the same fee was paid by Hugh's son John who died in 1361. In 1402 Edmund de Bibbesworth was probably living at Latton Hall married to Goditha who outlived him and their son John who died in 1449. It is recorded that Stephen Bugge *'held under John Bibbesworth 1 acre of land with a messuage in Latton by the device of paying yearly one Flaggon of oyl for maintaining a lamp before the image of the Virgin Mary in the chapel of the church of Latton'.*[1]

John and his wife Joan left only one surviving son, Thomas aged three. This necessitated an 'inquisition' into the inheritance of Latton manor which was conducted by John Skrene, 'the King's escheater,' who happened to be the first husband of Elizabeth Arderne of Mark Hall.

From the evidence of Sir Peter Arderne's will it seems that little Thomas Bibbesworth became his ward after the death of both parents and may possibly have been brought up at Mark Hall. In 1476 Thomas acts as one of ten witnesses to a grant of land by Sir Brian Rouclyffe to provide a stipend for Master Richard Haddilsey, perpetual chaplain of the Chantry of Sir Peter Arderne.

In 1485 when Thomas Bibbesworth died, leaving no direct heir, two cousins, Joan Barley, wife of Thomas Barley of Bibbesworth *'of the Warwickshire gentry'* and John Cotes, were the nearest relatives.

At this time the property under discussion consisted of *'One half of the manor of Latton Hall and 10 messuages, 1 mill, 100 acres land, 40 acres meadow, 12 acres pasture and 40 acres woods in Latton, Essex.'* This was first apportioned to John Cotes but after a 'recovery' Cotes conveyed it to Richard Harper, the second husband of Elizabeth Arderne of Mark Hall who was a receiver for Henry, Duke of Buckingham.[2] This transaction seems to have aroused controversy which led to another court case in 1548 when a grandson of Joan Bibbesworth disputed the Harper's right to the property.

As it is described as being *'in a ruinous state'* by 1485, it seems that Latton Hall may have been empty for many years. John's widowed mother Goditha could have moved back to the family home in Hertfordshire before her death in 1466.

---

[1] From the Holman MS in Colchester Castle quoted by John Fisher in *The Deanery of Harlow.*
[2] At this time Humphrey, Duke of Buckingham, held the half hundred of Harlow of the late king Henry VI.

5
The le Waleys family
Owners of Mark Hall 1317-1363

By 1317 Thomas de Merk has died. Augustine and Maud le Waleys become the owners.	1353/4 Augustine le Waleys dies, survived by his widow Maud (1290-1355). Maud le Waleys dies. Mark Hall manor is divided between two daughters.

See Chronology pages 150-51

Augustine was the son of Henry le Waleys who had moved to London from Chepstow as a young man. Henry had begun to trade in cloth and imported hides, but it was as a dealer in wine that he had made his fortune and attracted royal favour. Like Walter Bibbesworth he was granted the privilege for life of <u>not</u> being made sheriff against his will. By the end of the century he had become *'one of the leading figures in the government of London'*[1], exerting strict control over standards in the production of food, clamping down on strangers, fornicators and curfew breakers and setting up trusts to build or repair houses, markets and bridges. His interference with traditional rights and customs made him unpopular with many citizens of London but King Edward I frequently made use of his services, both in England and abroad and he dominated City life for quarter of a century. He held the position of Lord Mayor from 1273-4, 1280-1284 and 1298-1299, three years before his death.

It is impossible to gain any conception of the status of most of the owners of Mark Hall from the thirteenth century onwards without appreciating the central importance of the London guilds – usually described as the Livery Companies of the City of London. The City was – and is – unique in its peculiar form of government which is entirely based on a network of ancient Companies.

The story of the City's independent status begins in pre-Roman times with a thriving market conveniently situated for both home products and foreign imports. The Romans improved its accessibility and security and its prosperity rapidly increased.

Rather surprisingly, the guilds did not originate as unions of men practising the same craft, but as 'fraternities' – groups of neighbours who enjoyed each other's company and chose to celebrate special occasions and religious festivals together. As the only large rooms available were usually connected with the church, the fraternities developed close links with their local priests or monks, and adopted the local saint as their protector. The fact that almost all the old hospitals and many famous schools were founded by one of the guilds is explained by their origin, as is the central importance of banqueting and ritual. The significance of 'liveries', the brightly coloured robes and hoods worn by members on special occasions, was established in the fourteenth century.

Each guild became connected with a specific trade because the craftsmen who sought their fortune in the City preferred to set up their workshops near families in the same trade with similar needs and problems. Gradually, the business of satisfying those needs and solving the problems became the main purpose of the local fraternity but the social and religious functions survived, transferred to a large number of splendid halls. The fact that the promotion of a particular craft was not the original purpose of the guilds explains the fact that a businessman's guild does not necessarily define his occupation. Membership can be passed by 'patrimony' from father to son and defines social status rather than profession.

Membership of a livery company carries with it the right to vote annually in one of the City wards for members of the Common Council and for the two Sheriffs. Aldermen are chosen for life from the Council and the Lord Mayor is usually the longest serving Alderman.

Apart from owing a duty of allegiance to the reigning monarch, the Lord Mayor is completely independent, ranks next to the Queen in precedence and must be consulted if the monarch or her troops wish to enter the City.

Henry le Waleys made many enemies through his close cooperation with the king and, after the powers of the City had been seized by Edward II and then returned, it was decided that no Lord Mayor should retain that office for more than one year, though he might return after an interval.

---

[1] Dictionary of National Biography.

Augustine was Henry's only surviving son and the inheritor of most of his huge fortune except for large donations to the City's Franciscans and other mendicant orders.

The gift for money-making was definitely passed on from father to son in the le Waleys family. Like Henry de Seagrave, from whom he had bought Mark Hall, Augustine acquired land from owners in difficulties and, like his father, combined a lucrative government post with profitable trade.

Augustine's wife Maud or Margaret Conduit of Rothing[1] was probably the more enterprising of the two. Born about 1290 in Roding Saint Margaret, Essex, Maud's first partner was John de Shaddeworth by whom she had a daughter Idonea. Shaddeworth died in 1313 and, before marrying Augustine le Waleys c.1320, Maud had an illegitimate son John. After their marriage the le Waleys had two daughters Margery and Margaret. Wealthy spinsters and widows, unlike married women, could hold property in their own right and Maud made the most of this. She seems to have avoided marriage while living with Shaddeworth, made sure her name was associated with her husband's after 1320, and carried on managing her own affairs as a widow after Augustine's death. Throughout her life she accumulated property and fought repeated legal battles to retain it.

Having bought Mark Hall manor in 1317, when land prices were still depressed, Augustine and Maud would have ridden out from their home in Cornhill in the City and realised the potential of some of their land in the south of Latton parish as a fairground and market, if harvests and commerce should improve. As Henry le Waleys' son, the new squire would also have known all about the restrictive laws that prevented unlicensed trade but as 'Keeper of the Exchange' he had the ear of Edward III and understood how to present his case successfully. In 1332 the King granted his request for a charter for an annual fair in August, during the Feast of John the Baptist, the patron saint of Latton Priory. 'Bush Fair', as it became known, was set up to the south of Commonside Road near the woods known as Mark Bushes. Its existence stimulated trade and it soon developed into an important cattle and horse fair.

Bush Fair
Detail from 1616 map

Another important local product traded at the fair was pottery. There is evidence of Roman kilns in the Harlow area and, by the fourteenth century, domestic ware produced in Harlow and Latton was already finding a market in London. Bush Fair provided a valuable outlet and the industry expanded, reaching its peak in the seventeenth century. The importance to potters of displaying their products at the fair is shown in a clause in the will of John Wright, a Latton potter, written in 1636.

> *'I further give and bequeath to the said George or his assigns all my Bush Fayre stuff that is to say my poles, stretchers, Boardes plankes forms and one legg dormams and tressels whatsoever..'* [2]

The rents or 'tolls' paid by traders at Bush Fair were still being paid to the owners of Mark Hall five centuries later and may partially explain the attraction of the little manor to wealthy landowners.

Throughout the fourteenth and early fifteenth centuries, when Mark Hall changed hands several times, we have no idea whether the manor house was occupied or left empty. Bubonic plague,

---

[1] See Jack William, *Maud de Rothing c 1290-1355: a woman of means and ways.* Transactions of the London & Middlesex Archaeological Society, vol. 52. 2002.
[2] Quoted in Wally Davey's *Harlow Pottery Industries.* 2009.

'the Black Death,' which arrived from the Crimea in 1346 and wiped out a third of the population of England by 1350, had less effect in the sparsely populated countryside than in London. City merchants often moved their families out to healthier country estates but there is no evidence that the le Waleys chose Latton among their numerous properties. The dates 1348 and 1666 are often cited as marking the onset of plague epidemics in England but contemporary documents prove that there were frequent local outbreaks of 'the pestilence' in every century, though the exact nature of the fatal illness is not always clear.

Augustine le Waleys died in 1353 and was buried in Holy Trinity, Christchurch. By that time the family owned property in five counties as well as in six parishes in the City and one in the suburbs. Maud died two years later and the complications arising from the two separate and slightly differing testaments in which she stated her wishes occupied the lawyers for the next seven years.

6
Foxcote, Berlands, Bauds and Rokesburgh
Owners of Mark Hall 1363-1426

Margery le Waleys marries 1) Turk 2) Hunston 3) John Malwayn (d.1361).	Sir William's daughter Elizabeth marries John Baud.
Margaret le Waleys (b.1324) marries 1) William Carlton (d.1356).	They inherit Mark Hall.
2) John de Ludwick (d.1358).	1422 John Baud dies.
3) John de Foxcote.	His widow Elizabeth inherits Mark Hall in a ruinous state.
1363 John de Foxcote and Margaret (le Waleys) inherit Mark Hall.	John and Elizabeth's son William Baud marries Isabel Rokesburgh.
1374 Sir William Berland acquires Mark Hall.	William Baud grants Mark Hall to William Rokesburgh, Isabel's father.
He marries Christian, widow of John Fitz Eustace.	1426 William Rokesburgh conveys Mark Hall to John Tyrell.
two daughters – Joan & Elizabeth.	

See Chronology page 151-52

The Latton property was divided up between the daughters Margery and Margaret le Waleys, both of whom married three times. Margery's third husband, John Malwayn was an alderman from 1357 till 1361, the year of his death.

Margaret's second husband was John de Ludwick, a son of William de Ludwick of Hatfield who had travelled abroad with Aymer de Valence on King Edward II's service and been on a pilgrimage to Santiago. A complaint was made against him and his two sons John and Thomas in 1348 by Stephen de Bassingbourne who alleged that they *'broke into his close and house in Bishop's Hatfield, entered his free warren, carried away his goods and hares, rabbits, pheasants and partridges and assaulted his servant'*. John was presumably a reformed character later on as he became an MP in 1353, 54 and 57, the year before his death.

Although she was married three times, it seems that Margaret née le Waleys had no children. Her second husband John de Ludwick survived only two years after the wedding and though John de Foxcote, her third choice, became the guardian of a Richard Cavendish (son of a 'late draper') in 1365, he left no heirs. When the confusion caused by her mother's wills was finally sorted out, Margaret inherited Mark Hall and she and John de Foxcote held it for eleven years. Then, in 1374, it was sold to Sir William Berland and his wife Christian.

During the next fifty years the Hall passed by marriage through three families though it is very doubtful whether any of the owners lived there. Sir William Berland, who had become an MP in 1364, held land in several counties. In the 1380s he was residing in Prittlewell near Southend.

The second half of the fourteenth century was a period of unrest in Europe at every level of society. The shortage of labour caused by the 'Black Death' had enabled workers in many areas to demand more pay and more freedom, demands that were countered in England by an effort to freeze wages under a Statute of Labourers. This attempt, followed by the death of Edward III without an adult heir, the election of two rival popes and the imposition of the first poll tax, led to political and religious confusion and a widespread explosion of popular anger. The 'Peasants' Revolt', as it came to be called, though the participants included many craftsmen and men of some status, began in Essex and Suffolk and spread to Norfolk, Kent, Hertfordshire and Cambridgeshire. It is usually described as a march on London, led by Wat Tyler, but in many manors the attacks were concentrated on unpopular local lords and on buildings where court rolls were kept.

Judging by the number of Harlow citizens who were later indicted for taking part in the revolt, it seems that there were some very unpopular landlords in this area. Kitchen Hall was attacked and some of the manorial records were destroyed there and at Harlowbury. Dr Herbert Eiden has discovered the names of more than thirty men from Harlow, one from Latton and one from Netteswell, who were summoned to court. Some of the charges concerned attacks on a manor in North Weald belonging to Joan of Kent and others alleged attacks on property in London. William Ermyte of

Latton was apparently involved both in North Weald and London but John Sporyer (Spurrier?) junior of Netteswell only got as far as North Weald. It was interesting to discover that five of the surnames listed by Dr Eiden appear again in Wally Davey's long list of potters[1] who were working in the Harlow and Latton area through succeeding centuries. The modern versions of their names are: Taylor (1383 and 1391), Lock (before 1431), Clarke (1431), Fletcher (1618) and Baker (1674). John Tailleur, who lived and ran his pottery with his son Thomas in Foster Street in 1383, could have been the same man who had joined the Revolt two years earlier. Many potters were relatively prosperous citizens and by no means downtrodden peasants.

The Peasants' Revolt

No mention has been discovered of any attack on Mark Hall which may have been unoccupied at the time. We know that Sir William Berland of Mark Hall was in Prittlewell because his name was recorded in a case heard at Rochford, an interesting example of an attempt to involve some of the lords themselves in the rebellion. Dr Eiden writes: *'According to this indictment John Chandeler of Prittlewell tried to induce Sir William Berland and John Prittlewell senior to join the rebels in the early stages of the rising.'* The squires were not persuaded but they obviously failed to prevent Chandeler and his friends from fermenting the uprising. In his book on the history of North Weald, Stan Newens mentions a Richard Ballard who *'was involved in burning two bags containing records belonging to the Countess of Hereford at Little Wakering'*, a village near Prittlewell.

The revolt was short lived and petered out after the death of Wat Tyler but it had lasting effects. Apart from sporadic incidents of renewed violence and the disappearance of a great number of records all over the south east, 1381 proved the impossibility of maintaining the old feudal domination of lords of the manor. Service to the lord was increasingly commuted to cash payments and villeinage gradually withered away.

On 13 September 1383 Sir William Berland signed his will[2] leaving property including *'the vills of Prittlewell, Milton, Southchurch, Leigh Ashingdon, Goldhanger and Fambridge'* to Christian his wife and Joan and Elizabeth his daughters, administered by *'feoffees'* (trustees).
'They (Joan and Elizabeth) *should be married before the age of 15 or, if one or the other or both decide to be a nun or nuns by their free will and without compulsion I wish that she or they should have aid from the aforesaid lands after they are sold.'*

Elizabeth Berland apparently preferred matrimony to life in a convent and married John Baud of Hadham Hall.

The Baud Family

Baud

In 1076 William, Bishop of London, owned Hadham manor. When the Bishop died William I granted it to William le Baud of Normandy who had fought beside him in 1066. It was this William le Baud who built the first Hadham Hall. The family retained the goodwill of the king and in 1316 there was a crown grant by charter to William le Baud and his heirs forever of a market twice each week *'on Tuesday and Friday at his manor of Coryngham (in the parish of Storteford) and a fair each year for three days 20-22 September the day and the morrow of St Matthew the Apostle. Also a grant of free warren in all his demesne lands in Corringham provided that those lands are not within the bounds of the forest, so that none shall enter them to hunt or take anything pertaining to the warren without licence of William or his heirs, under penalty of £10.'*

The Baud family tree is very difficult to trace correctly because of their addiction to the names William and John.

In 1338 Sir William le Baud was mentioned holding land in Grantchester where John le Baud (brother or son?) was rector. In 1373 a William Baud is named as an MP and it was his son, another

[1] Herbert Eiden. *The Peasants' Revolt in Essex and Norfolk* Journal of the Historical Association. Vol. 83. 1998.
[2] Berland's will is quoted in *Women of the English nobility & Gentry 1066-1500* 1995 by Jennifer Ward. Manchester University.

John, who married Elizabeth Berland. By this time the family seems to have acquired Stortford, Stanstead Abbots and Great Parndon as well as Hadham and Mark Hall. It was probably during John's time as lord of the manor that some attention was paid to the state of the local roads. In 1404 and 1407 a certain Robert Webbe, with Grantchester connections, was among a group of men granted *'pavage for 3 years, in aid of paving the ways called "Tornohills" and "Newestrete" in Latton, North Weald and Harlow"*[1]. After John's death in 1422 the parish of Stortford was granted to 'Thomas Baud senior'.

John and Elizabeth Baud's son, another William, married Isabel Rokesburgh, a daughter of William Rokesburgh of Berwick near Standon and Elizabeth Fitz-Eustace. William Rokesburgh was MP for Hertfordshire in 1421 and escheator of Essex in 1430. He died in 1434, having lived in Great Parndon in later life.

In the tower of Stanstead Abbots church *'carelessly thrown amongst a number of hatchments'*,[2] lies the old window bearing the arms of Baud and Rokesburgh – removed in 1866 to make room for a new window.

By the 1420s Mark Hall was in a ruinous state and changed hands very quickly. John Baud's widow, Elizabeth, passed it on to her son who immediately granted it to his father-in-law William Rokesburgh. By 1426 it had become the property of John Tyrell.

Lady Alice Tyrell. Memorial in the Church of All Saints, East Horndon

---

[1] Market Privileges 1401-1410 URL 2006.
[2] J.J. Cussons Hist. of Herts. Vol. 1

Tyrell Family Tree

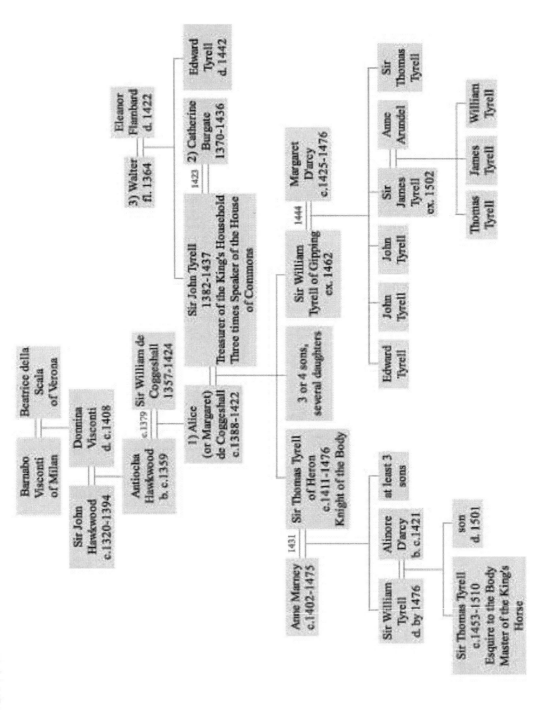

7
The Tyrell Family
Owners of Mark Hall 1426-1446

1426 William Rokesburgh conveys Mark Hall to John Tyrell. 1437 John Tyrell dies. His trustees name his brother, Edward Tyrell, as his successor.	1446 John Tyrell's son Sir Thomas quitclaims Mark Hall to Sir Peter Arderne.

See Chronology page 152

Tyrell

The fact that Mark Hall was described as being 'in a ruinous state' by 1422 suggests that it had either been left empty for years or was occupied by tenants who had no funds to keep it in repair while a succession of landlords ignored it. When John Baud's son passed it on to William Rokesburgh it was probably of very little value and was soon disposed of to another very wealthy landowner. Sir John Tyrell (c.1382-1437) who added Mark Hall manor to his extensive land holdings in 1426, was a member of an enormous Anglo Norman Irish family. His ancestor Sir Walter Tyrell (1) came to England from Picardy where he owned several estates. He fought at Hastings beside the Conqueror who chose him as one of seven commissioners for the county of Essex, a group that included a Baron Coggeshall.

Walter Tyrell (1) died in 1080 and it was his grandson Walter Tyrell (3) whose name appears in Domesday as the holder of Langham in Essex. This manor, which had previously belonged to *'Fin the Dane,'* was very small. The first Tyrell had apparently been granted other estates including Kingsworthy in Somerset though by 1086 this is described as owned *'by the King himself'*.

Sir John Hawkwood

According to one of many varying accounts, it was Walter Tyrell (3), a friend of William Rufus, who accidentally killed the king with a misplaced arrow when they were out hunting together in the New Forest on 2 August 1100.

By 1369 the Tyrells had acquired the manor of Heron in East Horndon which later became their main family seat.

Sir John Tyrell's first wife Alice, daughter and co-heir of Sir William de Coggeshall, had a much closer connection with a relation who killed, not by accident, but for a living. Her maternal grandfather was the notorious mercenary Sir John Hawkwood (c.1320-1394) who had joined the English army fighting in France in the 1340s and spent the rest of his life offering the services of his highly efficient company to any duke, king or pope who was prepared to pay him.

Geoffrey Chaucer, who had dealings with the adventurer while on a diplomatic mission in Lombardy, is said to have modelled his ironic *Knight's Tale* on Hawkwood.

Like the famous mercenary, Sir William Coggeshall had also set out as a young knight to seek his fortune on the Continent. He met Sir John Hawkwood in Italy and married his eldest daughter Antiocha before 1380. William brought his bride back to England to reclaim his Essex estate but Hawkwood decided to remain in Italy where he had acquired several castles. His employer at this time was Barnabo Visconti of Milan who had provided him with Donnina, one of his ten daughters, as a second wife. Soon after this marriage Hawkwood transferred his allegiance from Milan to Florence where he died naturally, aged seventy-three, after another decade of fighting. He has fine monuments both in Florence Cathedral (as Giovanni Achud) and in the church at Sible Hedingham in north-west Essex where he was born.

By 1411 William and Antiocha Coggeshall's daughter Alice had married John Tyrell who was later to become one of the richest landowners in Essex. She brought him Broomfield as her dowry to add to his manor of Heron and bore him five or six sons and probably as many daughters before her death in 1422.

Sir John Tyrell then remarried, choosing Catherine Burgate of Suffolk, another wealthy heiress, who had already been twice widowed, and they eventually owned estates in Cambridgeshire, Hampshire and Suffolk as well as his Essex home in East Horndon. Why he acquired Mark Hall in 1426 has yet to be explained.

John Tyrell provided valuable service for both the house of Lancaster and of York. Under the Lancastrian kings he fought at Agincourt with Humphrey, Duke of Gloucester who assisted him to appointments both as the duke of York's receiver-general and chief steward of the Duchy of Lancaster. In 1431 he was knighted and made treasurer of young King Henry VI's household. He sat in parliament twelve times, usually for Essex but once for Hertfordshire, and was chosen as Speaker three times, an office which he resigned two weeks before his death in 1437. Rather surprisingly, he left the major part of his property to his younger brother Edward and it was not until Edward died in 1442 that Thomas, John's eldest son, inherited a number of manors including Latton.

The fortunes of some of Sir John's sons and grandsons in the fifteenth century suggest that Sir John Hawkwood bequeathed his liking for violent action but not his unfailing good luck to his Tyrell descendants. Thomas Tyrell (c.1411-1476) and his brother William of Gipping both supported the reigning Lancastrian monarch Henry VI. Thomas was first appointed Sheriff of Essex in 1440 and MP for Essex in 1442, two posts which he held at intervals until 1459. During this period he sold Mark Hall to Sir Peter Arderne who became Chief Baron of the Exchequer in 1448. In 1450 Thomas was on active service for Henry VI in France, leading the siege of Lisieux and accepting the surrender of Caen. One month later, back in England, he was among the officers sent to arrest Jack Cade, the leader of another dangerous uprising in the south-east against high taxes and corruption.

By 1452 Tyrell had become a Knight of the Household and by 1453 he was on the King's Council. It was Sir Thomas Tyrell who is alleged to have been sent to Richard, Duke of York to deliver the summons to the king's Great Council – the summons that Richard denied receiving. King Henry's phase of insanity that enabled Richard to claim power in 1453 was the immediate cause of civil war. Richard of York was killed in an early battle but his claim to the throne passed down to his son Edward. In 1460, when Henry VI was captured by the Yorkists, Thomas Tyrell managed to survive by escaping from the Tower where he had hoped to withstand Edward's attack on the City. His brother William Tyrell of Gipping was less fortunate. He was executed for treason in 1462, the year after Edward IV was crowned in Westminster Abbey.

Throughout the next decade, while Edward IV struggled with the supporters of Henry VI, Sir Thomas Tyrell seems to have lived peacefully as a country squire with his wife, Anne Marney and their large family that included at least four sons. His name appears repeatedly *'on a commission of the peace for Essex'* but only once in connection with national government. That was in 1473 when he was *'at the mansion of the Keeper of the Rolls in London when he was delivered the Privy Seal by Henry Bourchier, Earl of Essex.'*

Both Anne, Sir Thomas Tyrell's wife, and William, his eldest son, died before him so he was succeeded in 1476 by his grandson, another Thomas, who managed to become *'an esquire of the body'* to both Edward IV and Richard III. This Thomas must have been aware of the rumours that linked his own cousin James, a son of the executed William Tyrell of Gipping, to the disappearance of the princes in the Tower. James was executed in 1502 but Thomas Tyrell (3) managed to retain a position at Court throughout the reign of Henry VII.

Arderne Family Tree

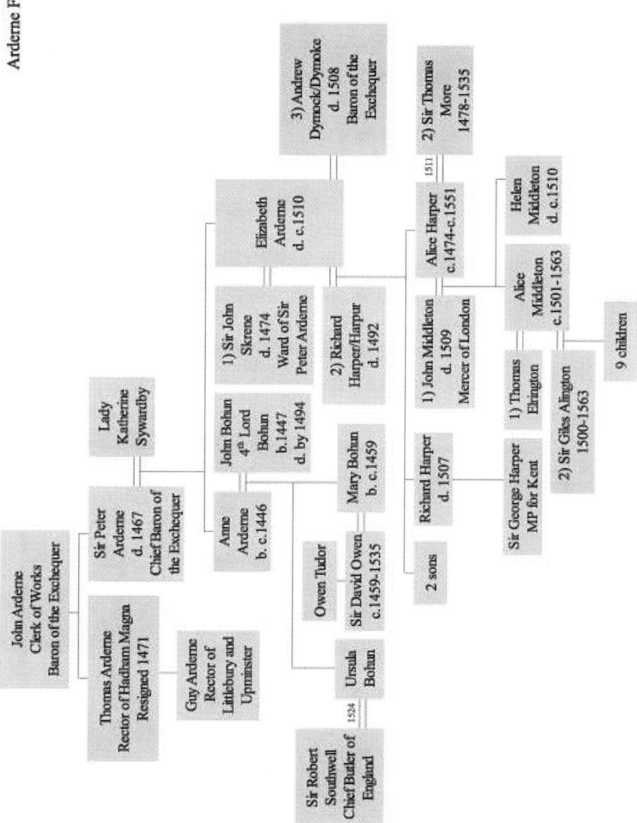

8

Ardernes, Bohuns & Harpers
Owners of Mark Hall and Latton Hall 1446-1548

1446 John Tyrell's son Sir Thomas quitclaims Mark Hall to Sir Peter Arderne and Katherine. Arderne daughters: Elizabeth marries 1) John Skrene 2) Richard Harper 3) Andrew Dymoke Anne marries John Bohun. 1466 Edward IV grants Sir Peter Arderne and his wife Katherine licence to found two chantries for two priests to say mass. 1467 Sir Peter Arderne dies. He leaves Mark Hall to his widow Katherine Arderne and his two married daughters.	1486 Latton Hall is conveyed by John Cotes to Richard Harper, Sir Peter's son-in-law. 1492 Richard Harper dies. Latton Hall passes to his son Richard (d.1507). By 1500 Anne Bohun owns Mark Hall. 1501 Sir John Shaa buys Mark Hall with 220 acres. 1507 Sir George Harper (grandson of Richard and Elizabeth Harper) inherits Latton Hall. 1548 Sir George Harper conveys Latton Hall to John Hethe.

See Chronology pages 152-54

In 1446 Sir Peter Arderne acquired Mark Hall manor and two years later he became Chief Baron of the Exchequer.

Sir Peter and his wife Katherine were probably the first owners to regard Mark Hall as their home. It was almost certainly they who restored the 'ruinous' manor house as well as extending and decorating the church.[1]

In 1465 Sir Peter was made Justice of the Common Pleas by the new king Edward IV, while retaining the post of Chief Baron of the Exchequer. In that same year, in the midst of the young king's struggle to retain the throne, he granted Sir Peter a licence *'to found two chantries for two priests to say mass, one dedicated to the Holy Trinity and St Mary, the other to St Peter and St Katherine in the same church.'*

Two 'perpetual chaplains' were to be appointed *'to celebrate divine service at the altar of St Peter and St Katherine in the same church for the good estate of the King and his consort Elizabeth, Queen of England, and their heirs, and of the said Peter and Katherine his wife, and their souls after death and the souls of the relatives and benefactors of the said Peter and Katherine and all for whom he is bound to pray, to be called the chantries of Peter Arderne, knight'.*

The first chantry was established[2] but it seems probable that the second was never created, possibly because of Sir Peter's death.

Arderne's efforts to extend and beautify his church continued until the last year of his life. In February 1466 he signed his will, appointing his wife 'Katherine Arden' and his brother 'Master Thomas Ardern' and others as his executors. The will is a fascinating indication of the values and preoccupations of a wealthy fifteenth century lawyer. Besides leaving handsome legacies, plate and furniture to his wife, his daughters and other relations, he carefully divides up his library, suiting the content and language of each book to the recipient and often describing the bindings.

Together with a crucifix and *'the furniture of a chapel'* Katherine receives his *'daily primer, his book of*

Sir Peter and Lady Katherine Arderne

---

[1] See *A History of Latton* by Jonathan Edmunds for a detailed description of Peter Arderne's additions to St Mary-at-Latton church.

[2] After the Reformation this chantry was used as a vestry but was restored as a chapel in 1970 when the new vestry was built to the west.

legends in English and his English translation of Bonaventura de vita et passione Christ' [The Life and Passion of Christ]. His daughter Anne inherits a 'mass book' and Elizabeth a book in French. One 'son' [son-in-law] John Bohun, receives armour and a book concerned with hunting and the other, John Skrene, is left volumes of statutes, *'a good boke compiled of Law with a yellow leather covering, a greate book of gramer, with the siege of Troy borded, a greate booke called Catholicon borded, and a good new bounden fair little book compiled of Assises.'*

Then comes an entry indicating Sir Peter's close interest in his *'ward'* Thomas Bibbesworth. The bequest begins: *'To my ward Thomas Bibbesworth his own marriage free to himself, and my best Register of Laws, my own gret compiled booke of Law covered with red leather...'* The books bequeathed to Thomas suggest that, having no son, Sir Peter hoped that Thomas, his neighbour's only son, left an orphan at the age of three and now twenty-one, would follow in his own footsteps and enter the legal profession A niece, Margaret Newport, receives *'a table of ivory with the salutation of our Lady in ymages of silver.'* Various garments including a cloak and a hood are bestowed on close relations. Sir Peter's brother and executor, Thomas Arden, receives a *'scarlet gown furred'* as well as a *Life of St Thomas of Canterbury* and other books.

Embroidery of Lady Katherine Arderne

The will was proved on 10 July 1467. One of the witnesses was John Leventhorpe of Shingle Hall, Sawbridgeworth, a member of the family that was to intermarry with the Althams of Mark Hall in the next century.

Both the Leventhorpe family and the Ardernes have well preserved memorials in the churches where they worshipped. Great St Mary's at Sawbridgeworth contains fine tombs and brasses of generations of Leventhorpes and in St Mary-at-Latton Sir Peter Arderne and Lady Katherine still lie beneath their undamaged brasses beside the chantry that they founded.[1]

Sir Peter also has a memorial in London. In the crypt beneath the buttery of the Inner Temple, the only part of the original building that survives, an angel stands on a bracket over the fireplace holding two coats of arms. One belonged to Sir Peter and the second to Sir Brian Rouclyffe, a relative and one of Sir Peter's executors, who followed Arderne as Chief Baron of the Exchequer in 1467. Ten years later it was he who willed that the rents of a messuage, somewhere in Latton, and the manor of Overall in Gilston were to go towards the stipend of the Latton chantry priest.

The story of Mark Hall and Latton Hall was linked by the Ardernes. Anne married Sir John Bohun and they became the owners of Mark Hall. Elizabeth, the joint heiress, married first John Skrene, the king's escheater, and next Richard Harper, who seems to have bought Latton Hall from Bibbesworth's descendants in 1489, though, according to C.C. Stopes in his book *'Shakespeare's Family'*, Sir Peter Arderne acquired not only Mark Hall but Latton Hall and Bobbingworth Hall near Ongar in 1446.

Alice, the daughter of Elizabeth and Richard Harper, married John Middleton, a wealthy mercer, and after his death she became the second wife of Sir Thomas More, an old friend of the family.[2] More had close connections with the owners of several manors near Mark Hall. John Colt, the father of Jane, More's first wife, owned Little Parndon as well as Nether Hall in Roydon. The church of St Thomas More now celebrates this connection. Moor Hall was owned by Thomas Bugge, More's brother-in-law.

Alice More's nephew Sir George Harper, who became MP for Kent in 1545, inherited Latton Hall and held it for forty years before conveying it to John Hethe, a member of the Guild of Merchant Taylors, in 1548. John Hethe also acquired the Priory in 1556 and then passed both properties on to John Titley who sold them to James Altham.

---

[1] Lady Katherine's maiden name, apparently deduced from the similar coats of arms of Sywardby and Bohun, is uncertain.
   In 1473 she is described in a legal document as widow of Peter Arderne and wife of Sir John Cheyne.
[2] See *In the Shadow of a Saint. Lady Alice More* by Ruth Norrington.

Shaa Family Tree

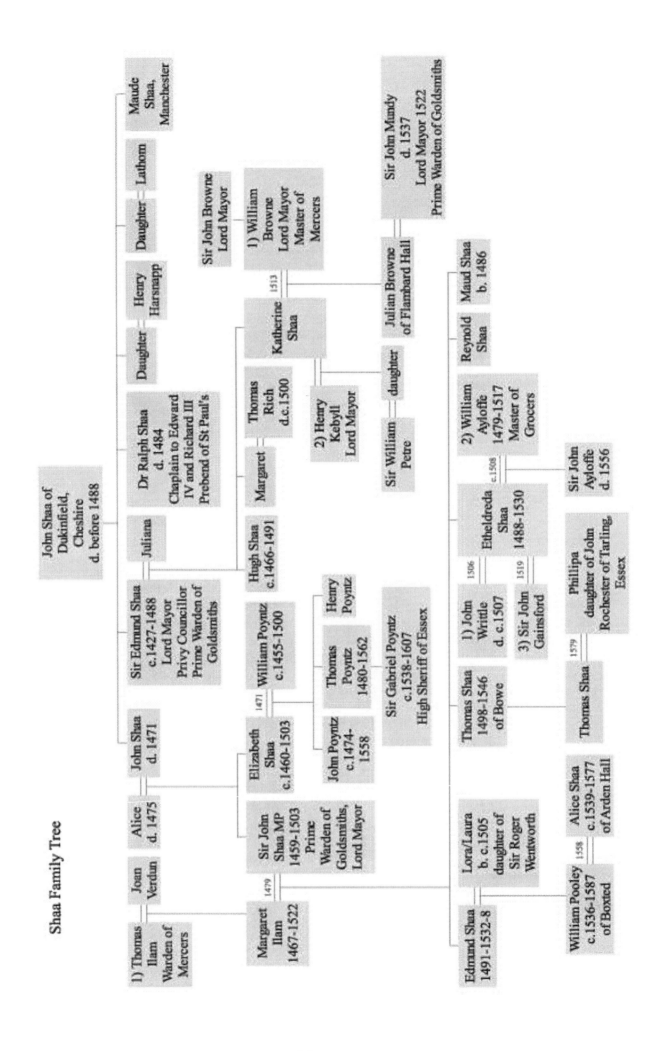

34

9
The Shaa Family
Owners of Mark Hall 1501-1538

1501 Sir John Shaa buys Mark Hall from Ann Bohun. 1503 Edmund Shaa (John's son) inherits Mark Hall.	1521 Henry Parker (Lord Morley) leases Mark Hall from Edmund Shaa for ninety-nine years. 1538 Thomas Shaa sells Mark Hall to Henry Parker.

See Chronology page 155

Shaa

John Shaa, who became the owner of Mark Hall manor in 1501, was a man of great wealth and influence. His uncle Sir Edmund Shaa or Shaw (c.1427–1488) was apprenticed to a goldsmith and by 1462 he had risen so high in that profession that the new king, Edward IV, appointed him *'engraver of the King's dies for all gold and silver money coined in the Tower of London or in England or in Calais.'* This post was granted for life but after twenty years Edmund passed it on to John Shaa whom he always described as 'cousin' but was almost certainly his nephew.

As an alderman of Cripplegate Ward in the City, Edmund would have been a leading member of the 500 city worthies who greeted Edward IV when he returned from fighting in France in 1473. Elected Lord Mayor of London in 1482, Edmund, the eleventh goldsmith to hold that title, continued the lucrative business of supplying the court and the royal family with loans, gold and silver ware and jewellery during the last year of the king's life. When the king died, leaving a twelve-year-old heir, another Edward, the Shaa family grasped every opportunity to profit from the crises that resulted from the determination of Richard, Duke of Gloucester, the late king's brother, to seize the throne from his nephew. As Lord Mayor, Edmund led the cavalcade that greeted young Edward V as he made his way towards the Bishop of London's Palace at St Paul's to await his coronation. Richard, who was popular after successful battles against the Scots, had been named with Buckingham as one of the boy king's Protectors and it was he who decided it would be safer to house the prince in the Tower of London with his nine year old brother Richard to keep him company.

Detail from the painting in the Royal Exchange of Edmund Shaa presenting the crown to Richard III

Both 'Protectors' then set about persuading possible allies, including the Lord Mayor and his brother Dr Ralph Shaa, to support Richard's claim to the throne. On Sunday 22 June 1483, nine days after Richard had fabricated a revolt requiring the immediate execution of Lord Hastings, one of the boy king's staunchest supporters, Dr Ralph Shaa preached his famous sermon at St Paul's Cross based on the biblical text *'Bastard slips shall not take deep root'*. By asserting that, because of a previous betrothal, Edward IV's marriage to Elizabeth Woodville was bigamous, Ralph Shaa set out to convince his audience that their sons were illegitimate and therefore had no claim to the throne. Two days later Edmund Shaa was summoned as Lord Mayor with all the aldermen and commoners of the City to a meeting at the Guildhall where Buckingham repeated Ralph Shaa's proof of Richard's right to the crown. If the Lord Mayor, who was now a Privy Councillor, made no move himself to lead the acclamation that Buckingham demanded, he certainly did nothing to quell it when a group of supporters shouted *'King*

Richard! King Richard!' Taking this as general consent, Buckingham led the way to Baynard's Castle where Richard was 'persuaded' to accept the throne. According to some reports it was Sir Edmund Shaa who presented the crown to King Richard III during the magnificent coronation ceremony in Westminster Hall. Sir Thomas More, relating the story forty years later, maintains that Shaa received his knighthood the day before the coronation. Shaa certainly acted as King's Cupbearer during the coronation banquet. An entry in the City Archives describes the occasion:

> *'After dinner ended the mayor offered to the said lord the King wine in a gold cup with a gold viol full of water to temper the wine. After that the wine was taken by the Lord the King the mayor retained the said cup and viol to his own proper use'.*

Soon after this resplendent occasion both princes disappeared from the Tower. The manner of their disappearance has never been the subject of impartial investigation. Sir Thomas More, a supporter of Henry VII, maintained that Richard despatched Sir James Tyrell (a nephew of Thomas Tyrell of Mark Hall) to arrange their murder and that they were suffocated and buried in the Tower.

Some believe that Buckingham joined the rebellion against Richard partly because of his horror at their murder, while others suggest that he himself was responsible, knowing that the boys would be an obstacle to his own ambition to gain the throne.

Whatever the truth of the matter, Sir Edmund Shaa remained firmly on Richard's side and mustered soldiers from within the Goldsmith's Guild to fight against Buckingham when he joined the southern shires in their rebellion against Richard, the usurper. For the remainder of Richard's brief reign Shaa acted as the king's banker and 'merchant', adding to his own enormous fortune. This he used to buy numerous estates in Essex.

The 'mayor of London' in Shakespeare's Richard III is said to be based on Edmund Shaa.

The power of great wealth is proved by the fact that, when Richard lost his crown and was killed at the battle of Bosworth, Edmund Shaa managed to find favour with his Lancastrian adversary, Henry Tudor. In less than four months Edmund, together with John Shaa, was granted custody of another large Essex estate and a writ for working gold and silver. At the same time Edmund gained the aldermancy of Cheap, filling a vacancy caused by the deaths of a succession of aldermen and mayors from the sweating sickness, a virulent form of malaria.

Sir Edmund's memory is still cherished in Stockport where he founded a free Grammar School which remains in close touch with the Goldsmiths' Company. He died in April 1488. His wife Juliana survived him but their only son Hugh died unmarried in 1491.

John, (who was said to be the son of a brother of Sir Edmund and Dr Ralph, though no clear evidence supports this claim) became even richer than his uncle. He was described as a man *'lytell of stature'* who possessed *'a sharp wit ... and a good and bold spirit by reason of the favour he stood in with the king and queen'.* In 1479 he married Margaret, the daughter of Thomas Ilam.

In 1491 John Shaa became Prime Warden of the Goldsmith's Company, then Joint Master of the Mint, investing most of his increasing fortune in property. In 1493, for example, he bought *'the manor of Old Ford and 14 messuages, 8 tofts, 14 gardens, 240 acres of land, 50 acres meadow, 50 acres pasture, and 2 acres woods in Old Ford, Stepney, Hackney and Stratford-atte-Bow, Middlesex.'* Two years later he was elected MP for the City of London and in 1496 he is described as 'alderman of the City of London' in a will written by William Paston of Norfolk, among a group of 'honourable folk'

St Paul's Cross, a pulpit built outside St Paul's Cathedral, was used from the thirteenth century until its destruction in 1643 as a gathering place for sermons and proclamations of national importance. It was rebuilt in 1910.

entrusted with looking after a faithful servant.

In 1497 John was knighted by Henry VII *'for his service at the battle of Blackheath'.*[1] His London home was *'at the upper end of Wood Street'* and the records suggest that he bought Mark Hall with 220 acres from Anne Bohun in 1501. Why he chose Mark Hall when he already possessed large estates elsewhere in Essex is not clear.

Elected as Lord Mayor of London in 1501, he led the procession that greeted Catherine of Aragon when she arrived from Spain to marry Arthur, Henry VII's eldest son. While Lord Mayor Shaa instituted a private court for the benefit of the poor which became the Court of Requests and another long-lasting innovation, the mayoral banquet at the Guildhall.

He died on Boxing Day 1503, leaving three sons and one daughter. Edmund, John Shaa's eldest son, inherited Mark Hall and several other estates. He married Lora, daughter of Sir Roger Wentworth, and had a daughter, Alice. In 1525 Edmund became insane. It seems probable that the custody of his estates then passed to his brother Thomas, though some historians identify the custodian as Sir Thomas More, soon to become Lord Chancellor. A letter from More exists enquiring about Edmund's welfare. By this time Mark Hall had been leased to Lord Morley who bought the manor outright in 1538.

---

[1] There were several uprisings that included a confrontation described as the 'Battle of Blackheath'. Jack Cade's rebellious followers camped there in June 1450 and in 1497 Cornish rebels were routed there by Henry VII's army.

Parker Family Tree

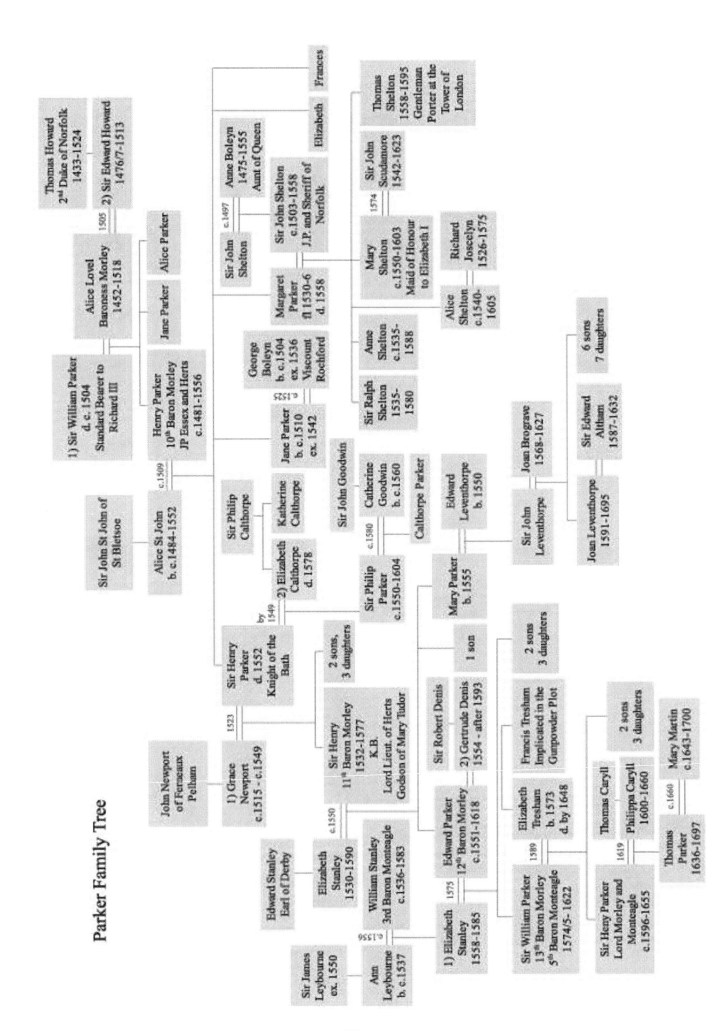

10
The Parker Family
Tenants and owners of Mark Hall 1521-1562

1521 Henry Parker, the 10th Baron Morley, leases Mark Hall from Edmund Shaa for ninety-nine years. 1534 Henry Parker is granted the Priory by the Crown. 1538 Thomas Shaa sells Mark Hall to Henry Parker.	1556 Sir Henry Parker dies. 1562 Mark Hall is sold to James Altham by Sir Henry Parker's grandson – the 11th Baron.

Chronology pages 155-56

Morley

The problems faced by law-abiding conservative Catholic noblemen in Tudor times are revealed in the contrasting fortunes of Henry Parker (d.1556) and his grandson, another Henry (d.1577) both of whom owned Mark Hall, by then an impressive collection of buildings grouped around a large courtyard. (These two Henrys are sometimes described as the second and third Lord Morley or the tenth and eleventh as there was a break in the succession).

Henry Parker senior was born in about 1481, the son of Sir William Parker of Hallingbury who gained his title and his fortune through his wife Alice Lovel, Baroness Morley. William Parker was not a favourite of Henry VII, having sided with Richard III, and Alice Lovel's second marriage to Sir Edward Howard led to further complications for her descendants. It was through the patronage of Lady Margaret Beaufort, Henry VIII's grandmother and the founder both of Christ's and St John's College, Cambridge, that the young Henry Parker was brought up in the outer circles of Court life. As a 'sewer' or attendant and cup bearer to Lady Margaret, Henry Parker developed a reverence and admiration for Henry VIII that was to be the guiding principle of his life.

Coupled with his love of royalty was Henry Parker's devotion to the English language. After his marriage to Alice St John and the birth of their first child, Henry was able to study at Oxford through the generosity of Lady Margaret, herself a great book collector, who both paid his expenses and housed his family while he was at college. From then on he worked constantly to help to build up the great body of English literature which he considered essential in the formation of an independent state. His work usually took the form of translations of Greek and Latin texts including Plutarch, Seneca and Cicero, each presented to the King, to Mary Tudor or to an important minister at the annual exchanging of New Year gifts at Court. Often the chosen text bore some message relevant to the political situation.

Henry Parker 1481-1556

In 1537, for example, when Morley was in some danger of being suspected of sympathy with the violent rebellion against Cranmer and Thomas Cromwell that started with the 'Pilgrimage of Grace', Morley sent Cromwell two of Machiavelli's works which included justifiable methods of dealing with insurrection.

It was during the 1530s, when Lord Morley could have been staying at Mark Hall while his great mansion at Hallingbury was being built, that Thomas Cromwell was trying unsuccessfully to lease Harlowbury House.

There is no end to the contradictions apparent in Henry Parker's writings and in the variety of individuals he regarded as friends. Before the Divorce he supported Queen Catherine but his was one of the signatures on the lords' letter to Pope Clement VII backing Henry VIII's request for a divorce.

He became devoted to Mary Tudor whom he frequently visited in Hunsdon and to whom he dedicated eight manuscripts, yet in 1525 he arranged the marriage of his daughter Jane to George Boleyn, later Lord Rochford, the wealthy brother of Anne Boleyn. As the Boleyns continued to rise in the King's favour a second daughter, Margaret, was married to John Shelton, Anne Boleyn's cousin. A member of the old Catholic aristocracy, Morley took part in the trials and made no objection to the execution of many of his fellow peers for treachery, a group which in 1536 included Lord Rochford, his own son-in-law. Jane, who gave evidence against her husband, remained in favour at Court for the next six years, only to lose her own head in 1542 when she was convicted of procuring for Queen Catherine Howard.

Less than a year after Jane's execution, Morley's gift to the King consisted of an elaborately bound translation of the first part of Boccaccio's description of the immorality of a number of women ranging from Eve to Helen of Troy. Even the rape of Europa by Jupiter is firmly blamed on the temptress not the god in Morley's carefully edited translation, designed to prove the writer's loyal approval of all his Sovereign's actions.

Before the accession of young Edward VI, a ruthless Protestant, Morley was able to reconcile himself to every royal attack on the old order by his belief in the English monarch's right, as the successor of Constantine, to total loyalty. His love of the old forms and ceremonies and his erudition were useful to Henry VIII who employed him on several diplomatic missions, including the presentation of the Order of the Garter to the Archduke Ferdinand. The purpose of this trip to Germany, when Morley deputised for the King, was to encourage the Archduke to stamp out Martin Luther's heresies.

The Dissolution of the Monasteries, the most fundamental and permanent attack on the old order, seems to have been welcomed by Morley. He acquired several church properties himself, including the deserted Priory in Latton and in 1544, as one of two King's commissioners, he was sent to Bishop's Stortford to assess the wealth of St Michael's church. Henry VIII rewarded him for his services by granting him the Wickham Hall estate at Thorley.

Henry Parker was about sixty-six when Edward VI, aged nine, succeeded his father. Dominated first by Edward Seymour and then by the Regent John Dudley, Edward's short reign revealed all the dangers of unswerving devotion to a mortal monarch. His last act, after six years of sustained attacks on lingering Catholic rituals, was to try to remove both his half-sisters Mary and Elizabeth from the succession in favour of Dudley's daughter-in-law, Lady Jane Grey. At this stage Henry Parker revived his old belief in the necessity of the Papacy, while still retaining his hankering for a supreme English 'Defender of the Faith'. Fortunately for him he survived long enough to welcome the accession of his beloved Mary Tudor and was buried in St Giles' church, Hallingbury with full Catholic honours in 1556. The inscription in the church tower wall still reads: *'Essex was made more illustrious by this hero living in it, for he was among the nobility like a gem of price shining with the splendour of all virtues.'*

Frontispiece of Cranmer's Bible

Thomas Butler (alias Scallon or Stallion) 1500-1556

At the same time as Henry Parker was writing his careful translations of the classics, his near neighbour on his Mark Hall estate, Thomas Butler of Harlow and Broom Lees (Bromleys) farm, was also compiling a work that would survive until the present day.

Between 1547 and 1554, while dealing in grain and woollen cloth at his shop at Bromleys, near Latton Mill, Thomas Butler or Scallon was compiling a 'Commonplace Book'[1]. This was a collection of household notes combined with a 'Manual of the Astrolabe', made up of planetary charts, family horoscopes and numerous quotations from medieval and contemporary astrological authorities. Perhaps the most interesting item enclosed in the book is a detailed map of England – a drawing that is confusing at first sight as east is at the top of the map. Unfortunately few of the multitude of place names are easily legible but great care has been spent on the planks and rigging of the large ship near the Wash.

Butler also compiled a list of *The ways from town to town unto London & the distaunce in myls'*. He notes that the figures coloured red show the distance from one *'bayting'* town to another – the sixteenth century equivalent of the gaps between service stations on our motorways.

Butler, who left a very informative will, must have been an educated man with access to manuscript and printed books and scientific equipment. Helped by his son and his wife Elizabeth, he ran his farm and store at Bromleys while living in Harlow, visited London where he held another lodging, and found time in the day or night to study, write and draw. His landlord, William Sumner, the tenant of Harlowbury House who served as overseer to his will, would probably have been interested in his work and it is possible that Lord Morley of Mark Hall encouraged his efforts and helped in his search for books.

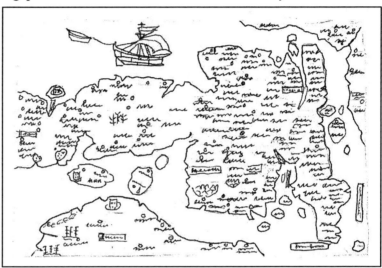

The Mape of Ynglonnd by Thomas Butler

Lord Morley's descendants

Henry Parker's only son died four years before him in 1552. He had married twice and left four children. By Grace Newport, whom he married when she was eight, he had two sons and a daughter, and by Elizabeth Calthorpe he had one son.

In contrast to the 10th Lord Morley, his eldest grandson and heir, another Henry Parker, retained his uncompromising allegiance to the Papacy and refused to subscribe to Edward VI's Act of Uniformity or to Elizabeth's Act of Supremacy. At first he tried to gain the favour of the young Queen Elizabeth and entertained her in 1561 at his splendid new mansion known as Morley House or Hallingbury Place. By 1570, however, suspicion concerning his connection with a plot involving Thomas Howard, Duke of Norfolk, forced him to flee to the Continent. He spent the last seven years of his life moving between Spain, Italy, Belgium and Germany, making periodic unsuccessful attempts to achieve a reconciliation with Queen Elizabeth. He died in Paris in 1577.

Tension between belief in the old faith and loyalty to the reigning monarch continued to complicate the lives of Henry Parker's heirs. His property was confiscated in 1572 and his eldest son Edward

Grace Newport

(Lord Morley 1577-1618) was confined in the Fleet prison. (By that time Mark Hall had been sold to James Altham so it escaped confiscation.) Shortly before his father's death, Edward conformed and was allowed to inherit the Morley title and property. He married Elizabeth, daughter and heiress of

---

[1] Butler's Commonplace Book was discovered in Beinecke Library (man.558) Yale University It has not been reproduced.

William Stanley, 3rd Lord Monteagle. Like his grandfather he took an active part in the trials of leading Roman Catholics with whom his family had close connections. These included Mary Queen of Scots and Phillip Howard, Earl of Arundel.

An interesting anecdote concerning a dispute between Edward Parker and a 'Mr Leventhorpe' was described in 1990 by Professor Joel Samaha of Northwestern University, USA. Both squires were magistrates and the argument, which took place in 1578 *'on a moat side of Morley's Essex estate'* concerned a tenant of Morley's named Smith who had fathered an illegitimate child with a maidservant and sent mother and child back to Ashwell, a village in Leventhorpe's parish. The Ashwell parishioners, anxious to avoid supporting the child on the poor rate, promptly returned them to Hallingbury. Smith sought and obtained Edward Parker's support and was granted a warrant to send them back to Ashwell but Leventhorpe refused to honour the warrant.

This story neatly illustrates the effects of Queen Elizabeth's poor law but the commentator also makes use of it to contrast the two Justices of the Peace: Lord Morley *'descended from a long line of aristocrats who would soon assume his place as head of one of the most prominent Catholic families in the county'* and *'Mr Leventhorpe, a puritanical Protestant, born without money or title who had achieved success by determination and hard work.'* In fact the two men were probably brothers-in-law. If this was (Sir) Edward Leventhorpe he married Mary Parker, Lord Morley's sister, and, though Leventhorpe may have been a puritanical Protestant, Lord Morley, already head of the family in 1578, was certainly not a devout Catholic.

William Parker (Lord Morley & Monteagle), the eldest son of Edward Parker and Elizabeth Stanley, married Elizabeth Tresham in 1589, gained a dowry of £3800 and continued the balancing act between loyalty to the Pope and to the Crown. While closely associated with the conspirators Robert Catesby and Francis Tresham, his wife's elder brother, William wrote to his new sovereign James I *'I was breed upp in the Romish religion and walked in that, because I knew no better'* but he had *'come to discerne the ignorance I was formerly wrapped in as I nowe wonder that ether myself or any other of common understanding showd bee so blynded'*.

Explanations vary of the circumstances in which the mysterious letter *'of an unknown and somewhat unlegible hand'* was given to Morley's servant in November 1605 by a man of *'reasonable tall personage'* but there is no doubt that William Parker profited considerably from his decision to deliver the letter to Whitehall in time to intercept the Gunpowder Plot.

The Parker, Leventhorpe and Altham families were all linked soon after this when Edward and Mary Leventhorpe's granddaughter Joan became the second wife of Sir Edward Altham of Mark Hall.

Hallingbury Place

11
The Architecture of Mark Hall in 1600

There is considerable uncertainty about the buildings which occupied the Mark Hall site before 1600, but fortunately a tiny contemporary drawing of the house as it was in 1616 has survived. Thanks to Stan Newens, a full size photograph of Jeremiah Bailey's map of the Altham estate, on which the house appears, now hangs in the Museum of Harlow and it seems probable that Mark Hall looked very much the same when the young Lord Morley owned it a century earlier and when the Althams welcomed Queen Elizabeth there in the 1570s.

The general pattern described on page 16 is clearly evident in Bailey's drawing of the manor house and in a second representation of the Mark Hall building, also dated to the seventeenth century and said to be taken 'from an old painting' (see page 50). Doubts have been expressed about the attribution of this illustration to Mark Hall, and suggestions that it may be a painting of Marks Hall, near Coggeshall, but its close resemblance to the estate map sketch indicates that it is genuine, though perhaps depicting the building at a later date.

The 'hall' structure, with open timber roof, porch leading to the screened passage and tall window lighting the high table, was now only one element in what had developed into an elaborate courtyard house, parts of which may have been brick-built. The layout comprised wings of lodgings, chapel, gatehouse, stables and a large barn; Mark Hall was not only a gentleman's residence but the headquarters of an agricultural enterprise. One feature which appears in the same position in both illustrations is difficult to interpret: a windowless turret-like structure, square or hexagonal in plan, that seems to have no specific function, unless it was an exceptionally large dovecote. In his *'Domesday Book and Harlow'*, Ian Jones includes a conjectural plan of the courtyard house in which he interprets the turret as a gatehouse.

When the Royal Commission for Historical Monuments visited the late eighteenth century Mark Hall in 1921 they discovered brick-walled cellars of the early sixteenth century (dated by four-centred arches over a doorway and a recess), indicating that some rebuilding or extension of the house took place at that time.[1] With such a succession of wealthy owners, it is probable that numerous alterations were made to the buildings both before and after Jeremiah Bailey drew his illustrated map.

The enlarged sketch of a section of the 1616 map shown overleaf includes both Mark Hall and Latton Hall with only the church, the old road and 'Church feilde' between them. The two Halls stood closer together than any others in the five parishes and it seems obvious that their Saxon founders would have been closely related. With the coming of the Normans, the manors were allotted to different overlords but by 1616 they had belonged to the same family for over fifty years. Bailey's map shows that Mark Hall was much the larger of the two and it was probably considerably older. Latton Hall, 'a small but elaborate' mansion, had been rebuilt in the sixteenth century in a completely different style. In 1616 it was still occupied by the family of Emanuel Wollaye, stepson of the first Altham at Mark Hall.

The precision of Bailey's drawing and its excellent state of preservation make the map a unique source of information, not only about roads, field boundaries and buildings, but also about sport and diet. Recreation for the occupants and their visitors in both Halls would have been provided by the bowling alley, south of Mark Hall, and the importance of meat from pigeons and rabbits (coneys) is shown by the large 'dove house' and the carefully illustrated 'cunnigre' or rabbit warren beside Latton Hall.

A clear, accurate impression of Latton life in the time of Shakespeare and Galileo can be gained by close examination of this remarkable document.

---

[1] See Chapter 19 for more recent exploration of the cellars.

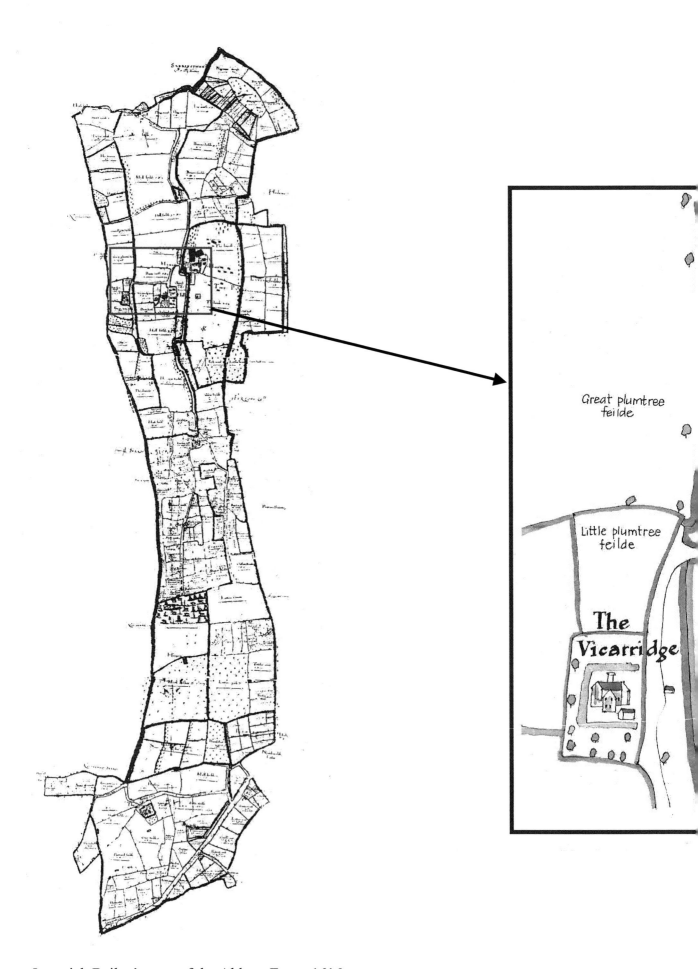

Great plumtree
feilde

Little plumtree
feilde

The
Vicarridge

Jeremiah Bailey's map of the Altham Estate 1616

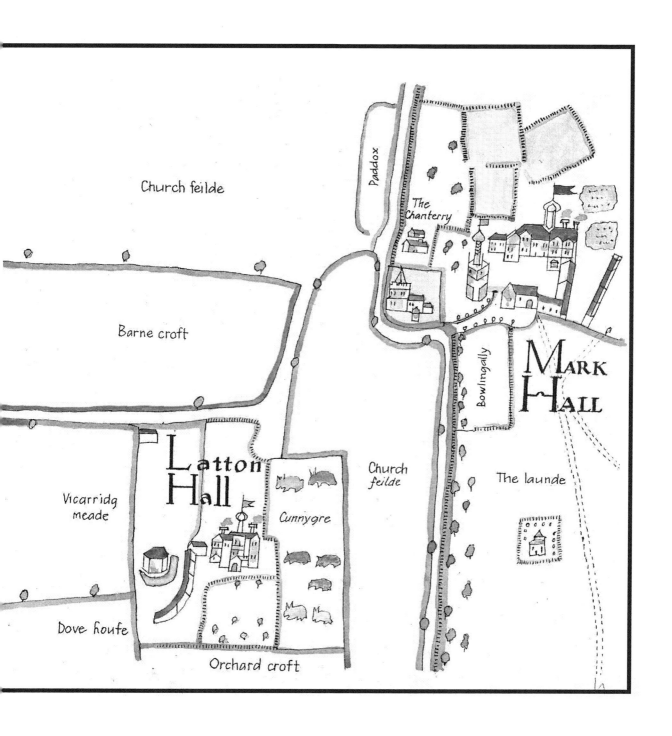

Church feilde

Paddox

The Chanterry

Barne croft

Mᴀʀᴋ Hᴀʟʟ

Bowlingally

Lᴀᴛᴛᴏɴ Hᴀʟʟ

Vicarridg meade

Cunnygre

Church feilde

The launde

Dove houfe

Orchard croft

Enlarged portion of the Altham Estate map

Descendants of James Altham

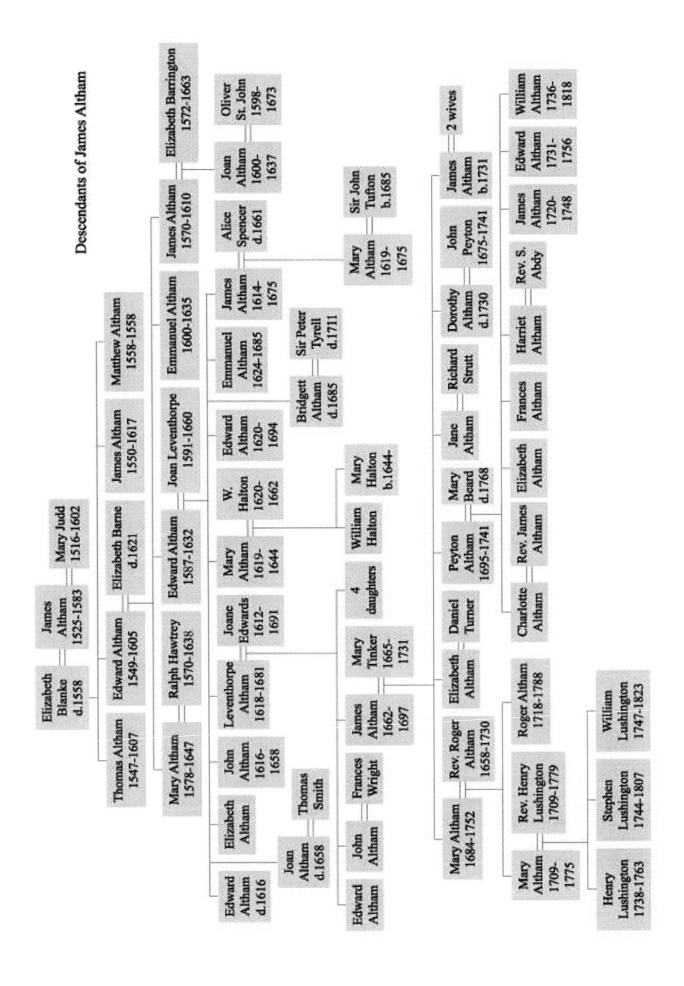

Mary Mathew's Marriages

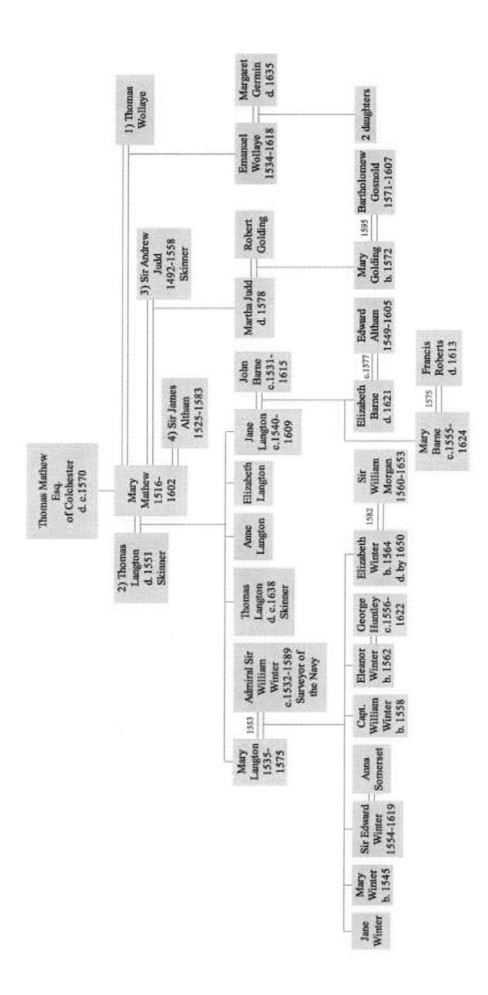

Andrew Judd's Marriages

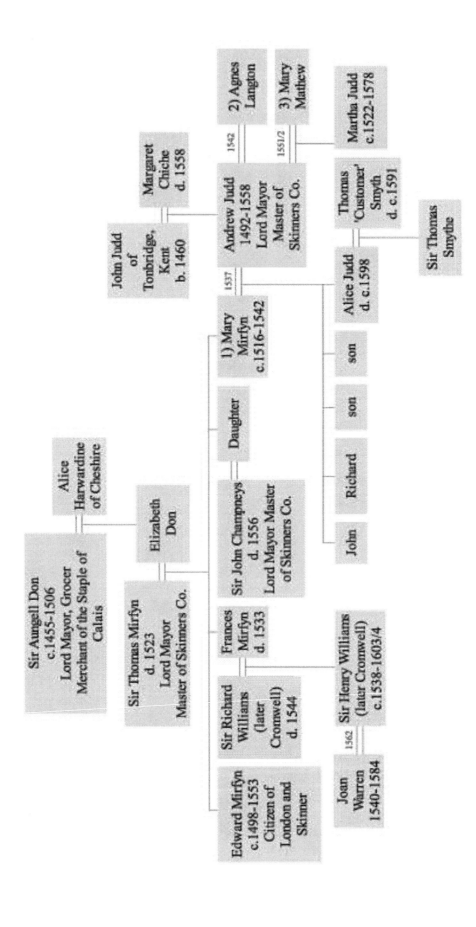

12
The Altham Family of Mark Hall & Latton Hall 1562-1776
Brenda Miller

1562 James Altham buys Mark Hall from Sir Henry Parker (Lord Morley). His wife is Dame Mary Judd. James also buys Latton Hall from John Titley.	1632 Sir Edward Altham dies. James Altham succeeds.
1566 Latton Hall is occupied by Emanuel Wollaye, Lady Judd's son, and his wife Margaret.	1635 Margaret Wollaye of Latton Hall dies.
1571, 1576, 1578 Elizabeth I visits Mark Hall.	1675 James Altham dies. His brother Leventhorpe Altham inherits Mark Hall.
1583 James Altham dies.	1681 Leventhorpe Altham dies. James Altham inherits.
Edward Altham (second son) succeeds. He marries Elizabeth Barne, Dame Mary Judd's granddaughter.	1697 James Altham dies. Peyton Altham holds Mark Hall for forty-five years. He marries Mary Beard.
1602 Dame Mary Judd dies.	1741 Peyton Altham dies, succeeded briefly by sons James and Edward.
1605 Edward Altham of Mark Hall dies.	
James Altham succeeds his father. He marries Elizabeth Barrington.	1756 Third son William Altham inherits Mark Hall.
1609 James Altham is knighted.	1768 Mary Altham dies.
1610 Sir James Altham dies. James' brother Sir Edward Altham inherits. Edward marries Joan Leventhorpe.	1776 William Altham sells Mark Hall to his cousin William Lushington.
1616 A map is made of the Mark Hall estate by Jeremiah Bailey for Sir Edward Altham.	

See Chronology pages 157-161

JAMES ALTHAM (1525-1583) was possibly Harlow's first 'EastEnder'. His father, Edward Altham (d.1548) was a citizen of London and member of the Clothworkers' Company. Like other merchants of the time he had acquired land at Hamme (now Newham) previously held by the Cistercian Abbey of Stratford Langthorne, founded in the twelfth century by William Mountfitchet of Stansted in Essex. James and his brothers Thomas (b.1527) and Edward (b.1529) each inherited one-third of half their father's estate; the remainder was left to James after all other payments had been made, including a 'recreation' for the Clothworkers' Company and gifts of money and coal to 'the poor people of London'. He also inherited money and property from his mother's relatives.

James has been described as an ironmonger, but archives from the Clothworkers' Company show that he was also made Free of that company by Patrimony. He became Quarter Warden of the Company in August 1550 and Third Warden in September 1554.

His first wife was ELIZABETH BLANKE, daughter of Sir Thomas Blanke, a wealthy haberdasher, and at the time of her marriage, sister of the Lord Mayor of London. There were five children of that marriage but only four sons, THOMAS (b.1547), EDWARD (b.1549), JAMES (b.1550) and MATTHEW (b.1558) survived – their mother died in childbirth. In 1557 James was elected Sheriff of London and an Alderman for Aldersgate. In 1561 he became a Member of Parliament but in July of that year he was deprived of his Aldermanship for 'contemptuous disobedience' of a Court order and was fined 100 marks (about £70). In 1562 he purchased Mark Hall and moved there with his second wife, Dame Mary Judd(e).

This was DAME MARY'S fourth marriage – she retained her courtesy title by virtue of rank. Her late husband, Sir Andrew Judd (1492-1558) was Mayor of London in 1550 and also Mayor of Calais. He was a Master of the Worshipful Company of Skinners, and also a prominent member of the London Merchant Adventurers, mostly trading in wool. The expeditions he helped to finance were extremely dangerous – one was an early but disastrous attempt to find the now famous north-west passage through the Arctic to Asia. In England his philanthropic works included the foundation of Tonbridge Grammar School.

Although there were no children of Dame Mary's marriage to James Altham, a bloodline between the two families was established when her granddaughter Elizabeth Barne married her stepson Edward Altham. By 1566 the Althams had also purchased the lands of Latton Priory and Latton Hall, virtually owning all of Latton parish together with other properties in Essex, Hertfordshire and Kent. James served as Sheriff of Essex from 1570-1571 and in September of that year Queen Elizabeth I made the first of three visits to Mark Hall, now considered 'fit for a queen'.

The Judd memorial in St Helen's Church, Bishopsgate, London, was commissioned c.1600 by his children. The female in the right-hand panel is thought to be his second wife.

A sketch of Mark Hall based on an old painting

Weeks of preparation were needed for a Royal visit and 'harbingers' were sent on ahead to inform all concerned about the necessary procedures. As the royal progression numbered at least 500 people with their animals and equipment it is extremely unlikely that they could all be accommodated at Mark Hall. Other large houses in the vicinity were taken over for the nobility. Latton Hall, then tenanted by Emanuel Wollaye, Dame Mary's eldest son, would certainly have been crowded and many of the servants, craftsmen and artisans would have been housed outside in large tents or marquees.

Amongst those present on the first occasion was Lord Burghley, Chief Secretary to the Queen. He supervised and sent out from Mark Hall important letters in code, relating to the Ridolphi plot to overthrow Queen Elizabeth and place Mary Queen of Scots on the English throne. Incriminating documents had been seized and three minor Court officials were imprisoned in the Tower of London awaiting interrogation and trial. In a personally signed letter to Sir Thomas Smith and Dr Thomas Wilson at the Tower of London, the Queen wrote on 15 September 1571:

> '...we will and by warrant hereof authorise you to proceed to the further examination of them upon all points that you think by your discretions meet for knowledge of the truth...if they shall not seem to you to confess plainly their knowledge, then we warrant you to cause them both or either of them to be brought to the rack...and if that shall not move them with fear then you shall cause them to be put on the rack and to feel the taste thereof until they speak plainly or you think meet...'

This letter, one of the rare occasions when the Queen ordered the use of torture, was countersigned by Lord Burghley at Mark Hall and endorsed by him in a separate letter on the same day. Barker, Bannister and Higford were later joined in the Tower by the Duke of Norfolk, the premier English peer and cousin to the Queen. He was found to have been sending gold to Mary's supporters and writing letters to her in cipher. He was charged with high treason and beheaded in June 1572.

Torture on the rack 1586

The second royal visit in 1576 was the shortest. The Queen and her party arrived on the 10 August 1576 and moved on to stay with Edward Parker at Great Hallingbury the next day. The timing of this visit to the Morleys' great mansion is very interesting. Lord Henry Morley, who had sold Mark Hall to James Altham, and whom Elizabeth had last visited in 1561, was still alive and living on the Continent, where he had fled to escape punishment for his refusal to give up his Catholic beliefs. His son and heir Edward Parker had been allowed to return when he agreed to conform. During this visit to Hallingbury, which lasted for three days, Elizabeth would have had ample time to check on Edward's recent conversion.

On 23 July 1578 Mark Hall was chosen as the location for a meeting of the Privy Council. In a letter written for the Queen on that occasion, she refers to 'this most dangerous world' in connection

The Altham Memorial

with a rumour that the brother of the French King, one of her own many suitors, was paying attention to the daughter of the Prince of Orange. This visit lasted three days and the Queen moved on via Standon to Audley End, home of Thomas Howard, son of the executed Duke of Norfolk.

James Altham died in 1583 – the executors of his will were his wife and three sons, two of whom were to receive some money in addition to goods and property given to them earlier. His bequest to his remaining brother Thomas was a *'basin and ewer of silver gilt with a rose upon it'*. After all additional bequests and payments had been made the remainder of his estate was to be divided into three equal parts, one third for his wife and the rest to be shared between his sons. Dame Mary remained in residence at Mark Hall until her death in 1602. The Altham memorial in St Mary-at-Latton church is dedicated to both James and Mary – the lower panels were added by her children after her death.

Dame Mary's will, written in 1596 gives a detailed and clearly itemised account of the furniture, fittings and layout of Mark Hall at that time. The listed items were her personal possessions, but there are references to at least fifteen large rooms and three small ones. Some rooms seem to be interconnected to form separate apartments for various members of the two families.

Queen Elizabeth's routes to Latton

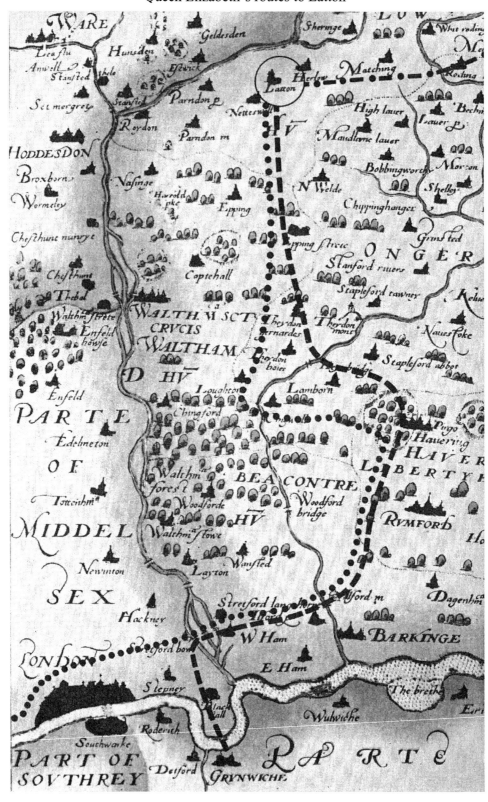

Part of Saxton's map of Essex, 1576
Queen Elizabeth I's routes to Latton
1571 ■━●━●━■━●━■
1576 ●●●●●●●●●
1578 ■━■━■━■━■━■

Scala Miliarium
1 2 3 4 5

Saxton's scale is based on the old English
mile of 2,140 yards, not 1,760 yards.
Saxton shows deer parks, but not roads,
which were not marked on any county
maps until the 1590s.

The 'Great Parlour' was furnished with rugs and Turkish carpets, upholstered furniture and cupboards. The 'New Parlour' contained a bed, cupboard, three stools and five chairs. Other rooms are referred to as 'the Queen's Chamber', the 'Chapel Chamber' the 'Iron Bar' chamber and 'My Lady Wynter's Chamber'. As well as furniture and furnishings there was a large quantity of household, personal and table-linen, gold and silver plate, jewellery and lavish embroidery, such as *'one long pillow of cloth of silver which hath Mr. Altham's arms and mine in it'*. The main recipients were family and household members, including her eldest son Emanuel Wollaye and his wife Margaret, tenants of Latton Hall, whose memorial brass is also in the church of St Mary-at-Latton.

The Arms of James Altham & Mary Judd

Emanuel and Margaret Wollaye

Bequests were made to all of James Altham's children. Non-family members, household servants and estate workers were also given mourning clothes or material to make them, as well as money where applicable:

> *'I give unto forty poor women gown of cloth at 6s. 8d. the yard to be worn by them at my funeral, and my will is that my poor neighbours specially those of Latton and Harlow should have those gowns. I give to the poor of Much Parndon three pounds; I give to the poor of Latton four pounds; I give to the poor of Harlow four pounds and I give to the poor of Netteswell three pounds.'*

A sixteenth century funeral was a very formal occasion with everyone in appropriate costume taking their correct place in the cortège. Poor people were given money to buy mourning clothes and bring up the rear of the retinue.

Traditionally THOMAS ALTHAM (1547-1607) as James's eldest son should have succeeded his father, but as he had become a Roman Catholic he was unable to inherit. He agreed to surrender his estates in return for a modest pension. He then left Essex and moved to the west of England with his wife Madeleine, son James, and daughter Mary, who subsequently became a nun. EDWARD ALTHAM, the second of James's sons then became heir to the estate.

The third brother JAMES ALTHAM (1550-1617) attended Trinity College Cambridge in the 1570s and practised Law at Gray's Inn. He was made a Baron of the Exchequer, and occupied a high legal position, Sergeant at Arms, in the Court of James I. He was one of the Judges present at the trial of nineteen witches at Lancaster Assizes in August 1612. Sir James lived with his third wife Helen and family at their home at Oxhey, Hertfordshire, where he built his own private chapel in 1612.

James Altham at Lancaster, August 1612

Internal and external views of the Altham Chapel at Oxhey

EDWARD ALTHAM (1549-1605) was educated at Clare College Cambridge in the late 1560s and entered Lincoln's Inn in November 1570. He married ELIZABETH BARNE, Dame Mary Judd's granddaughter, and they had four children.

    i.   JAMES (c.1570-1610) m. Elizabeth Barrington (1593-1663)
    ii.   MARY (1578-1647) m. Ralph Hawtrey (1570-1638)
    iii. EDWARD (1587-1632) m. Joan Leventhorpe (1591-1660)
    iv. EMMANUEL (1600-1635) unmarried

Edward Altham

Edward Altham inherited the estate in 1583 while Dame Mary Judd was still living at Mark Hall and both his younger sons were born at Mark Hall during her lifetime. Although the last years of his life saw the death of Queen Elizabeth, the accession of James I, the union of Scotland and England and the Gunpowder Plot, there are very few recorded events of local interest during Edward's time at Mark Hall. The church was given a new tower and the keeping of Parish Registers became obligatory – those from Latton record a cluster of several deaths in December 1603 attributed to an unspecified 'plague'. The bubonic plague prevalent in London during that summer may have spread out this far, but did not usually attack in the winter months.

In his will, dated 1605, Edward Altham bequeathed all his leases and profits of Mark Hall and Latton to his eldest son James; Edward was to have a farm in Kent and Emmanuel was to be paid £400 at the age of twenty-one. His own brothers received £20 each. Thomas Denne, Vicar of Latton received a remembrance of £3 and Emmanuel Wollaye and his wife had £10. Remembrances in the form of *'rings with death's heads upon them'* were to be purchased for his parents-in-law and his daughter's husband Ralph Hawtrey of Ruislip.

Mary and Ralph Hawtrey of Ruislip

Edward's third son EMMANUEL (1600-1635) did not follow the usual family traditions of entering Law or Commerce – he chose to seek his fortune in the Americas. He became an investor in, and eventually an agent for, the Company for Adventurers in New Plymouth. He made his first crossing of the Atlantic in the summer of 1623 as Captain of the *'Little James'*, which was being sent out for fishing and fur-trading. He stayed in New England for a year, making several expeditions up and down the coast. During that time he sent several long letters home describing his adventures, the places he had explored and the people he had met.

Letter to Sir Edward Altham dated September 1623:

> *'...and now I will speak of the savages in the country about; I mean the native Indians. The nearest that any dwell to Plymouth is fourteen miles and their town is called Manomet. The king of this country is a great emperor among his people; upon the occasion of the Governor's marriage, Massasoit was sent for to attend, where there came with him his wife, the queen, although he hath five wives. With him came four other kings and about six score men with their bows and arrows. When they came to town we saluted them with shooting off many muskets and so all the bows and arrows and muskets was brought into the Governor's house. They brought the Governor four bucks and a turkey. We had very good pastime in seeing them dance, which is in such manner, with such a noise that you would wonder. And now to speak of Massasoit's stature. He is as proper a man as ever was seen, and very courageous – he is very subtle for a savage and goes like the rest of his men all naked but only a black wolfskin upon his shoulder and beads about his middle. I craved a boy of him for you, but he would not part with him; but I will bring you one hereafter'.*

Unfortunately on the return journey his ship was impounded for non-payment of debts incurred by two members of the ship's company. He then undertook a second expedition on his own, but this also resulted in failure. Again his trials and tribulations are recorded in his long letters home. He returned to England, rather disillusioned with the Merchant Adventurers and found employment with the East India Company, with whom he spent two years sailing around the Indian Ocean, visiting Madagascar and Mozambique where he was hired to 'intercept' the cargo of Portuguese ships. It was during this period that his brother Edward received two very strange letters, written on the same day – in the first he writes: '...you shall receive a strange fowle, which I had at Mauritius, called by ye Portingalls (Portuguese) a Do Do, for which the rareness thereof I hope will be welcome to you...'

The second letter, possibly another version of the first has the added words '...if it lives...' There are no records of the said bird arriving at Mark Hall, alive or dead. A present-day descendant of the Altham family, Mme Jane Lagesse has written a delightfully illustrated children's book about the adventures of 'The Oldest Dodo in the World'. It tells the story of a Dodo named Joseph, brought home to England by Emmanuel, as a pet for his nieces and nephews at their 'very old house – it had pointed roofs and many small windows, with big dark wooden beams – the carriage drove up a long drive with tall shady trees growing either side of it, and there waiting by the front door was Emmanuel's family – his brother Edward with his wife Joan and all their children...'

All Emmanuel's letters home are available online and extracts are published in a book entitled 'Three Visitors to Early Plymouth' edited by Sydney James Jr., 1963. Copies of the transcribed versions are in the Museum of Harlow archives. The two following illustrations are by John White, a 'limner' who accompanied Walter Raleigh to North Carolina in 1584. The illustrations are very similar to those described by Emmanuel – they were the subject of an exhibition at the British Museum (March 2007) marking the four hundredth anniversary of the first landings in Virginia.

Contemporary artist's impressions of the native population

After a further visit to England in 1630 Emmanuel was sent to Armagon, about sixty miles north of Madras. He was Factor and Captain of the Fort and made a good life for himself with the East India Company. He was making plans to return home permanently when he was taken ill and died at Goa in 1635. His will, written in 1630, begins '...whereas I Emanuell Altham am undertaking a voyage for East India and my return being doubtfull, I do commend my soule and bodie into the hands of the Almightie...' He asks that a payment of forty shillings should be made to 'one Mrs. Thomson of Newe England, which I doe of conscience owe her although she knoweth it not'. He left his brother-in-law Ralph Hawtrey £40 – everything else was to be divided between his nephews.

But Emmanuel Altham was not the only member of this large extended family to seek adventure abroad. The Latton Register for 1595 records the marriage, at Mark Hall, of Dame Mary Judd's granddaughter MARY GOLDING to BARTHOLOMEW GOSNOLD (1571-1607) of Bury St Edmunds. Very little is known of Bartholomew's early history except that he studied law at Cambridge University before entering the Middle Temple where his contemporaries included Sir Walter Raleigh and Sir Francis Drake. In 1602 Bartholomew sailed across the north Atlantic with the intention of starting a small settlement or trading station. Although his main search was for gold he also saw the potentially rich rewards of trading in furs and sassafras, a new 'wonder drug', believed to cure syphilis and obtainable only in the New World. His journey was encouraged by wealthy patrons such as Sir Richard Hakluyt, Geographer to the Queen, and part funded by Henry Wriothesley, Earl of Southampton, and patron of William Shakespeare.

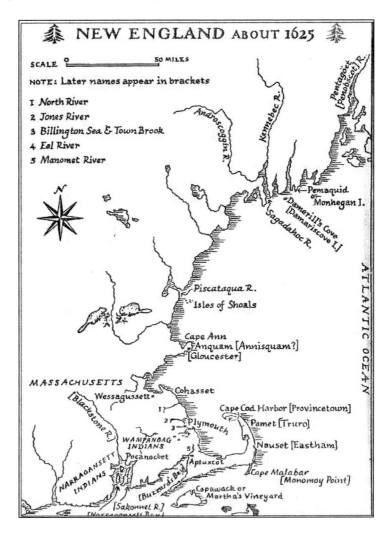

Bartholomew's ship, the *'Concord',* described by one of its passengers as *'a leaky bark only 13 paces long and six wide',* carried thirty-two people, including twenty would-be settlers, a chaplain, a journal-keeper, a goldsmith, a lawyer and an herbalist. Off the coast of Massachusetts Gosnold is credited with naming 'Cape Cod' where he was impressed by the seemingly inexhaustible marine harvest. He also 'found' a small island which he named 'Martha's Vineyard', probably in memory of his infant daughter, who died in 1598. This is one of the very few places in the United States of America that is allowed to have an apostrophe in its name.

This first journey was not a success and the *'Concord'* set sail for England three weeks later. Back home Gosnold spent much time recruiting further sponsorship. In 1606 King James I granted two exclusive charters for lands stretching from the Hudson River in the north to the Potomac in the south. Bartholomew was made a Vice-Admiral of the London fleet, and almost immediately set sail for Virginia in the *'Godspeed'.* Unfortunately the settlement was surrounded by swampy land with poor drinking water and by the end of the first winter only fifty colonists of the original 144 had survived. Bartholomew Gosnold died of dysentery and malnutrition on August 22 1607. Four hundred years later American archaeologists and historians, together with representatives from Channel 4's 'Time Team' began searching for a defensive 'fort' which had been built on Gosnold's instructions. During excavation of the site, a tomb, containing a skeleton, was unearthed.

Forensic examination of the bones and grave goods gave almost conclusive proof that this was Gosnold's body, buried with his staff of office. The facial features were later reconstructed and Bartholomew Gosnold now appears, as large as life, in the *'Living History'* Centre at Jamestown.

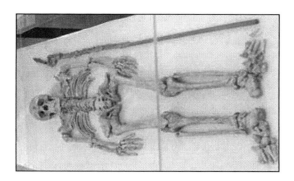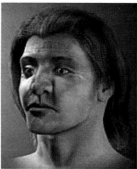

Skeleton, grave goods and facial reconstruction of Bartholomew Gosnold

No doubt news of these two adventurers was eagerly awaited and discussed at Mark Hall and other estates to which the numerous family branches had spread.

JAMES ALTHAM (c.1570-1610) inherited Mark Hall in 1605.

He became a Justice of the Peace and was knighted by King James I at Whitehall on 9 November 1609. His wife was ELIZABETH BARRINGTON (1572-1663), of Barrington Hall, Hatfield Broad Oak, daughter of Sir Francis Barrington and Joan Cromwell. He died on 15 July 1610 leaving one daughter, JOAN, (1600-1637), but no male heir. His widow remarried two years after James Altham's death becoming Lady Masham of High Laver.

EDWARD ALTHAM (1587-1632) inherited Mark Hall and its estates from his elder

brother in 1610. He married twice – by his first wife Mary he had two daughters, Jane (or Joan) d.1620, and Margaret, d.1625. His second wife, JOAN LEVENTHORPE, (1591-1660) was the daughter of Sir John Leventhorpe of Shingley Hall, Hertfordshire, related through her paternal grandmother to Lord Morley, Lord Derby and the Duke of Norfolk. Edward and Joan Altham spent the twenty-two years of their married life at Mark Hall. They had ten children, six sons (one died in infancy) and four daughters:

    i.   JOAN (d.1658) m. Sir Thomas Smith of Horum Hall & Hill Hall.
    ii.   ELIZABETH (Betty) (d.1647) unmarried – died of a chronic illness.
    iii.   BRIDGETT (Biddy) (d.1685) m. Sir Peter Tyrell, died childless.
    iv.   JAMES (Jack) (1614-1675) inherited Mark Hall, m. Lady Alice Spencer.
    v.   Edward (d.1616) – died in infancy.
    vi.   JOHN (1616-1658) – barrister, died unmarried at Grays in Essex.
    vii.   LEVENTHORPE (Lev) (1618-1681) merchant, m. Joane Edwards of Oswestry.
    viii.   MARY (Molly) (1619-1644) m. Sir William Halton, died in childbirth at Sampford.
    ix.   EDWARD (Ned) (1620-1694) religious ascetic – died abroad.
    x.   EMMANUEL (Manuel) – (1624-1685) soldier, died unmarried.

Edward Altham was knighted by King James I in 1613. One of the responsibilities that came with this honour was the organisation of the local militia, of which there was an annual muster of each 'hundred'. From 1613 to c.1620 Sir Edward was joint Captain, with Sir Henry Lee, of the Harlow half-hundred muster who met at Epping and Brentwood. They numbered 160-200 men, half of whom had muskets and other weapons.

It was during this period that Sir Edward commissioned the detailed plan of his entire estate that Jeremiah Bailey completed for him in 1616 (see pages 23, 44-45, 132-133). This invaluable source of information shows that at that time there were nine potteries on the Mark Hall estate and includes the names of the potters: William Brown, William Cattrowle, Thomas Hill, John Prentice, Thomas Prentice, Edmund Reeve, Emmanuel Emmyngs, John Starkys and John Wright. By 1650 there were twenty-five potters working in the area and the output of Metropolitan ware, the yellow and brown pottery produced mainly around Potter Street and Latton Common, reached its peak. The improvement in the roads and the rapid expansion of London increased the demand for household ware and the industry continued to bring some prosperity to Latton until after 1700[1].

Metropolitan ware plate

The Worshipful Lady Altham was a constant and prolific correspondent, who loved *'Mark Hall more than any other place'*. Lady Joan continued to live there until 1638 when she retired to her farm at Feltwell, near Thetford in Norfolk. However, she kept in close contact with letters and lengthy visits to her own children and other relatives almost up to the time of her death in 1660. It is from letters to and from Mark Hall, London, and the Continent, that much of the information about family and contemporary events at home and abroad is derived. But, before Lady Altham died, England had experienced an upheaval so fundamental in its long term effects that it can be compared to the arrival of the Normans.

KING JAMES I died at Theobalds Park, Hertfordshire in 1625 and his son Charles was crowned at Westminster Abbey in 1626. Charles's rigid insistence on the 'divine right' of absolute rule for the monarchy eventually led to civil war and regicide. During the first years of his reign Charles dissolved Parliament three times, ruling without it from 1629-40, and began to introduce anti-Puritan reforms, led by William Laud, whom he appointed as Archbishop in 1633.

Although the residents of Mark Hall and the surrounding estates escaped the plague and smallpox epidemics prevalent in London and other parts of the country during the seventeenth century, the family was not free from personal loss. Edward and Joan's first son, Edward (b.1616) died in infancy. Their youngest daughter, Mary, (Molly) Lady Halton, died aged twenty-five, shortly after giving birth to her second child, a daughter, named Mary by her grandmother who was present at the birth. The orphaned children were later brought under the guardianship of James Altham at Mark Hall. Bridgett, (Biddy) Lady Tyrell, (d.1685) also died childless, possibly during pregnancy and Elizabeth (Betty) (d.1647) died of a chronic illness from which she suffered throughout her life.

In an undated letter to an unnamed pregnant daughter (probably Joan), a worried Lady Altham writes:

> *'...good daughter, I was glad to hear that thee and thine were all in good health and I wish I could send the like from us here but I cannot do at this time by reason of extreme colds and coughs which have seized upon most of your brothers and sisters and both your aunts and some of our servants have been very ill with it. I pray God to keep you and yours from the like for a cough would come ill to you now being so big and near your time...'*

The family continued to worship at Latton Church, where the new vicar, Thomas Denne, held benefice from 1632-1680. Like his father, installed by Lady Judd, he had strong connections with the Puritans, supporting protests by members of the Essex clergy against liturgical changes imposed by William Laud, who became Archbishop of Canterbury in 1633. A cruder form of protest, assisted by alcohol, occurred during Denne's tenure. On New Year's Day 1641 a group of drunken villagers arrived at the church for bell-ringing practice. One member began to pull down the altar rails, newly installed on Archbishop Laud's instructions. All the rails surrounding the communion table and Altham monument were thrown out of the church, chopped up and set alight. The defence offered by William Skynner, the spokesperson of the group, was extremely well organised and had obviously been structured by someone, possibly Denne, who knew which terms of mitigation would be most

---

[1] See *The Harlow Pottery Industries*. W. Davey & H. Walker

acceptable to the Church leaders. In spite of his personal theological beliefs Thomas Denne continued on good terms with the Althams and retained his living after the Restoration of the Monarchy. The church at Latton did not remain unscathed. On 26 March 1644 Lady Altham wrote to her son John:

> *'...all ye news here is that the cross on our steeple is taken down, and the sanctus belfry*
> *also taken away ... all our trained bands warned to go with all speed to Walden, but what*
> *to do or whether to go is not yet known to us.'*

Another example of the close links that existed between many Royalist households and their political opponents is provided by the marriage in 1630 of JOAN ALTHAM (c.1600-37) to OLIVER ST JOHN

Oliver St John

(1598-1673). Joan was the only child of James Altham and Elizabeth (née Barrington), who was Oliver Cromwell's first cousin. Known to both Republicans and Royalists as the 'Dark Lanthorn', Oliver St John was regarded by the King's supporters as something of a shady character. He had been briefly imprisoned and brought before the Star Chamber in 1629 for suspected sedition and there were doubts about the legitimacy of his birth and the honesty of his intentions, both political and marital. Apart from these suspicions, neither his financial position nor his career prospects appealed to the bride's mother, now Lady Masham of High Laver. After pressure from the wealthy and influential Barrington family, plus financial support from the St John's employer, the Earl of Bedford and from the Earl of Warwick, the marriage did take place though St John and

Sir Edward Altham continued to wrangle over money. Joan and Oliver produced three children during the seven years of their marriage, but Joan died in childbirth in 1637.

Soon after becoming widowed, St John remarried, this time to Elizabeth Cromwell, another Barrington cousin and a great friend of the future Lord Protector. In 1640 St John became MP for Totnes, again with the backing of the Earl of Bedford who consistently supported his political advancement. By 1641 he had become the King's solicitor and throughout the Civil War continued to retain considerable influence over the course of events, while still supporting the Cromwellian cause. From 1648 till 1653 Oliver St John was Lord Chief Justice, eventually supporting the accession of Cromwell's son Richard to the position of Lord Protector.

After the Restoration of King Charles II in 1660, St John attempted to justify his political activities in print. Although no treasonable evidence could be found against him, he was excluded from holding any public office and died in exile in 1673.

JAMES (Jack) ALTHAM (1614-1675) attended Emmanuel College, Cambridge and

inherited Mark Hall in 1632. He married LADY ALICE SPENCER, (d.1661) daughter and heir of Sir John Spencer of Offley, Herts. in 1638. They had one child, Mary, known to her many relatives and doting parents as 'Sweet Moll' or 'Little Black Eyes'. Mary became Lady Tufton but the marriage was not a success and the couple separated. James enjoyed the life of a country landowner – he purchased a hound called 'Mounter' with two puppies, and took a keen interest in the boundaries of his 'enheritance'. He wrote to Sir William Masham of High Laver in very disgruntled terms about the felling of some trees on Thornwood Common:

> *'...as you were informed they were anciently set there as marks to distinguish the*
> *parishes of Latton and Weald, and have been so reputed to be for above 60 years ... till of*
> *late years the inhabitants of Weald, desiring to alter the bounds of their parish have cut*
> *them up (as they pretend at your command) and made a way there where never was any*
> *before, which being a great prejudice to my enheritance, I pulled up, with an intent to*
> *plant trees there. For this, we are presented at Quarter Sessions ... I crave that Weald*
> *men may mend their own ways and not encroach upon mine enheritance ...'*

Although as a landowner he was exceedingly angry and disgusted at the continuous demands for money imposed through taxation, James was a staunch Royalist. During the events leading up to and during the Civil War he was absent from Mark Hall for long periods of time on the orders of the *'higher powers'* about which his wife complained in a letter to her brother-in-law John:

'... I would do anything to get that little allowance which is allotted to me by the higher powers, that so I might go to my dear husband ... for I have not heard from him this five weeks...'

Alice had written to her husband on several occasions and was desperately concerned for his safety:

'... sweet heart, though I have no reason to write to you yet I cannot let so fit an opportunity pass but I must let you know that I was exceeding glad to hear by my brother of your welfare and that your business goes so well forward. I hope it will not be long before you have accomplished it and then I shall promise myself the happiness to see you here till which time I shall be yours most constantly. I send these lines to assure thee that I am and ever will be thy constant and loving wife ... as for news there is none. The soldiers are still in the town but as yet they are orderly and quiet so with my dear love to you I rest yours most faithfully A.A. Moll craves your blessing.'

On 12 January 1644 James eventually wrote to his wife from an undisclosed destination:

'...my dearest, to the many letters I have sent thee, I have at last received an answer. I cannot believe I have been so much neglected, or forgotten, but that thou hast writ more, though I have been so unfortunate as to receive but one, 'tis possible that mine might fall under ye same fate that I believe yours have. I confess we have both cause to lament the sad obstructions of these times in that particular as well as in many other.'

He goes on to explain that his reputation has been prejudiced by someone close to him, and that until his name has been cleared *'...my design of seeing thee must yet a while be suspended. I sent so large a remembrance to little black eyes in my last letter, that I question whether they be all delivered yet, therefore now I shall send her nothing but my blessing...'*

After their sister Mary (Molly) Halton died in 1644 James and Leventhorpe Altham assumed responsibility for William and Mary, her two orphaned children, as their father seemed to be *'too much occupied with his new wife'*. In 1662 he died en route for Virginia and James Altham was formally appointed the boy's official guardian, with Leventhorpe taking responsibility for the day-to-day living arrangements. The young Sir William was a very wilful and extravagant *'knight errant'*. His Uncle Edward, resident in Rome, had been warned of a proposed visit and told not to *'furnish him with money or assist him to any extraordinary garb'*. His taste in clothes had also caused problems with his Uncle Leventhorpe who in 1663 wrote to James at Mark Hall:

'... it was all about a hat. I told him it was too fantastical for him, and thought it fitting he should be clothed fashionably, yet considering the condition he did intend to put himself into, he ought not to mind every new-fangled fashion, it would make him ridiculous. Upon which he flung away, taking his sword and coat, mumbling something to himself. My wife saw him not today, neither did he say anything to the maid when he went a-running...'

He appears to have lived a dissolute life. He died on 4 March 1675 and was buried at Latton. Nothing more is currently known about his sister Mary, who may not have survived infancy.

Lady Mary Bankes

One member of the Altham family became famous for her courage during the Civil War. Mary Altham (b.1578) and Ralph Hawtrey (b.1570) had one daughter, MARY (b.1591). She married SIR JOHN BANKES, of Corfe Castle, Dorset, in 1614.

Like James Altham, the Royalist Sir John Bankes spent much of his time in London, where he held high office at Court. In 1640 he accompanied King Charles I from Westminster to York. His wife remained with their children and household servants at Corfe Castle, which was twice attacked by Cromwell's soldiers. Lady Bankes' organisation of her troops and defence of her home, which she was eventually forced to leave in 1646, led to her being recognised and named by both rebels and royalists throughout the kingdom as *'Brave Mary'*.

In 1648 General Sir Thomas Fairfax, the leader of Cromwell's army, besieged the city of Colchester, imprisoning many of the local Royalists within the walls of the castle.

Lady Joan Altham, who had been staying with relatives in London, stopped for two nights at Mark Hall on her way to Little Sampford, from where she sent the following letter to James, who was still absent from home:

> 'good son, according to my promise and yr. desire, I shall give you an account of our journey and safe arrival the first night at Mark Hall where we found all well and quiet I thank God... Mr. Denne and others think there is no danger but yet you may come down and stay without disturbance. We finding all quiet made Sir John (Leventhorpe) willing to rest his horses one day, for they had a very bad journey and found the ways very bad, and the waters very high at Stansted and Roydon, but past them through safely. On Saturday we went to Stamford where I thank God we arrived safely and found no trouble but the foule ways, and they were worse now than ever I see them, but Sir John's horses carried us very well through them ... I pray send such news as is stirring, for whether it be good or bad it will help to pass way the time in this solitary place, where there is no taking of horses now, nor any other trouble but sending away provision, which it is feared will make great scarcitie in these parts if the siege continue much longer. But it is certainly reported by many that hath lately been at Colchester that they are in a very good condition and want nothing but peace and love with their enemies, which I beseech God send in all places in his good time...'

The following August Lady Altham wrote again to James at Mark Hall:

> '...Jacke, hearing you were to come to Mark Hall this week I congratulate you on your happy return there, where I hope I shall hear you are all safe and well, though troubles still continue in the county and we may fear it like to do so still, for Colchester is not yet taken nor like to be yet ... the news is that they can take it, but Sir Thomas in mercie still spares them ... how true it is I leave it to you and others to judge...'.

A few days later the beleaguered town was forced to surrender to General Fairfax. Local legend has it that 'Humpty Dumpty' of nursery rhyme fame was actually a large Royalist cannon, placed on the city ramparts. During the 'thump, thump' of the ensuing battle it was dislodged from the breached wall and smashed to the ground, where 'all the King's horses and all the King's men couldn't put Humpty together again!'

General Thomas Fairfax

The breached Roman Wall

Humpty Dumpty

Sir James was made a Knight of the Bath after the Restoration of the Monarchy in 1660 and died in 1675. In a work entitled 'Worthies of England' one of his contemporaries wrote, 'He addeth with his accomplished civility to the honor of his ancestors'.

JOHN ALTHAM (1616-1658) was Edward's third son. He attended Sidney College, Cambridge, before becoming a barrister with Chambers at Gray's Inn. He gave counsel and advice to all the members of his immediate and extended family as well as receiving and passing on detailed first-hand information about events at Court and in Parliament. On 7 March 1638 John wrote to his brothers at Mark Hall:

> '... the Army will not disband. Yesterday a letter from the General to the House imparts as much as we are in a very great amaze here. Today I hope will compose them and make them willing to submit to reason ... yesterday the House of Commons had a long debate concerning the eleven members. When the debate began they modestly withdrew.

It continued till near four at night, therefore the house cannot suspend these men without a high breach of those laws they have so oft bound themselves to maintain. The debate ended, they returned again, and then Mr. Hollis in the name of the rest, desired that they might have leave to sequester themselves (yet promising to attend the house when they should be called upon) and that those of them that had a desire to travel, might leave ...'

John's Uncle Edward Leventhorpe was also *'in a great amaze'* when he wrote to Mark Hall from London a few weeks later *'...on Thursday last was the Thanksgiving, but truly if you ask me for what I cannot tell you, no man can I meet...'* In June 1647 there was a pause in the Civil War while Cromwell tried to mediate between the two sides. He was not successful and the Army demanded the expulsion of eleven members of the Commons on the grounds that they were causing serious disagreements between the Army and Parliament. During the same month John wrote to James:

'... The King is resolved to go to Scotland ... the royal household goes away on Monday next. Mr. Charles Cotton killed Sir John Hunt in the Strand. My Lord Leicester is coming out of France, the cause is unknown...'

In 1647 John Altham was called upon to give legal advice to his second cousin, Mary, the only surviving child of Thomas Altham (1547-1607). Thomas had been disowned by the family because he was a Roman Catholic. He had two children, James who died widowed and childless in 1647 and Mary, a fifty-eight-year-old nun in a Belgian convent. James had named his sister as his sole executrix but as a nun in a closed order she was not allowed to inherit. John was asked by Mary to arrange for the various properties to which she assumed she was entitled to be *'resigned'* to James Altham. All she asks in return is that he should contribute towards her maintenance as her brother had done. John had to make several visits to Bruges where he attended meetings with the public notary, his cousin, and the Mother Superior of the Convent, who signed and countersigned affidavits relating to the transaction in English and French. The London lands and tenements were assigned to Sir William Halton and William Smyth Esq., for the use of James Altham in his lifetime, but some eventually came into Leventhorpe's possession when he inherited the Mark Hall estate in 1675.

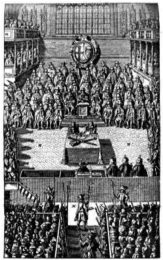

The imprisonment, trial and execution of King Charles I in 1649 are not recorded in any correspondence to and from Mark Hall, but on 6 July 1653 John wrote to his mother at Horum Hall:

'.... I received your Ladyship's letter last week with the enclosure, which I delivered to my brother to be sent forward by the first opportunity ... the letters to Ned were likewise delivered to him. Madam, here is little news, only that the Great Council met at White Hall upon Monday. The General made a speech near two hours long; and for that day they broke up when that was ended. They agreed to meet yesterday at the House of Commons in Westminster and sought God by prayers for a blessing upon their Council. This day they are to meet

Trial of Charles I

again to choose their Speaker and appoint other officers. My Lady Smith is nearing Stowe, and my Lady Bankes went out of Towne last Saturday and I believe she is this week for the West... J. Altham.'

Oliver Cromwell

This letter refers to the *'Barebones Parliament'*, also known as the Nominated Assembly which was formed in July 1653 as the last attempt to find a stable political forum before the installation of Oliver Cromwell as Lord Protector of the Commonwealth. It was an assembly entirely nominated by Oliver Cromwell and the Army's Council of Officers, acquiring its name from the nominee for the City of London, Praise-God Barebone. The members of the assembly voted to dissolve it on 12 December 1653 and it was succeeded by the first Parliament of the Protectorate.

When John Altham died in 1658, two years before his mother, he was living at his home at Grays, Essex. In his will he asked to be buried at Latton church: his beneficiaries were all his remaining siblings, his cousin Jane Leventhorpe and the two Halton children as well as his household servants and 'ten poor ministers' to whom he left £50. James Altham, who also inherited the residue of the estate, was to be sole executor.

LEVENTHORPE (Lev) ALTHAM (1618-1681) inherited Mark Hall when his brother James died in 1675. His wife JOANE EDWARD(E)S (1612-1691) came from Oswestry in Shropshire. They married in 1633 and had at least seven children but only four are recorded as having survived infancy. Confusion has also arisen over names as some girls were christened 'Edwardes' after their mother's maiden name:

i.   JAMES ALTHAM (1662-1697) m. Mary Tinker (1665-1731)
ii. THEODOSIA ALTHAM (b.1665)
iii. JOHN ALTHAM (b.1666) m. Francis Wright
iv. JANE ALTHAM (b.1668)
v.   Edward Altham
vi. Edwardes Altham
vii. Mary Altham

Leventhorpe spent his childhood at Mark Hall, but later moved to London where he was a merchant trader, dealing in wine and furs. He also spent a number of years in Rouen, from where he sent most of his letters home during 1645-48. In the first of these, dated 3 March 1645 he apologises to his mother for the long delay in replying to her letters, in which she has expressed her concerns for his safety and continues:

> 'Madam, my joy is exceeding great to hear of the continuance of your health and preservation in these troublesome and distracted days - the which God in his Mercy continue to you and all our near and dear and in his good time convert these days of mourning and affliction into days of joy and peace that once more I may have that happiness to see your Ladyship, the which I know wages[?] despair of, but trust in God I shall...'

Two years later Leventhorpe is still in France. In 1647 he was informed through long-delayed letters from his family that his *'dear sister Betty'* had died in the winter of the preceding year, and on 11 April 1647 he wrote a long letter of condolence to his mother. In a letter to John, dated a few weeks later, he expresses very forcefully all his anger and frustration about the situation in England at that time:

> '... I perceive the impeachment that hindered your coming hither must have patience until, please God, I shall see you in England. Which is very uncertain yet to be; not withstanding my great longing and desire, the which is still frustrated by the broils and unsettled posture at home, which frustrates all my hopes ever to see a calm where I may be so happy as once - to have the encouragement to venture the shallop of my credit upon the waves of a propitious trade, until which I shall rather choose to live in obscurity abroad than return to live promiscuously at home, so with my best and most dearest salutations to all our friends, I rest in haste, your own Lev. Altham...'

On the 27 November in another letter to his mother he still laments *'these distracted times'* but also thanks God for the *'joys and comforts'* he is able to enjoy in France. Presumably his wife and children were able to join him at Rouen. By 1665 the Monarchy had been restored, and Leventhorpe and his family were living in Hackney, then a small rural community. An epidemic of the Plague had broken out in London, and he wrote to Mark Hall on 29 September:

> '...I am very much afflicted to understand the Contagion is dispersed amongst your neighbours; it is so with us here, yet my family and myself enjoy good health and I go to London as seldom as I can ... the bill of mortality that came out yesterday specifies the decrease of 1,837, which doeth make us hope the Contagion hath been at the height. Upon Tuesday last the Court removed to Oxford, where the Parliament is to meet on the

9 October. The Fleet is all come in, with quantities of rich prizes, which might have been more had somebody pleased ...'

Further letters from Leventhorpe to Mark Hall during this period are mostly concerned with news from London and the impact of the Dutch Wars on the economy in general and continental trade in particular. These wars which took place during the seventeenth and eighteenth centuries between the Kingdom of Great Britain and The United Provinces of the Netherlands were about control over the seas and their profitable trade routes.

Battle between English & Dutch ships on the River Medway – Peter Cornelisz Van Soest 1667

Leventhorpe Altham seems to have been a more extrovert character than his older brothers. He obviously had an eye for fashion and was frequently asked to obtain or sell items of clothing and jewellery for his family and friends. On 30 March 1640 his brother-in-law Thomas (Tom) Smith wrote to John Altham at Gray's Inn:

'... good brother, my brother Altham told me this last week that my brother Lev has sent 4 beaver hats out of France and that amongst other of his friends I am to have offer of one of them for my money ... I desire you to reserve one for me of the largest brims and fullest crown. I must confess the extremity of this foolish fashion that is now used I do not affect...'

Two ladies' watches sent to 'Lev' by his mother in October 1640 for *'exact mending'* were received back *'safe and well and they go yet pretty right'* and in November 1640 Leventhorpe wrote to her regarding another errand for his sister-in-law Alice Altham:

Seventeenth century watches

'... pray will you tell my sister Altham I cannot get any thing for her pearl nor diamond – the next time my brother Altham comes to town I will send them her; I do desire to know whether she intends to have the crystal watch she spoke to me for – pray please to tell her it will cost her at least eight pound if she thinks fitting. I will do my endeavour to help her with one as cheap as I can but there is no hope that her pearl and jewel should purchase a watch as she expects they should ...'

Items of food and drink frequently made their way from one household to another, ranging from venison and other game joints, seafood, poultry, various pies and puddings, marmalade and other preserves, exotic sweetmeats and wine. In an undated note to *'John at Grays Inn'*, his mother writes *'I have sent a box of marzipan for Lev and you to eat together'* and in August 1647 James Altham, at Mark Hall, received *'this keg of sturgeon'* from his Uncle Edward Leventhorpe, who signed himself *'the pudding eater'*.

Leventhorpe also seems to have made himself responsible for looking after various family matters in London, arranging tenancies on property, collecting rents and settling other accounts. He inherited Mark Hall after his brother's death in 1675 and stayed there with his family for the next ten years. During that time Thomas Denne died after forty-eight years as the Vicar of Latton.

Leventhorpe Altham then appointed the first of the four Altham Vicars, namely his cousin Michael, already Rector of nearby Eastwick. The exact relationship of Michael's family to the Althams of Mark Hall has yet to be traced. A new Register for Latton was started in 1683; Michael Altham died in 1705 but was not buried at Latton. Leventhorpe's death in 1681 preceded by a few years the beginning of a new reign when JAMES II became King of England, ruling for almost four years.

Both Leventhorpe's younger brothers, Edward and Emmanuel, caused their family considerable worry and financial hardship. While John was at college at Cambridge his mother wrote:

'could you bring some pretty civil young scollar down with you that would be willing...
this summer time... to teach your two brothers, who else I am afraid will loose their time,
by reason Mr. Denne has given over school...'

EDWARD (Ned) ALTHAM (1620-1694) attended St Catherine's College, Cambridge. Like his great-uncle Thomas he was attracted towards Roman Catholicism and asked his brother James, his *'patron'*, to use his influence in securing the living of Buckland, Herts. However, this placing did not materialise and a very disappointed Edward left to continue his studies abroad, mostly at the University of Groningen, Holland, from where he wrote to James in 1644 about his change of plans:

'... Sir, you may justly think by change of wind that I now set up sails for another port
than I first intended. I confess the weather has been cold and dark, sufficient to beat a
young midshipman off from his compass, yet my comfort is hope I have for an anchor at
which I will lie till a calm or prosperous gale appears on our coasts ...'

He is still determined to become a *'minister of God'*, yet is unable to come to terms with what he called *'the foul corruptions of the vulgar that trouble our Church and will destroy it'*. Edward met up with Leventhorpe several times on visits to France and sent messages home through him. Although at one time he was confined at Calais with an attack of *'the stones'*, he continued to travel abroad, learning Hebrew, Greek and other languages. He joined the Catholic Church in 1650 while living in Rome, where he spent the rest of his life. Although he seemed to have made influential contacts in artistic and religious circles, he was not a happy man: in 1681 he wrote to Leventhorpe at Mark Hall:

'... I should be glad to see you and yours and the rest of my unknown relations, for few of
my acquaintances, I suppose are living, yet I cannot promise myself that happiness in the
condition I am in and as things now stand in poor England ... we are become a
laughingstock to all nations ...'

Portrait of Edward Altham by Salvator Rosa
1665

Mr Altham as a Hermit

Both these portraits are at Kingston Lacy, Dorset, the ancestral home of the Bankes family, now administered by the National Trust. The *'Hermit'* picture with its wealth of metaphysical imagery is now thought to be a possible self-portrait. A catalogue from a Rome art gallery dated 1783 records three landscapes and four seascapes by 'Monsieur Altham' – other of his artistic works are recorded in his will: landscapes, still lifes, and portraits, also figurative and religious subjects. Unfortunately none can be traced today.

In the 1670s Edward was commissioned by Lord Cheyne of Chelsea to supervise ongoing work on the effigy of Lady Jane Cheyne, by Antonio Raggi, one of the sculptor Bernini's most important collaborators. He was also responsible for shipping the piece back to London where it finally arrived in *'thirty great cases'* in January 1672. Leventhorpe Altham acted as the middleman for payments and transport, and also dealt with the customs authorities. Although earlier problems about reconciling the sculptor's measurements using the Italian 'palm', which was smaller than the English 'foot', were eventually resolved, a major problem occurred when the various parts were unpacked and reassembled. Edward had either misunderstood instructions about the statue's location in Chelsea Old Church or had been wrongly informed by Lord Cheyne, who later queried *'the posture of the figure lying with the feet to the West'*. The effigy had been made 'back to front' and, instead of standing in the Chancel facing the altar, the monument was placed on the north wall, looking out of the church door!

Edward Altham died a religious recluse in Rome c.1694.

EMMANUEL (Manuel) ALTHAM (1624-1685) As the fifth son there was little chance of Emmanuel inheriting any of the Altham estates. His brother Leventhorpe was asked to find him a situation in which he could both pursue his studies and help to support himself. In a letter to his mother dated 10 July 1640 Leventhorpe wrote:

> *'this is to certify to your Ladyship that I have acquainted my Master how you will stand affected in disposing my brother Emmanuel with him, whereupon he wished me to write to your Ladyship to send him up but I told him I thought you would desire to speak with him before you did resolve to send him ... He desires to send my brother Emmanuel into France as soon as is possible where he may practice his writing and get the French tongue, that it may be capable to do him service. He shall be placed with a very honest merchant in Rouen who is in the same way of trading as my Master and where he shall be employed ...'*

Unfortunately Emmanuel did not stay long in employment with the *'very honest merchant'* but cut away, drifting about the Continent with various mercenary regiments. This did not please Leventhorpe, who was also living in France at that time, or his mother. In a letter to John, dated March 1644, Lady Altham writes:

> *'.. I received many letters and bills from your brother Emmanuel which I have sent here enclosed that so you may see what he saith in excuse for his great expenses, which gives me but little satisfaction, knowing how extravagant he has been heretofore. I fear he goes on still in his idle expenses, which is a continual grief to me to think of. I beseech God in mercy look upon him and give him a sign of his vain and idle courses and grace to amend them. I pray you to advise where I were best to let him have this £10 he writes to earnestly for or no, for though money goes very short with me, if it might conduce to his good and not his hurt I would find some means to provide it.'*

By 1662 Emmanuel was back in England with one of the new King's regiments, again asking for money from his family. After a request for £50 per annum and the plea *'let me not sink'* was rejected by his brother James, Emmanuel wrote: *'... I know my follies have been great ... I am come up on purpose against this good time to ask God forgiveness for them all and to lay them also before me, if for the future I may endeavour never again to be acquainted with any of them.'*

James Altham did eventually promise Emmanuel *'anything he should want at Mark Hall'*, but apart from a short letter about Queen Catherine's health at the end of 1663, nothing more is known of his whereabouts – it is thought that he died abroad, unmarried.

JAMES ALTHAM (1662-1697) was nineteen years of age when he inherited Mark Hall and only thirty-five when he died. His wife, MARY TINKER (1665-1731), was reputed to be a great beauty. They had six children:

  i. MARY ALTHAM (1684-1752) m. Revd Roger Altham (1658-1730)
 ii. PEYTON ALTHAM (1695-1741) m. Mary Beard (d.1768)
iii. JAMES ALTHAM
 iv. JANE ALTHAM m. Richard Strutt
  v. ELIZABETH ALTHAM m. Dr Daniel Turner
 vi. DOROTHY ALTHAM m. John Peyton

MARY ALTHAM, their first child, married Michael Altham's son, the Revd Roger Altham, more than twenty-five years her senior. They had two children, Mary (1709-1775) and Roger (1718-1788).

In 1908 a Mr P. Griffiths found a piece of embroidery rolled up in an attic cupboard at Latton Vicarage. It was thought to be an altar frontal, probably Mary Altham's work, embroidered with the initials M.A. and dated 1700. He had it restored and framed, and offered it back to the church. As it was felt that it could not be properly conserved there it was sent to the Colchester and Essex Museum in 1926. It is now displayed in the Museum of Harlow, on the site of its original home. The piece is in three parts with an unfinished bottom edge; it is assumed that it had been put together from a wall-hanging or curtain of Mediterranean, possibly Italian origin, as Mary Tinker's father had spent some time in the Republic of Venice. However, there are also references in various Altham wills to rich continental furnishings and hangings from which the piece might have been cut.

PEYTON ALTHAM (1695-1741) was only two years old when his father died and there had to be a special dispensation from Queen Anne to allow him to inherit. He was named after Sir Yelverton Peyton, a distant relative of James Altham and close family friend. Dorothy Altham, Peyton's sister, married Yelverton's brother John. Yelverton Peyton was a great help to James's widow, who stayed at Mark Hall with the six children for twelve years – at St Mary's Church there is a memorial tablet to him on the south wall of the chancel. An incident occurred on 16 October 1698, a year after her husband died, that illustrates the type of problem with which Mary had to cope:

> *'James Marshall, tailor, Thomas Clarke, labourer, both of Epping and John Labanck of Netteswell, labourer, did fish without license in the fish pond of Mary Altham, widow in Latton. Witness James Oakley'.*

The case was recorded in the Sessions Roll, 1700 and Labanck was discharged. What happened to the other two poachers is not recorded.

Peyton Altham took over the estates officially in 1717 three years after GEORGE I of Hanover, was crowned King of Gt. Britain & Ireland, twelve American colonies, seven Caribbean islands, Gibraltar, Minorca and New Brunswick. In 1720 Peyton married MARY BEARD (d.1768) the daughter of SIR JOHN BEARD, PRESIDENT OF BENGAL and an administrator of the English East India Company. Another major event of 1720 which not only affected the Altham family but also had wider implications was the bursting of the 'South Sea Bubble'. The Treaty of Utrecht (1713) granted Britain a monopoly contract to supply slaves from Africa to the Spanish territories of South America. The South Sea Company took advantages of the new freedom from taxation and restrictions, promising rich rewards to investors. This started a wave of reckless speculation which spread throughout society from the King downwards. Few City men could resist the temptation and enormous fortunes were made and lost. In Harlow we know that New Hall and Kitchen Hall were bought up from the Lamb family by Sir Robert Chester, a director of the famous Company, but there is no record of how many other families were involved. When the inevitable crash occurred, New Hall and Kitchen Hall went into the hands of the receivers, Sir Robert Chester departed elsewhere, but still nothing hindered the lucrative slave trade. Parish registers show that several local mansions employed black 'servants' and Mark Hall was no exception.

Peyton and Mary Altham had nine children but only seven survived infancy and most were very short-lived.

i. JAMES ALTHAM (1720-1748) died childless
ii. EDWARD ALTHAM (1731-1756) died childless
iii. WILLIAM ALTHAM (1736-1818) died unmarried
iv. CHARLOTTE (c.1725-1763) m. Revd James Altham, her cousin, (1733-1787)
v. ELIZABETH died unmarried
vi. HARRIET ALTHAM m. Stothard Abdy, Rector of Theydon Garnon
vii. FRANCES (d.1749)

In 1705 when the 'squire' was still only ten, the death of the vicar, Revd Michael Altham, necessitated the appointment of his successor. Peyton, presumably advised by his mother and possibly Yelverton, presented the living to Michael's son Roger, who had married Peyton's elder sister Mary. Control of all parish affairs continued to be held by the Altham family and when Roger died in 1730 the living was then presented to Peyton's brother James.

During Peyton's tenure of Mark Hall life at Latton seemed to proceed much as usual, with farming as the main occupation, carried out by the principal landowners and their tenants. Generally, villagers did not travel far beyond their immediate location, but London was growing rapidly. Although most of his parishioners' interests might be concentrated on local activities and events Peyton Altham did add his name, together with those of other family members, to a subscription for a coach map of the area published in 1741.

In his will Peyton asked to be buried in any part of Latton Church but *'without show, pomp or pallbearers'*. He left all his *'land, messuages, tenements and hereditaments in parishes and precincts of Latton, Harlow, Epping and Sawbridgeworth in Essex and Hertfordshire'* to his eldest son James. To his wife he left for her lifetime all the Mark Hall furniture and fittings, household goods, jewellery, etc., together with *'coach horses, saddle horses, coaches, chariots and chaises'*. After her death they too would revert to James. He also instructed that the £6000 charged on his estate by his marriage settlement should be used for the support and education of his younger children. His wife was appointed sole executrix. As there were no witnesses to Peyton's signature on his will, an addition of 1741 included an affidavit from *'Mary Haynes and Roger Altham'* that *'they were well acquainted with Peyton Altham Esq., late of Mark Hall, Latton, being nearly related to him and that they were well-acquainted with his handwriting and having viewed the will and signature believed them to be in Peyton Altham's handwriting.'* The will was proved on 10 January 1742 when Peyton's eldest son James was twenty-two, Edward seventeen and William six.

WILLIAM ALTHAM (1736-1818)

Because of the early deaths of both his brothers, who left no heirs, William unexpectedly inherited the estate in 1756, when he was only twenty. He had attended Mr Hildesley's school at Hitchin, Herts, before going up to Trinity College, Cambridge in 1754, two years before his brother Edward died. None of his four sisters had children: Frances and Elizabeth died unmarried, Harriet Abdy was childless, and Charlotte, who had married her cousin, the Revd James Altham, died in childbirth. This meant that, when his mother died in 1768, William was left alone.

It is recorded that in 1771 William made a few *'peculiar innovations'* to the manor house, but suddenly, at the age of forty, he decided to dispose of the whole estate and move away from Latton. His cousin WILLIAM LUSHINGTON, recently returned from India, became the new owner in 1776.

No obvious reason has emerged for William Altham's decision. Isolated in a large old mansion badly in need of repair, William may simply have made up his mind to leave Latton and find a more interesting life for himself elsewhere. It has been suggested that he wanted to keep Mark Hall out of the hands of his cousin and ex-brother-in-law, the Revd James Altham (d.1787) but this seems unlikely. James was the eldest son of William's Uncle James, the late vicar, and brother of the Revd

Thomas Altham, who had succeeded his father at St Mary-at-Latton. After his first wife Charlotte Altham's death, James had twice remarried. From 1776-7 he was given the living of St Mary and St Hugh in Harlow as well as St Olave's, Old Jewry, London but in his later years he acquired a most undesirable reputation. In 1782 he was tried by the Episcopal Court at Doctors' Commons for *'adultery, defamation and obscenity'*. Reports of the trial were reported in the *'Daily Universal Register'* together with popular pamphlets and broadsheets of the time but this was six years after Mark Hall was sold. In the absence of any other direct heir and no will, it is possible that James might have had some claim to the estate, but certainly not in William's lifetime.

Charlotte Altham c.1762

After leaving Mark Hall, WILLIAM ALTHAM moved to Thetford, Norfolk. The Altham family had held property at Feltwell, Norfolk in the late seventeenth century, and it is possible that this influenced his choice of a new home. He was elected Mayor in 1784 and two years later was knighted by King George III. In February 1789, when he was living at Kilverstone Lodge, a complaint concerning his *'abuse of office in the Thetford Corporation'* was recorded. This must have been dismissed as he was chosen as Mayor of Thetford again in 1794. In 1802 the *'Bury & Norwich Post'* recorded that, after selling some cottages and their contents, Sir William was leaving Thetford and moving to Bath. In 1818 he died, unmarried, aged eighty-three, at Kensington House, Middlesex. He was buried at Latton, the last Altham to own the manor that had been in his family for over 200 years.

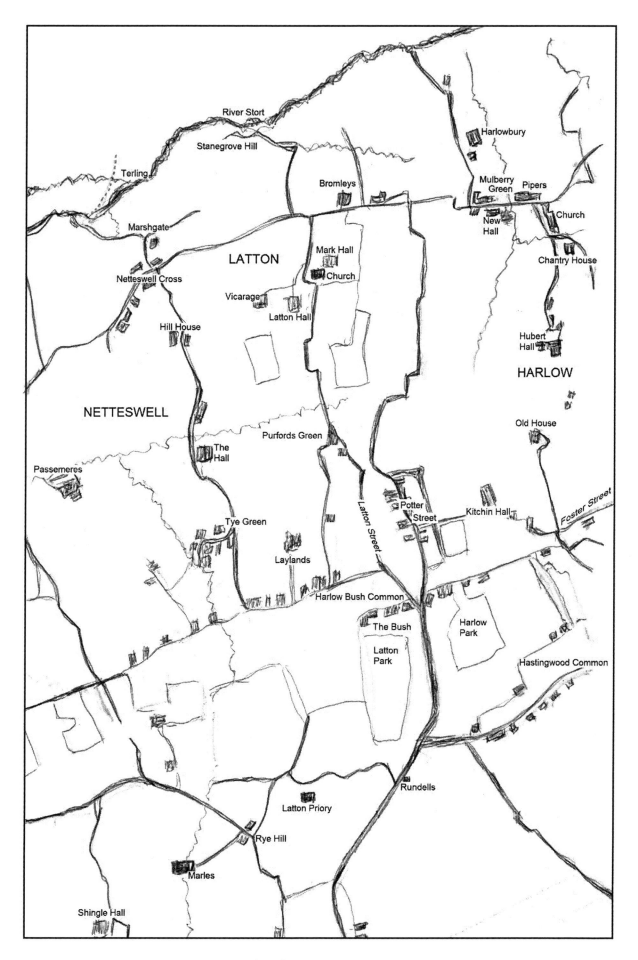

Roads and estates around Latton in 1777

Altham Family Connections

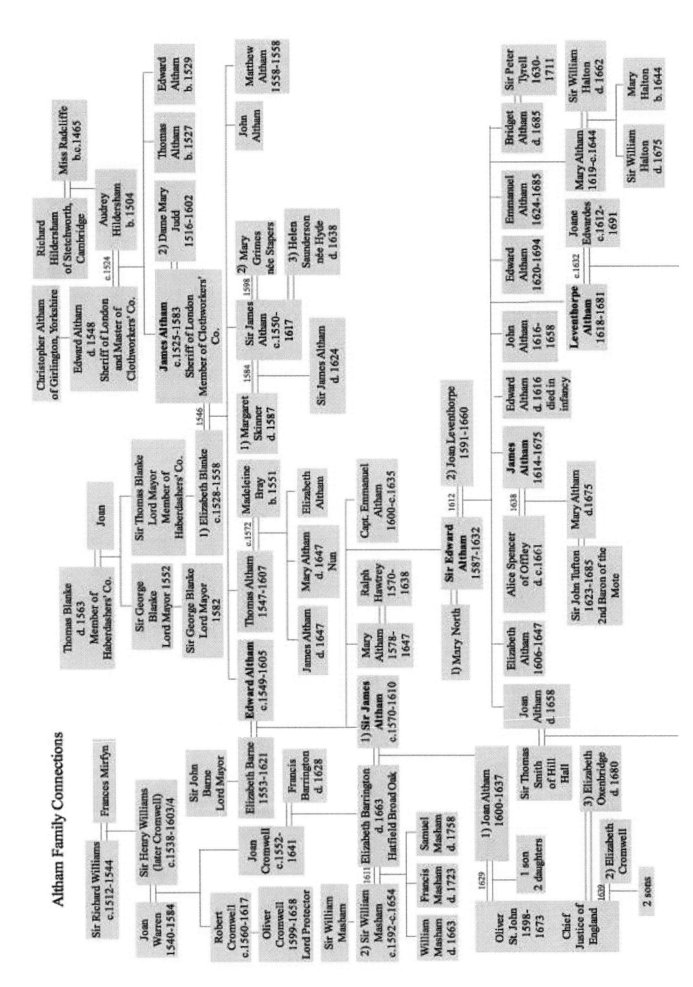

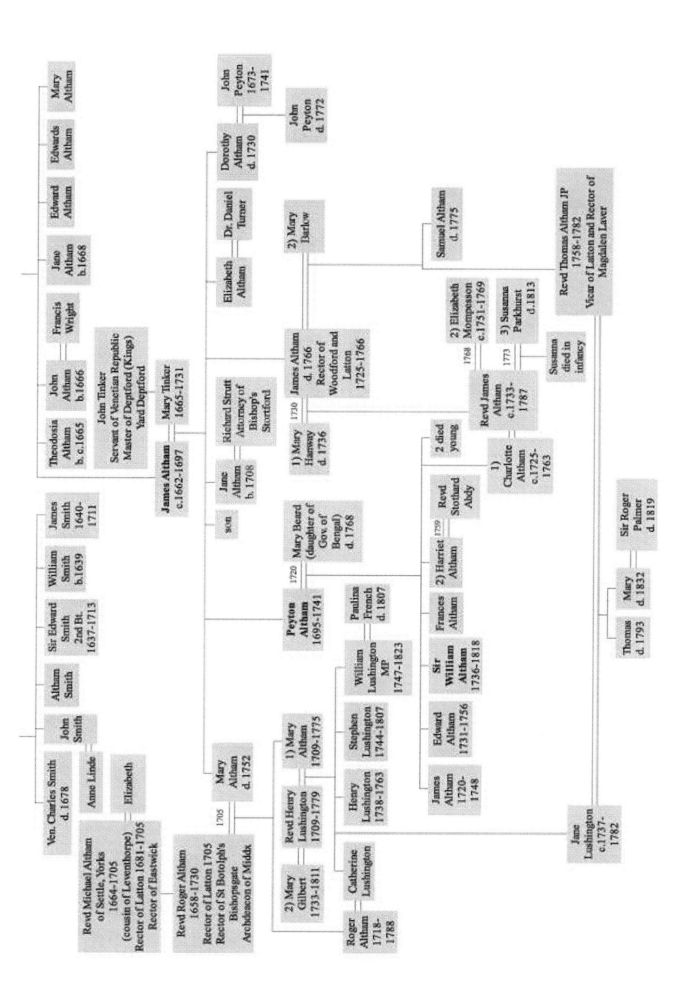

Lushington Family Tree

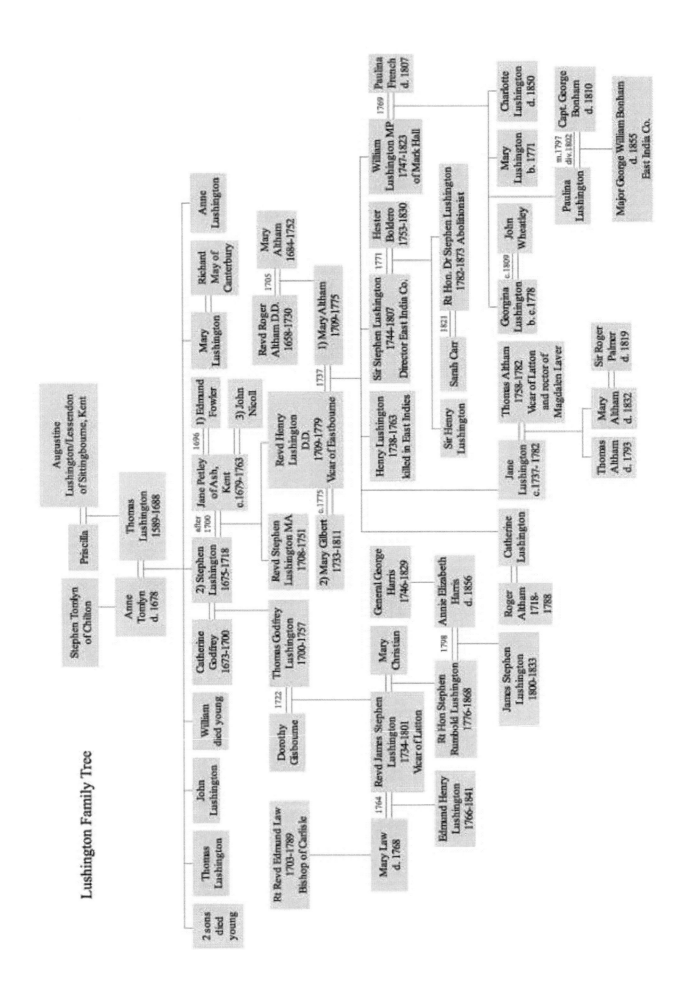

13
The Lushington Family
Owners of Mark Hall c1776-1786

By 1777 William Lushington has bought and begun to demolish and rebuild Mark Hall. 1778 Dr Henry Lushington (father of William) buys the Priory and land in Latton and Netteswell from William Altham of Mark Hall.	1782-1801 Revd James Stephen Lushington is vicar of Latton. 1786 William Lushington sells Mark Hall to Montagu Burgoyne.

See Chronology pages 161-62

Cartoon of William Lushington's election as MP for the City of London 1795
by Isaac Cruikshank

The Lushington family, who were established at Sittingbourne in Kent by the early seventeenth century were minor gentry characterised by high child mortality and a tendency to become or to marry Anglican clergymen. Their family tree is complicated by double and triple marriages, several of which involved members of the Altham family.

The earliest Lushington memorial in Latton church is dated 5 November 1751. Erected by his mother in memory of the Revd Stephen Lushington MA, aged forty-two, it reads somewhat cryptically:

> *'If Death ever spared the Man who was admir'd and lov'd*
> *He had not died'.*

Stephen was a curate appointed by Peyton Altham after he had bestowed the Latton living on his own brother James Altham. Stephen's mother was Jane Fowler née Petley, the daughter of Ralph Petley, Sheriff of Kent in 1680. Jane was the second wife of Stephen's father, another Stephen Lushington, who had died in 1718. They had four sons and three daughters. The Revd Stephen's younger brother Henry, who became vicar of Eastbourne, had married Mary Altham, a niece of Peyton Altham. Katharine, one of Jane's daughters, married another Altham, a barrister at law. Jane was already a widow when she married Lushington and after his death she became Mrs Nicholl. Before Mr Nicholl's death they apparently joined Jane's favourite son Stephen in Latton, where she chose to remain. Mrs Jane Nicholl died in 1763 aged eighty-four.

Jane's third marriage would account for two odd names in the Latton parish register of 1740.

'Mark Hall, a negroe of about 30 years of age a servant of Peyton Altham Esq. was baptised July 6ᵗʰ.'

'Kent Latton, a negroe boy of about 7 years of age belonging to Mr Richard Nicholls was baptised July 6ᵗʰ'.

Which member of the Altham or Lushington family brought the slaves back to England is not clear

Mary Altham
Henry Lushington's
first wife

but 'Mark Hall' obviously worked for Peyton and Mary Altham at the manor house while 'Kent Latton' belonged to Jane and Richard Nicholl who hailed from Kent.

By the time Peyton Altham's son William decided to leave Mark Hall, the Revd Henry Lushington of Eastbourne had fathered eight children, lost one daughter and two sons and decided to marry again after the very recent death of his first wife, William Altham's cousin Mary.

In 1776 it seems probable that Mark Hall was the scene of a family gathering attended by William Altham the unmarried squire, the Revd Henry Lushington and his new bride-to-be, Mary Gilbert of Eastbourne, Henry's son William Lushington and Paulina his wife, heiress of Thomas French of Calcutta, and their six-year-old daughter Mary Elizabeth. Guests invited to dinner would almost certainly have included the vicar Thomas Altham MA, another cousin of the squire. Thomas had married Jane, one of William Lushington's sisters.

William Lushington had given up his post in the East India Company in 1773, returned home and was planning to erect a brand new country mansion for his growing family.

The Revd Henry Lushington and Mary his second wife

At the same time William's father, the Revd Henry, was investing in land in the Latton area.

The Lushingtons represent a typical example of an enterprising upper middle-class family acquiring prestige and wealth through the Church and the Empire but also encountering violent death and financial disaster. The Revd Henry's brother Franklyn was the captain of a man of war and was killed on board his ship at the siege of La Guyra in Venezuela in 1743. In the next generation most of the sons in the extended Lushington family served in India. Three of Henry and Mary's sons joined the East India Company in different capacities. Henry survived the 'black hole of Calcutta' but *'was massacred by Cossim Ali Cawn at Patna, in the East Indies'*. Matthew died aged fourteen, Stephen, the third son, prospered and became a Director and Chairman of the Company and William, the youngest, held an East India Writership from 1763, acted as Persian interpreter to the Commander-in-

Chief, and returned home to an undistinguished political career after his lucrative marriage in 1769. William and Paulina lost at least two infant sons before they returned from India with Mary Elizabeth. Their three younger daughters, Paulina, Georgina and Charlotte were born in England.

William Lushington's father, the Revd Henry, did not long survive his second marriage. He died in Eastbourne in 1779, leaving most of his property, including his land around Latton, to his son Stephen. His second wife inherited the large mansion her husband had recently erected in Eastbourne. She died in 1810, bequeathing her home to her sister Susanna, a spinster, who changed her name from Gilbert to Lushington in 1811, the last year of her life. The Lushington mansion later became the Towner Art Gallery until 2005.

Having engaged the services of the surveyor Benjamin Armitage and decided to buy the Altham estate, William Lushington left his family in his London house in Portland Place and set about planning his new domain.

Accounts of this enterprise vary. An historian studying the Altham letters in 1884 states *'The Lushingtons rebuilt the house on a new site, in modern fashion. The old house, a sketch of which is at Timbercombe in the Quantock hills (the home of William Surtees Altham) was more of a fortification surrounded by a wall, with towers for defence, utterly unlike the modern mansion built by the Lushingtons.'*

How much of the Tudor or Jacobean building was still standing is not recorded. William Altham had already made unspecified alterations to the old house and it is possible that Lushington made use of some of his work. Members of the Gilbey family were under the impression that part of the old structure was encased in a brick skin and incorporated in the new mansion, a technique often used at the time, but if there was any evidence of timber framing predating 1777 it disappeared in the 1947 fire. The usual assumption is that Lushington swept everything away. Demolition on this scale would have produced quantities of building material, some of it capable of being re-used. Recycling of good timber was common practice and bricks laid in lime mortar could be cleaned easily. Rotten timber would be burnt on site and damaged bricks used for ground-fill. Some of the brick-built cellars were incorporated under the new house.

Reconstruction of Mark Hall c.1800

Once the ground was cleared, the new building arose, designed in the strict Classical style, which was undergoing a revival at that time after the freer interpretations of classical motifs used in the earlier Baroque period. Built at a cost of £30,000, the new Mark Hall had a compact rectangular plan – though one of Lushington's plans shows an irregularly shaped block attached to the back. The south-facing entrance front was distinguished by a portico with four Ionic columns surmounted by a broad pediment and flanked by two-storey bays with windows on three sides.

A building of this character would have required the services of an architect and Lushington may have engaged one on the recommendation of a relative or a London neighbour. John Johnson the County Surveyor was the most prominent country house architect in Essex at that time. He had worked for Sir Stephen Lushington, William's brother, in Wimbledon and for John Archer Houblon at Great Hallingbury, but there is no definite evidence to connect him with Mark Hall. The house was built in the local yellow-grey brick. By the late eighteenth century, to meet a growing demand, building materials in the Essex area were becoming readily available from commercial sources: Portland and Purbeck stone, red and 'white' bricks, chalk lime, pit sand and seasoned oak and fir could now be ordered in bulk and delivered to the site at competitive prices. Architectural features such as columns, capitals, mouldings and statuary were being fabricated in a new material called 'Coadstone' at a fraction of the cost of stone carving. This product may have made an appearance at Mark Hall in the classical elements of the entrance portico.

It was impossible to provide a suitably spacious setting for the new house without altering the position of the Latton Street boundary. The solution was to move the thoroughfare a good quarter of a mile to the west, demolishing the old Latton Hall at the same time. The parish church and the new manor house were now isolated within the park. The Lushington estate maps add to our uncertainty about the changes actually made to the landscape before it was resold. One shows a large lake or 'canal' between the house and the walled garden and a twisting water course dug through the park land north west of the house.

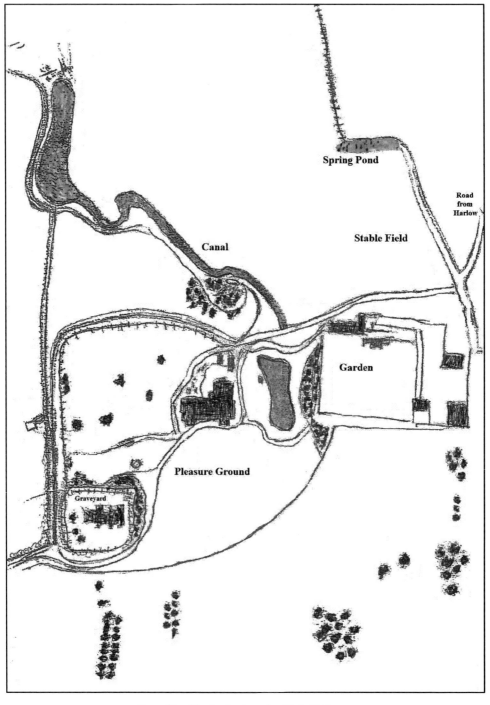

One of Lushington's plans for Mark Hall

In 1786 Lushington's ambitious plans for landscaping the estate were left unfinished when he sold the property to Montagu Burgoyne. Why his enthusiasm waned when the new mansion was still incomplete is not recorded. Perhaps Latton did not appeal to Paulina after Calcutta and London, and the Lushingtons felt unwelcome as wealthy incomers among the local aristocracy. The final demolition of both the old Mark Hall and Latton Hall, and the alteration of the road to the west of Mark Hall, may well have caused resentment among local people.

One link between the Althams, William Lushington and Latton ended in 1782 when William's sister Jane died in the same year as her husband, Thomas Altham, the vicar. William Lushington gave the Latton living to another of his relations, the Revd James Stephen Lushington, but his name does not appear in the records until 1786. As he had been Prebendary of Carlisle since 1777 and became vicar of Newcastle-on-Tyne in 1783, it seems probable that a curate or neighbouring vicar looked after Latton until Charles Miller, the vicar of Harlow, took on the Latton living officially in 1801 when James Stephen Lushington died.

William Lushington's political career followed the usual arc from mildly liberal to nationalistic and conservative, typical of young Englishmen in the French Revolutionary years followed by the Napoleonic wars. In the first flush of liberal anti-Bourbon enthusiasm he became a member of the Society for Constitutional Information and, very briefly, of the radical Friends of the People. At about the same time he was involved with James Law, a distant relative, in the running of a sugar, coffee and cocoa plantation in Grenada covering 254 acres and employing 164 slaves.

After William Pitt was finally pushed into war in February 1793, Lushington became a captain of the Loyal Essex Fencibles and wholeheartedly supported the young Prime Minister. He was elected as an Alderman in the City of London in 1795 and secured a seat in Parliament for Billingsgate in a City by-election while serving as a member of the Honourable Artillery Company.

During the years leading up to and after the abolition of Britain's part in the slave trade in 1807, William Lushington took part in various enterprises connected with shipping and trade with the West Indies. His name appears in the lists of investors in the new West India and the London Dock companies and he owned several ships. In 1799 there was an account in the press of an armed attack on a merchant vessel, the *Benjamin and Elizabeth, 'one of the most valuable of this season from Grenada belonging to Alderman Lushington'*. The ship was boarded in fog off Dover by the crews of two French Luggers and retaken by H.M. Sloop *Racoon*.

In 1800 William Lushington acquired property in Frinton which was later passed on to his daughter Charlotte. At the same date the firm of William Lushington and Co. is listed as one of Lloyd's underwriters. In 1808 William published an article entitled *'The Interests of Agriculture and Commerce are inseparable.'*

William's brother Stephen married into the Boldero family who had old-established enterprises in Jamaica, Trinidad and Granada. A document issued in 1813 connects William with 'slave stock' on the Camden Plantation, Trinidad, in which the Boldero family were involved and which ended in collapse. Unlike his father, Stephen Lushington's son and namesake became a leading Abolitionist.

Paulina Lushington, William's second daughter, was not fortunate in her marriage which ended in divorce in 1802. Her husband, Captain George Bonham of the East Indiaman *True Briton*[1], remarried within three months and disappeared with his ship in the China Seas in 1810. Paulina and Bonham had one son, George William, who became a captain in the East India Company.

William Lushington outlived his wife Paulina by seventeen years. On 6 May 1823 he made his will at Mount Pleasant, Tunbridge Wells leaving *'all unto my beloved daughter Charlotte'*, his sole executrix. It was proved on 13 October 1824.

In the lists of compensation payments to plantation owners and others who lost property in the form of slaves by the Act of 1833, the name of Charlotte Lushington appears.

---

[1] *The True Briton* was built for Sir Robert Wigram, Joseph Arkwright's father-in-law at Wells Yard, Deptford.

Burgoyne Family Tree

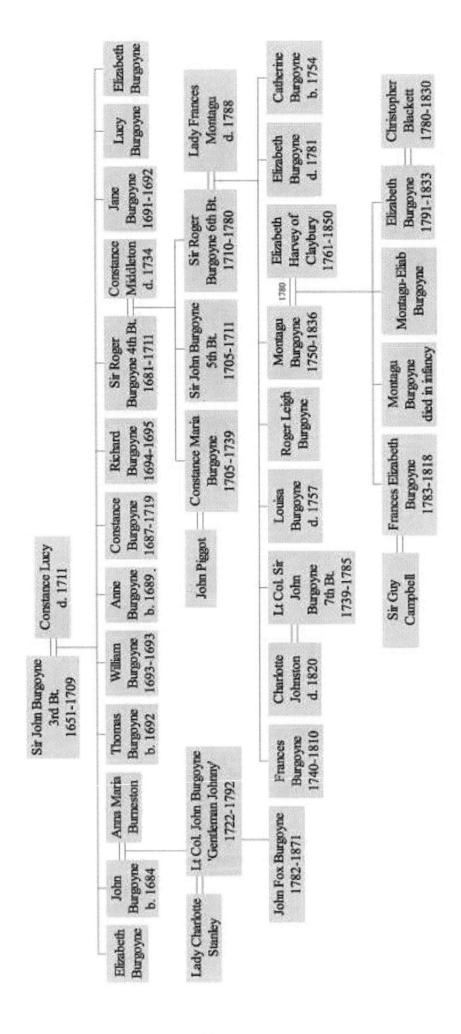

14
The Burgoyne Family
Owners of Mark Hall 1786-1819

1786 Montagu Burgoyne buys Mark Hall and completes the new building. Married to Elizabeth Louisa Harvey of Claybury. Two daughters survive infancy. 1803 John Batt sells New Hall and Kitchen Hall to Montagu Burgoyne.	1819 Richard Arkwright buys Mark Hall and all Burgoyne's estates. 1836 Montagu Burgoyne dies.

See Chronology page 163

When he bought Mark Hall from William Lushington, Montagu Burgoyne was an energetic man of thirty-six, happily married to Elizabeth Harvey, a wealthy heiress. He received a comfortable income as 'Chamberlain of the till office', a sinecure requiring no exertion which he had obtained from his cousin the Prime Minister Lord North. A further £400 was added in 1774 when he was made 'Inspector of duties upon tea and coffee' and commented *This great act of kindness will enable me to go through life in a most easy and comfortable manner'.*

In 1782 Burgoyne's portrait appeared in a cartoon by Gillray entitled *'The victualling committee framing a report'* which also includes Samuel Whitbread, a radical politician and Bamber Gascoyne, Lord of the Admiralty. Burgoyne had led the case against Christopher Atkinson MP, a grain merchant who had cheated both the Treasury and the Victualling Board over the price of wheat for the troops during the America War. Atkinson was expelled from the House and imprisoned but Burgoyne's constant attempts to expose corruption met with little enthusiasm from board members and he soon resigned in disgust.

Montagu Burgoyne

In 1786, the year in which Burgoyne bought Mark Hall, he joined Granville Sharp and Jonas Hanway in their attempt to help destitute black families in London. After the American war a large number of 'Loyalist' ex-slaves had been promised support by the British and had managed to reach England, often via Canada, but had failed to find work. For a brief period Burgoyne became chairman of the Committee for the Relief of the Black Poor which collected funds from wealthy businessman and distributed food to an ever-increasing number of applicants. Before long the numbers became overwhelming and the idea of exporting the problem to a new settlement in Sierra Leone was conceived. As far as we know, Burgoyne took no part in this questionable enterprise but concern for the poor remained a constant element in his activities. In 1814 he was involved in helping to raise money *'for ameliorating the situation of the Irish poor in the metropolis and educating their children'.* This was at a time when most wealthy landowners and industrialists regarded the indigent poor as a menace to be repressed by vicious vagrancy laws.

The Burgoyne family came from Bedfordshire where they owned the parish of Sutton. Montagu and Elizabeth had a house in Grosvenor Square where their first three children were born: two sons who died in infancy and one daughter, Frances Elizabeth. By the time she was three her father had satisfied his hankering for a house in the country by purchasing Mark Hall, possibly at the suggestion of Lord North, who owned Harlowbury House. A second daughter, another Elizabeth, was born in Latton. Unlike most earlier squires of Mark Hall, Burgoyne was interested in planning his country estate as a productive farm as well as a stately home. How much of the final result was due to him is not recorded but he certainly took a more lively interest in the details than his predecessor.

In 1789 he invited Humphrey Repton to advise him on landscaping his park. The only evidence for this visit is one entry in an account book and Repton's tiny sketch of Mark Hall in the 1792 edition of *Peacock's Polite Repository.* Lushington had already created a spacious setting for the

East Lodge

North Lodge rebuilt by the Arkwrights

house by demolishing Latton Hall and moving the road so it seems probable that Repton's advice to Burgoyne concerned details such as tree planting, screening, walks and lodges. The picture described as *'Mark Hall the home of Mr Montagu Burgoyne'*, which Humphrey Repton included in the list of drawings he provided to decorate the pages of the Peacock diary, has caused some controversy. If this does in fact represent Mark Hall, it is the only existing picture of the back of the building. The water in the foreground could be explained as Repton's vision of the scene as it might have appeared if Lushington's plans had been completed.

Montagu Burgoyne considered himself an authority on building matters and frequently crossed swords with the County Surveyor when he took his place on Council committees. It would be interesting to know how much notice he took of Repton's suggestions.

Drawing listed as Mark Hall by Humphrey Repton 1792

After the new Mark Hall was completed, Burgoyne acquired more estates in the locality including New Hall and Kitchen Hall and greatly improved production on all his land by introducing new farming methods and the latest agricultural machinery and equipment. As well as improving the drainage and fertilising by digging a number of cesspools at strategic points and pumping the dung water into a cart for use where it was most needed, he was a pioneer in the use of an early seed drill and a threshing machine. Like other progressive farmers at the time he turned to Southdown sheep of which he kept a large flock. By 1793 he had helped to interest sufficient numbers of local farmers in his methods to take part in founding the Essex Agricultural Society.

In his *General View of the Agriculture of Hertfordshire* (1805) Arthur Young includes information from Mr Montagu Burgoyne concerning *'a very luxuriant crop of potatoes grown in 6 foot ridges by Mr Plummer of Gilston in whole fields around Harlow'*.

The Burgoynes were a family with strong military and naval connections: Montagu's brother Sir John Burgoyne served in India and his first cousin once removed, 'Gentleman Johnny', was the unfortunate Commander forced to surrender to the Americans at Saratoga. Mrs Burgoyne's first cousin Eliab Harvey distinguished himself as captain of the *Temeraire* at the battle of Trafalgar and the Burgoyne's son-in-law, Sir Guy Campbell, was described by his proud relations as *'the hero of Waterloo'*. Montagu himself was too much of an individualist to adapt easily to military discipline and his sympathies were with the French revolutionaries rather than the invading Prussians and Austrians in 1792. His name appears among a group of Whig protesters who described the war as *'A shocking effusion of human blood designed to re-establish French monarchy and to subsidise the King of Prussia.'* Yet he took the lead in raising a regiment of local cavalry in 1794, designed *'for the defence of the country and the suppression of possible domestic commotion'*. The rise of Napoleon, bent on conquering Europe, removed his doubts about the war and in response to the threat of invasion he mustered more local troops under his own command and drilled them in Mark Hall park. He then made himself colonel of the Loyal Essex Regiment of Fencible Cavalry which served in Scotland and elsewhere but never on the Continent. Friction with some of his junior officers led to charges of embezzlement and two courts martial but the charges were mostly dismissed and he retained his command.

In 1815, during the crisis caused by Napoleon's triumphant return from Elba that ended at Waterloo, Montagu Burgoyne made another effort to recruit local volunteers to defend Britain. A poster appeared on trees and walls around Harlow, headed by the royal crest and bearing the following invitation:

To **WEAVERS**
And other Manufacturers.
An Opportunity offers to you of immediate
Employment and good Encouragement
There are a few Vacancies
In a Regiment of Light Horfe,
Commanded by
MONTAGU BURGOYNE, Esq,
Of Mark Hall, Essex
Who engages that you shall not be fent out of the
KINGDOM
And be *discharged at the End of the WAR*
When you may return to your old Occupation

The wording of the poster suggests that Burgoyne was as concerned with finding jobs for unemployed craftsmen as he was with repelling Napoleon, as long as the Emperor stayed on the other side of the Channel.

Throughout the long war with France, Montagu managed to combine soldiering with his many other interests. In a period when most wealthy landlords concerned themselves with the poor only when threatened by uprisings, Burgoyne was one of the leaders in promoting Sunday Schools and helping to finance 'Schools of Industry' to equip children with alternative methods of earning a living, as well as acquiring habits of diligence and obedience. Sewing, hand spinning and straw plaiting were taught to children who were given free meals. Harlow women were also encouraged to take up hand spinning and a local Wool Fair was set up to help local farmers to get a fair price for their produce.

In 1802 Burgoyne started a free school in Harlow High Street and by 1819 his Sunday and day school at Purford Green had forty pupils. Montagu was constantly aware of the problems faced by the poor and, as well as condemning the *'pernicious consequences'* of enclosures, he was an early champion of the allotment movement. His published works include letters and addresses on defects in public charity schools, the reform of Parliament, *'a statistical account of the Hundreds of Harlow, Ongar and Waltham'* and *'Thoughts on the causes of the present discontents'*.

The diaries of the daughters of William Smith MP, who lived at Parndon House from 1785 till 1820, provide several glimpses of life at Mark Hall at the beginning of the nineteenth century. Parties or 'balls' were frequent events and early in 1803 sixteen-year-old Fanny Smith lists the company present on one occasion.

'Mr Johnson of Pardon, [vicar of Great Parndon] *father of 10 children*
Master William Towers the youngest of 10
Mr Wakefield [land agent] *note – it is to be hoped he is a better agriculturalist than dancer or he will make nothing of his farm.*
Chamberlayn of Rys, foxhunter and not v. genteel.
Mr Ralph Palmer – young gent.
Mr Sotheby man of large estates in Essex
Mr Petre a pretty young boy about 6 years old.
Lord & Lady Petre staying at Mark Hall
Everybody admired Joey [Joanna Smith aged 13] *and her dancing. She looked uncommonly pretty and skipped away with such life and spirit that the dullest caught new animation and imitated her capers.'*

At this time, for some reason never explained, Mrs Frances Smith seems to have regarded Montagu Burgoyne as a dangerous influence on her eldest son Ben, then aged twenty. In August 1803 when she and most of the children were travelling north, leaving Ben behind with his father, she wrote an anxious note to her husband:

> *'Aug. 27 re Ben – He cannot be at Parndon alone. He cannot have <u>anything to do with Mr Burgoyne.</u> Are not these things clear?'*

The Smiths and the Burgoynes frequently visited each other but Julia Smith and her sisters found Elizabeth a somewhat patronising young lady. Describing a visit to Bush Fair on 4 August 1817 Julia wrote:

> *'I saw a monkey wipe his nose upon his sleeve and a very beautiful woman who carried all the custom and sold bad gingerbread – a man in women's clothes – I wanted very much to see the lion who attacked the Exeter mail. Elizabeth Burgoyne was not quite so condescending as usual. She used it all up on the ineffable courtesy with which she accepted my Uncle Harry's gingerbread nuts'.*

William Smith and Montagu Burgoyne were both supporters of the Whig party but they differed in their attitude to bribery as a method of winning a seat in the House of Commons. As a middle-class nonconformist Smith knew that he had no chance at all of success without bribery and he saw no other way of achieving enough influence to lead the fight against illiberal laws. Burgoyne, who also had political ambitions, refused to bribe anyone and was heavily defeated on the only two occasions when he stood as a candidate to represent Essex in 1810 and 1812.

Burgoyne's scruples concerning bribery apparently did not apply to his method of achieving the position of a Verderer of Epping Forest, an honour he fervently desired and for which he paid £10,000.

In May 1818 the Burgoyne's eldest daughter Frances Elizabeth Campbell died after the birth of a daughter in Florence. Soon after this the family decided to sell Mark Hall and return to the Burgoyne estate in Sutton. Later that year Mrs Smith referred to this sale in a letter to her daughter and son-in-law, Fanny and William Nightingale, who were also in Italy.

> *'Mark Hall isn't yet sold I believe. Though very likely to be so. Lady Vincent writes Patty* [Smith] *that there are various competitions. That Mr Burgoyne hopes to get £120,000 which by agreement of the Trustees Lord Rocksavage, Mr Neville, Mr Leigh, Mr Duncan is to be vested in the funds. Mr & Mrs B will have a very fine income. I hope they will be happy – we have been neighbours for 36 years'.*

Details of the Lushington/Burgoyne mansion have fortunately survived in the sale catalogue printed in 1819 when the Mark Hall property was put up for auction. By this time the estate included a large number of other properties. (Both Burnt Hall and New Hall are listed as if they were two different houses.) Mark Hall itself is described as *'one of the most perfect houses in England'*.

Judging by later plans of the ground floor, there would hardly have been room for an adequate kitchen, if this was included in *'Offices of every description.'* The small plan that was attached shows several outbuildings down the slope to the east of the house, and it is possible that some of the *'offices'* were situated in these or in the basement.

Out of doors, the flower and vegetable gardens, hot-houses, fruit-houses and ice-house, lodges, lawns, trees and rides through the extensive grounds combined to make it *'a suitable Residence for a distinguished Family'*.

An ice-house, one of the features mentioned in the catalogue, was often found in well-appointed country estates from the seventeenth to the nineteenth centuries. The location of the Mark Hall ice-house, some 165 yards from the house, is shown on the Latton Tithe Award map where it is named 'The Great Ice Cellar'. They were usually brick-built, wholly or partly underground with ramped access. At Mark Hall the building was reached by a footpath along which blocks of ice, obtainable in most winters from the large pond within the park, would be wheeled to the kitchen. The walled kitchen gardens, stables and farm buildings were situated to the east of the house.

An impression of the appearance of the new mansion can be gained from an engraving entitled 'Latton Church & Mark Hall, the Seat of M. Burgoyne Esq.' which was published in 1818 by Longman & Co for the series *'Excursions through Essex'*. The church and part of the house front are glimpsed through a heavy shield of mature trees. Cattle and sheep in the foreground denote a working agricultural estate and complete the romantic scene.

ESSEX AND HERTFORDSHIRE.

CAPITAL FREEHOLD MANORS AND ESTATE, ADVOWSON,
&c. &c.

CONSISTING OF

MANY CAPITAL FARMS,

A SPLENDID

MANSION-HOUSE, WITH GARDEN, HOT-HOUSES, LAWN, &c.

AS PER PARTICULAR.

Particulars and Conditions of Sale

OF THE VALUABLE

MANORS,

OR REPUTED MANORS,

OF

MARK HALL, LATTON HALL, BURNT HALL, NEW HALL, AND KITCHEN HALL,

THE TOLLS OF HARLOW-BUSH FAIR, LARGE CORN-MILL, TWO PUBLIC-HOUSES, AND THE CELEBRATED MANSION-HOUSE, CALLED MARK-HALL, AND ADJOINING ESTATE; OF THE VALUE OF £4000 A YEAR, AND UPWARDS, LAND-TAX REDEEMED.

WITHIN

A SHORT DISTANCE OF THE TOWN OF HARLOW,

IN THE

COUNTIES OF ESSEX AND HERTFORD,

AND

THE ADVOWSON OF THE PARISH OF LATTON,

WHICH

Will be Sold by Auction,

BY

MR. WAKEFIELD,

AT

GARRAWAY'S COFFEE-HOUSE, 'CHANGE ALLEY,

CORNHILL, LONDON,

On Tuesday, the 1st of June, 1819

AT TWELVE O'CLOCK—IN TWO LOTS.

To be viewed by Tickets only, which may be had at Mr. WAKEFIELD's, Land Surveyor, No. 42, *Pall Mall, London*; and Particulars had of him, and of Messrs. GRAHAM, KINDERLY, and DOMVILLE, Solicitors, *Lincoln's Inn*; of Messrs. ODDIE, ODDIE, and FORSTER, Solicitors, *Carey Street, Lincoln's Inn Fields*; of JOHN FOREMAN, Esq. Solicitor, *Harlow*; of T. HALL, Esq. Solicitor, *Saffron Walden*; of Mr. JACKSON, Auctioneer, *Hertford*; of TIMOTHY HOLMES, Esq. Solicitor, *Bury St. Edmund's*; of Mr. WAKEFIELD, *Brook Street, Ipswich*; of Mr. LAKE, Land Surveyor, *Colchester*; of Messrs. MEGGY and CHALK, *Chelmsford*; of Mr. MORTON, Land Surveyor, *Lampitts, Fyfield*; and at GARRAWAY's.

LOT I.

MARK HALL,

Upon which, with its adjoining Grounds, the present Owner has of late years expended above £30,000.

	A.	R.	P.
Scite of House, Gardens, Farm-Yard, and Roads . . .	10	0	34

IT CONSISTS OF

A large Entrance Hall; Dining-room, 40 Feet by 17; Drawing-room, 38 Feet by 25; Ante-room by Drawing-room, 24 Feet by 18; second Dining-room, 27 Feet by 18; Library, and Offices of every description, on the Ground Floor. A Drawing-room, 24 Feet by 17; Five spacious Bed-chambers, Six ditto of a good size, Three Dressing-rooms with room for occasional Beds in them, on the First Floor. In the Attics are One Bed-room, and Seven Servants' Rooms. Stabling for Eighteen Horses and standing for Six Carriages, with Men Servants' Rooms over them; capital Kitchen and Flower Gardens, and spacious Green-house, Hot-houses, Fruit-houses in the centre of a spacious Lawn.

Also, a large Water Corn Mill on the River Stort, called LATTON MILL; Two Public Houses; the Tolls of Harlow Bush Fair; Land immediately joining the Town of Harlow, of very great value as Accommodation Land to the Inhabitants, of capital Feeding Pastures; Meadows, and Arable Land, with Woods and Plantations, tastefully stored with Timber and Young Trees: the whole of which have been laid out so as to adapt the place for the Residence of a distinguished Family.

The Estate is perfectly compact; the Timber, which probably will not exceed in value 10,000l. is tastefully distributed, so as to prove most ornamental to the property; the high road from London to Norwich passes for three miles through the Estate; the high road from Harlow to Hertford crosses it in another direction; the Parish Church of Latton is in the Park, at a pleasing distance from the Mansion; the Town of Harlow is at one end of the Property, and, from the Wealth of its Inhabitants and great thoroughfare, adds to the local value of this fine Property,—it is partly bounded by the navigable river Stort, which conveys produce to London,—at the other end of the Estate, and upon the Manor with the Tolls payable to the Lord, the celebrated Harlow Bush annual Fair is held, at which time the Grass-land, at that end of the Estate, generally produces 30s. per acre, for the week, for the Maintenance of Cattle brought to that Fair. As a Gentleman's Residence it unites one of the most perfect houses in England, 23 miles from the Metropolis, at the end of the Royal Forests of Epping and Hainhault, adjoining a good Post-town, through which a Mail-coach passes, and Stage-coaches nearly every hour; contiguous to the best side of Hertfordshire, with Fox-hounds, belonging to Mr. Conyers or Mr. Hanbury on either side of it; in a Neighbourhood abounding with Gentlemen's Seats; the Place itself celebrated for the tasteful and elegant way in which it has been laid out, replete with every possible convenience of the best Kitchen-garden, with Pleasure-grounds, Green-houses, Hot-houses, Ice-house, &c., the Lawn surrounding the House forming the appearance of a Park, with elegant Lodges, &c.; rides through the whole Grounds of many miles; that it may be truly said, that this Property unites Consequence, Convenience, Pleasure, and Profit, to an eminent degree.

The sale was completed in June 1819. Richard Arkwright of Willersley Castle, described in the Annual Registry of 1843 as *'probably the richest commoner in England'*, paid 100,000 guineas for it, plus the value of the timber, and entrusted it to the care of his youngest son Joseph.

Memorial for Frances Elisabeth Burgoyne

Among the correspondence of Joseph Arkwright is an exchange of letters with Montagu Burgoyne concerning the problems of moving house. Three wagonloads of Burgoyne property had been despatched to their London home in 1819 but Joseph is becoming rather irritated by 1821 when his house is still not completely clear of Burgoyne books and pictures. A letter written in 1823 by Montagu Burgoyne concerns the memorial for his daughter Frances Elisabeth that can be seen in the church of St Mary-at-Latton.

Soon after Burgoyne's arrival in Sutton he became embroiled in a series of court battles with Dr Edward Drax Free, the notorious Rector of Sutton, who had been antagonising everyone by his obscene and illegal activities since his appointment in 1808. An account of this extraordinary affair was published in 1997 by R.B. Outhwaite entitled *'Scandal in the Church'*.

Montagu and his wife both outlived their only remaining daughter and her husband Christopher Blackett. Montagu died in 1836 and his widow lived on until 1850 when she was almost 90.

Mark Hall, the Seat of M. Burgoyne, Esq.
From a drawing by J Greig

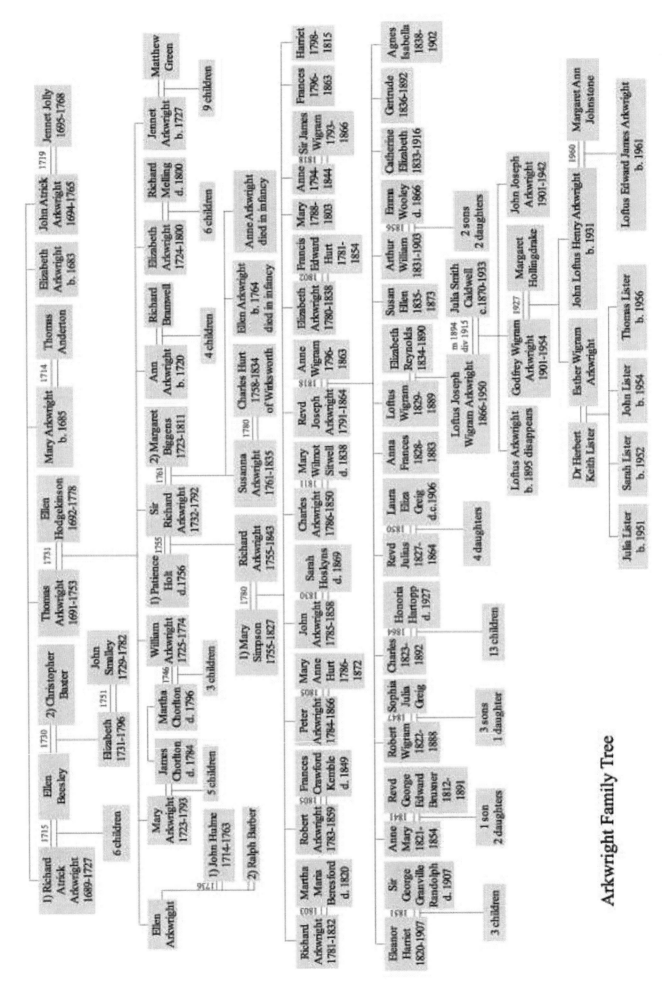

Arkwright Family Tree

15
The Arkwright Family
Owners of Mark Hall 1819-1953

1819 Richard Arkwright of Willersley Castle, Derbyshire buys Mark Hall, New Hall and Kitchen Hall for his youngest son Revd Joseph Arkwright and his wife Anne Wigram.	1889 Only son Loftus Joseph Arkwright, inherits Mark Hall, Parndon Hall and all the local Arkwright estates.
1820 Joseph Arkwright becomes vicar of St Mary-at-Latton.	1890 Elizabeth Arkwright dies.
1843 Richard Arkwright dies. Joseph Arkwright inherits Mark Hall. Twelve children.	1891-94 Loftus lets Mark Hall, first to Josiah Caldwell then to Newman Gilbey. The Gilbeys rent Mark Hall until 1943.
1850 Joseph buys Little Parndon manor and makes his fourth son Loftus Wigram manager.	1894 Loftus Joseph marries Julia Caldwell. Three sons.
Loftus Wigram Arkwright marries Elizabeth Reynolds. One son – Loftus Joseph.	1915 Julia divorces Loftus Joseph.
1864 Revd Joseph Arkwright dies. Loftus Wigram Arkwright inherits Mark Hall and all his father's estates.	1943 The Women's Land Army occupy Mark Hall.
1867 Loftus Wigram and family move into the new Parndon Hall.	1947 Fire destroys Mark Hall except for the Victorian wing.
1889 Loftus Wigram Arkwright dies.	1950 Loftus Joseph Arkwright dies. Son Godfrey inherits.
	c.1947-51 The New Town Corporation buys the Arkwright estates.

See Chronology pages 162-66

Arkwright

Richard Arkwright junior was already a very successful businessman and mill owner when his father, Sir Richard Arkwright, died in 1792 leaving his many cotton-spinning mills to his only son. Willersley Castle near Cromford, which Sir Richard had started to build in 1786, was at last completed four years after his death and Richard moved in with his wife Mary and their eleven children: six sons and five daughters. By that time many competitors were producing cheap cotton thread and Richard decided to sell all his mills except Cromford and Masson, investing the proceeds in a variety of profitable enterprises. Peter, the second son, became a partner with his father in the Cromford mills and each of the other sons was made manager of a large estate. These included Normanton Turville in Leicestershire, Sutton Scarsdale in Derbyshire, Hampton Court in Herefordshire, Dunstall Hall in Staffordshire, and finally Mark Hall in Essex, one of the less expensive of Richard's manors.

Willersley Castle

Joseph, the youngest son, was twenty-eight when he moved into Mark Hall. As part of the process of converting the grandsons of a completely uneducated northern industrialist into country gentlemen, Richard Arkwright had sent all his sons to Eton and all except Peter to Trinity College, Cambridge. Joseph, whose passion was hunting, was destined for the church. Although his studies were not allowed to interfere seriously with his sporting activities, he managed to acquire a BA degree and was ordained in 1814. Four years later he married Anne Wigram, the seventh child of Sir Robert Wigram and his second wife Eleanor. Sir Robert Wigram of Walthamstow, whose twenty-third child would have been six by this time, was a wealthy Irish ship-owner and an MP.

The Wigram and Arkwright families continued to intermarry for at least two generations. Joseph's younger sister Anne married Sir James Wigram, Sir Robert's eleventh child and their son married Margaret Helen Arkwright, one of Peter's daughters. Margaret Helen's sister Susan Maria Arkwright complicated relationships still further by marrying the Revd Joseph Cotton Wigram, Bishop of Rochester and Sir Robert Wigram's fifteenth child.

One advantage that Richard Arkwright could enjoy by acquiring old manor houses was the right to appoint the next vicars as soon as the posts became vacant. Mark Hall may have been chosen partly because the Latton vicar, the Revd Charles Miller, was also vicar of Harlow and was willing to concentrate on that parish. The age of the Latton vicar and the small number of his parishioners were included in the sale catalogue as inducements to attract prospective purchasers.

LOT II.

ADVOWSON OF LATTON.

---

112 ACRES OF GLEBE LAND,

WITH AN

EXCELLENT PARSONAGE HOUSE,

VIZ.

	£.	s.	d.
Nine of Grass, five of Woodland, and ninety-nine of Arable, at 40s. .	224	0	0
Tythe on 1317 acres, in the highest cultivation, at 6s. 6d. per acre .	428	0	0
	£ 652	0	0

Supposed to be rated so low in the King's Books as to be tenable with any preferment, as the last Incumbent, the Rev. W. LUSHINGTON, held the Living of Latton, with the Living of Newcastle upon Tyne.

The ADVOWSON HOUSE is a very good one, with Barns, Stables, &c. in the midst of the Glebe of 112 acres, which surrounds it. There are not 300 persons in the Parish, and the Incumbent 59 years old.

The agent has confused the name of the last owner with the name of his vicar. It was the Revd James Stephen Lushington, not William, who held Latton and Newcastle on Tyne.

'The Incumbent', Charles Miller, did in fact give up the Latton living soon after Joseph arrived. This left the post free for the new squire and by 1824 Richard Arkwright was able to present his extravagant youngest son with a second living at All Saints church, Thurlaston, near his brother Richard's mansion in Leicestershire.

In 1826 Joseph would have been consulted by Mr John Barnard junior of Harlow about the foundations of very strong walls that had appeared on Stanegrove Hill within Mark Hall manor. This discovery, which Mr Barnard described in a letter to the Gentleman's Magazine, seems to have awakened interest in the *'elevated field which was formerly almost surrounded by the water of the river Stort, hitherto unnoticed by antiquarians.'*[1] The idea that this was the site of one of four Roman forts built along the Stort from Harlow to Stansted Mountfitchet began to gain acceptance.

Joseph and some of his rapidly increasing family often spent months every year at Normanton Hall with his brother Richard, a widower whose children all died very young. After Richard's early death in 1832 Joseph became manager of the Normanton Turville estate where he revelled in the excellent hunting. As a Cambridge undergraduate Joseph had kept four horses and throughout his life horses and dogs remained his obsession. Disagreements with H.J. Conyers of Copped Hall, Master of the Essex Foxhounds until 1852, partly explained his preference for Leicestershire, but in the later years of his life, having resigned from both livings, Joseph became the Essex Master, built new Kennels near Hubbards Hall, and devoted most of his time to hunting, varied by horse racing, shooting, archery and cricket.

---

[1] *The History and Topography of Essex* Vol. 11 Thomas Wright 1835.

The Meet at Matching Green

The grounds of Mark Hall were cherished by farm-workers and gardeners who formed their own cricket team; a custom that descended to Joseph's son and grandsons at Parndon Hall. Fruit-growing interested Joseph and his correspondence includes orders for nectarines, pears, apricots, plums and cherry trees. The holes made by nails to support wires for his figs and other fruit can still be seen in the old walls of Mark Hall. An invoice from James Lee of the Vineyard, Hammersmith, dated March 1822, lists all kinds of vegetable seeds and eleven fruit trees despatched in '1 basket and 1 bag' at a total cost of £6.1s 8d.

Joseph's sporting activities in Essex and Leicestershire might appear to leave little time for his pastoral duties but his parishioners, both in Latton and Thurlaston, were well used to an absent vicar, helped out by a hard working curate. The Latton curate before 1850 was the Revd David Lewes who lived in Potter Street. Julius, Joseph's third son, who was ordained in 1848, may have become a curate in Latton shortly before being presented with the living when his father gave it up. The Thurlaston living was bestowed on the Revd George Bruxner, a widower who had married Joseph's second daughter Anne in 1841.

In that same year, in spite of Joseph Arkwright's petition to the House of Commons to stop the railway from invading his land, the Northern and Eastern line from London was successfully completed as far as Harlow. Joseph had based his objection on information that the line was to be completed only as far as Bishop's Stortford and argued 'the same therefore cannot be of any public advantage sufficient to justify the proposed invasion of the property of your Petitioner.' He was persuaded to waive his objection by an offer of £7,800 for thirteen acres (he had hoped for £10,000) and the line continued on its expensive way towards Cambridge. Everyone, except the owners of canal boats and stage coaches, benefited considerably, including both landlords and tenant farmers.

When Richard Arkwright died in 1843, Joseph inherited both Mark Hall and Normanton Hall in addition to a legacy of £120,000 and an equal share in the residue with his four surviving brothers – a precise calculation that worked out at £263,745.17s each. This enabled him to invest more freely in land and new buildings in the Harlow area.

By this time Burgoyne's original mansion with its twelve main bedrooms no longer satisfied Joseph and Anne and they decided to extend the house, reserving the grander rooms for themselves and their visitors. The old outbuildings which may have housed the kitchen and 'domestic offices', were removed and replaced by a two storey wing with a basement. Most of the boys were then accommodated in the new east wing where the land slopes steeply down towards the stables. Writing a century later, a visitor to Mark Hall was rather disgruntled to find himself 'relegated to the former nursery, now the bachelors' wing which had been added much later to accommodate the sons of the house, interspersed with some housemaids' cupboards. Bathrooms were few and there were pantries, lamp room and other offices below.'[1]

Bathrooms were not only few but virtually non-existent in 1819. In one letter Joseph wrote: 'For several months no water comes even to the base of the house that is fit for the most common household purpose'.

---

[1] Jack Gold in *Alfred Gilbey. A Memoir by Some Friends*. Ed. David Watkin 2001 Michael Russell (publishing) Ltd.

Mark Hall depended on water pumped from wells for its water supply throughout its existence.

If J. Grieg's drawing of Mark Hall in 1818 is accurate, it is apparent that Joseph Arkwright changed several features of the original building as well as adding a new wing. The pediment feature was retained but the attached Ionic columns were removed and the plain windows were surmounted by new decorative embellishments. The small semi-circular window in the pediment was replaced by a circular one and a bay-window, absent from Lushington's plan, was added on the west side of the house.

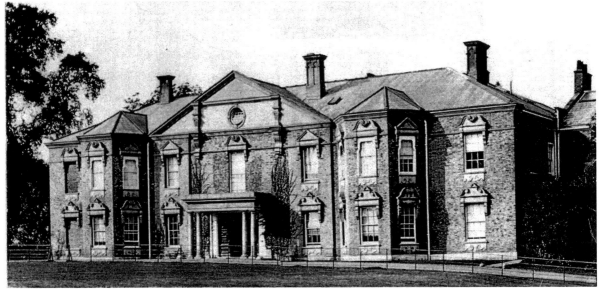
Mark Hall after 1850

In White's Directory of 1848 the description of Latton includes the information that *'the Rev. Joseph Arkwright, the lord of the manor, is both patron and incumbent, and has recently restored and beautified the interior of the church'*. He also spent a good deal on building a new rectory. The old moated rectory had been in a very bad state of repair for years and Joseph planned a much finer establishment for his son, the Revd Julius and Laura his wife. Now renamed Moot House, the Community Centre in the Stow, this simple elegant building is one of the few remaining indications of Joseph Arkwright's taste in architecture, apart from the Clock House at Purford Green and the school building opposite it.

Joseph and Anne had five sons but only two of them remained in Latton. Robert and Charles, the two eldest, both joined the Dragoon Guards after attending Eton and Trinity, served in South Africa and spent very little time at Mark Hall.

Julius who, as the next in age and vicar of Latton, might perhaps have expected to inherit Mark Hall, was already ill with a wasting disease when Joseph made his will, shortly before his death in February 1864. Mrs Anne Arkwright had already died and Julius himself died a month later, leaving a widow and four daughters. He

Moot House in 1996

was described by his temporary successor, the Revd William Shilleto, as *'the late rector whose holy life and premature death still lives green in the memory of his former parishioners'*, but his father left him very little, with no provision for his family. This may have been because there was a developing rift in the Arkwright clan over Roman Catholicism.

Both Julius and his eldest brother Robert had married into the Grieg family, several of whom converted to Catholicism, and Joseph abhorred the idea of Mark Hall being inherited by 'bloody Papists'. Although Julius remained the vicar of Latton until his death, the Census of 1861 shows that he and Laura no longer lived at the rectory with their four daughters. That building was occupied by Samuel Lloyd, *'curate of Latton'*, his wife Catharine, one son, two stepsons and five servants. Julius may already have been ill and unable to perform his duties several years before his death and the family could have gone abroad seeking a cure. Alternatively, their departure from the rectory may have marked the beginning of the rift in the family that was to last well into the next century. The new rectory was soon occupied by the Revd William Pitt Wigram, a nephew of Mrs Anne Arkwright, and no more is heard of Laura and the children in Latton. One daughter became a Benedictine nun and the marriage of another took place in a Catholic church.

Loftus Wigram Arkwright

In 1901 Laura, aged seventy, was living in Kensington with two unmarried daughters. She died aged seventy-five and was buried in the Catholic cemetery at Mortlake, followed by her daughters in 1911 and 1934.

Charles, Joseph's second son, was still unmarried when his father died, and had a rather wild reputation while Arthur, the youngest, had settled in Leicestershire and devoted himself to medicine. Apart from five unmarried daughters still living at Mark Hall, this left only Loftus Wigram, the fourth son, who shared all Joseph's interests. Like his Uncle Peter, Loftus Wigram had gone home to help his father as soon as he left Eton. Together they had hunted and supervised the Kennels and when Joseph acquired the Little Parndon estate Loftus Wigram was made manager.

Since the Amherst family had moved away, the old Parndon House had been demolished and the little parish had no manor house. Loftus Wigram lived at Rundells, later an antique shop, on the road to Epping, and it was there that he brought his bride in 1862. She was Elizabeth Reynolds, the daughter of a horse dealer who had owned livery stables in

Kensington, and she shared the Arkwrights' passion for hunting. When their first child, Loftus Joseph, was born four years later the couple were living at Gladwins, now the home of a doctor, between Sheering and Hatfield Heath.

Faced with the prospect of sharing Mark Hall with Anna, Catherine, Susan, Gertrude and Agnes, who had all been given the right to remain there for life, Loftus Wigram decided to build a new home for his family in Little Parndon.

The new Parndon Hall was completed in 1867 and Elizabeth was able to make use of

Parndon Hall in 1900

her considerable talent for painting as she decorated the doors, walls and ceilings of the new mansion. Now encircled by Princess Alexandra Hospital, the house has so far survived threats of demolition and the paintings are still admired by visitors, though it was as a huntress, rather than an artist that Elizabeth was well known in her time.[1] Loftus Wigram had taken on the position of Master of the Essex Foxhounds after Joseph's death and, though he could no longer ride after breaking his back in 1868 while hunting in Epping Forest, he always followed the hunt in a phaeton and retained control of the Kennels until his death in 1889.

---

[1] See *The Huntress who lived in a Painting* by Carole Murray. Unpublished notes. Museum of Harlow.

No account has been preserved of the lives of the five sisters at Mark Hall after the death of their parents. Their grief over the loss of their brother Julius, so soon after Joseph's death, is commemorated in the east window of his church but it seems that no contact was maintained with Laura, his widow. As Laura's sister Sophia had married Robert Arkwright, by then well established at Knuston Hall in Northamptonshire, his sister-in-law probably stayed there for a while with her children. Sophia's enthusiastic Catholicism continued to rankle at Mark Hall and communication ceased between the household at Knuston and their relations in Latton and Little Parndon. The Arkwright sisters' high Anglican religious leanings may be assumed by their generous contributions to the rebuilding of the church of St Mary Magdalene in Potter Street, but Joseph's daughters would have no dealings with Rome.

One of the few contemporary references to the sisters at Mark Hall is included in a lecture on the history of Latton[1] given in the Latton Street schoolhouse by the Revd William Shilleto, the Locum Tenens, in October 1865. His work, he says, is based on researches into the parish registers *'...and I derived further light and information from Morant's History of Essex, a copy of which now rare book I have through the kindness of the ladies of Mark Hall been allowed to use during nearly the whole of my sojourn in Latton. This I am glad to have the opportunity of publicly acknowledging'.*

There was probably frequent contact between the Misses Arkwright and Eleanor, their eldest sister, at Hadham. Eleanor had been thirty-one when she married Vice Admiral Sir George Granville Randolph in 1851 and the couple had three children. Lady Randolph lived to be eighty-seven, but her sister Anne, the second wife of Revd George Bruxner, had died aged only thirty-three and lies buried at Thurlaston, next to Bruxner's third wife.

Anna Frances, who was one year older than Loftus Wigram, seems to have been his chosen companion. They were both staying at the new rectory, as guests of Julius and Laura, when the rest of the family were in Leicestershire in 1851, and her initials are among those engraved on the wall of his new home in Little Parndon. Maybe she sided with her brother over his choice of a wife. Family legend suggests that, in spite of her ability in the hunting field, Elizabeth Reynolds was not considered a suitable match by some of the family.

For the next twenty-five years, while Loftus Wigram carried out the duties of the squire in both Latton and Little Pardon, life at Mark Hall probably followed the pattern set by Joseph Arkwright, but with less exuberance. Susan died in 1873, aged only thirty-eight, and Anna ten years later in 1883. An entry in the local newspaper in September 1880, describing the harvest celebrations, indicates the part the sisters played in parish life.

'After the service [at Little Parndon church] *the Harlow band marched the congregation to a barn that had been prepared for the occasion. Tables were laid for about 150.*

The provisions consisted of enormous rounds of cold roast and boiled beef, pies, plum pudding, etc. with hot vegetables and an abundance of nut brown ale. Grace was said by Mr Earle who presided. Mrs and the Misses Arkwright, Hemming and the other ladies waited on the party. The choir enlivened the afternoon with songs and glees until tea was served, shortly after which Mr Arkwright and his friends retired,'

The picture presented is of rural prosperity but the 1870s, 80s and 90s brought a prolonged period of depression to British agriculture. In his *History of Latton* (1970) Jonathan Edmunds described the causes of this slump in some detail.

'Cheap corn from the American prairies hit arable farmers and later came refrigerated meat from Australia, New Zealand and the Argentine. But the farmer's worst enemy was the weather. Between 1875 and 1878 there were four wet and cold summers producing poor harvests and causing shortages of hay. In 1879 it seemed to rain almost without ceasing from early spring until late in September while the following winter was very cold. 1880 saw great losses of sheep because of rot in their feet and even more were lost in January 1881 following a fierce blizzard. Yet 1885 and 1887 suffered from droughts. The last decade of the century started with snow drifts 20 feet deep followed by a wet harvest.'

---

[1] Lecture on *The Parochial History of Latton* by Revd William Shilleto. Locum Tenens 1865. Manuscript and copy. Museum of Harlow. This manuscript was sent to the Museum by Mr Ralph Gilbey in 2007.

Rents and wages fell and even opulent landowners began to look for less risky investments. For many farm labourers, poaching became the only method of obtaining an adequate meal and Arkwright had to protect his coverts with forty men during the annual Bush Fair. In 1879 Loftus Wigram and other local magistrates had the fair closed down and the Assembly Rooms, where Joseph Arkwright had entertained his parishioners and practised archery, gradually slid into disuse.

During these years, while his mother hunted and painted and his father supervised their large estates and managed the Kennels, Loftus Joseph, who had intermittently attended both Eton and Charterhouse, left Cambridge and sought the company of the sons and daughters of the local landowners. He excelled at racing and shooting, went hunting with Edwin Bowlby of Gilston and sometimes shared the company of Lady Warwick of Easton Park with Edward, Prince of Wales. It could have been at Easton Lodge that he met the Caldwells, *'a distinguished Connecticut family'* who frequently visited England and were friendly with the Warwicks. This carefree period was interrupted in 1889 by the death of his father.

Loftus Joseph Arkwright

On 6 May 1889 the Times reported that *'Mr Loftus Wigram Arkwright J.P. of Parndon Hall Essex died suddenly at his residence early on Saturday morning in his 60th year. He had long suffered from paralysis, but his death occurred quite unexpectedly at last.'* Later the Essex Herald reported that, at about the same time, *'his wife Elizabeth was severely injured by being thrown from her trap near the Burnt Mill Brass Factory* [Kirkaldy's] *and it is possible that she never really recovered from the shock she then experienced.'* Almost immediately after her husband's death Elizabeth moved out of Parndon Hall and the house was closed up. She went to London, possibly to stay with her brother James, a wine merchant, and Loftus Joseph, then aged twenty-four, moved down to share Parndon Hall farmhouse with one servant. In May, 1890, almost exactly a year after his father's death, Loftus Joseph became solely responsible for all the Arkwright estates when his mother collapsed and died while staying at the Great Eastern Hotel at Liverpool Street Station. Mark Hall was still occupied by Loftus Joseph's three aunts and their servants. The 1881 Census lists seven maids, a footman and a butler in the house, as well as several men in the outbuildings. The Laundry, a building near Bromleys, was occupied by two Irish sisters, Margaret and Maria Lanagan.

Since her brother's death, Catherine had taken on his duties as churchwarden of St Mary-at-Latton and Gertrude and Agnes continued to concern themselves with the rebuilding of St Mary Magdalen.

Suddenly the situation changed. Instead of anticipating a peaceful old age in the mansion where they had been born, the sisters were informed that the Mark Hall estate was to be let and they must move out. What suggestion, if any, Loftus Joseph made about a possible new home for his aunts is unknown but it was certainly not Parndon Hall. That was soon reopened and let to a solicitor and his family.

Loftus Joseph stayed on at Parndon Hall Farmhouse and in 1893 he became joint Master of the Essex Hunt with Mr E.S. Bowlby of Gilston Park[1]. The Kennels had been sold to Mr Charles E. Green in 1890.

Little more is recorded about the Misses Arkwright. Their eldest sister Lady Randolph was in a position to help them and their brother Arthur had become a successful doctor. Charles, who had belatedly married Honoria Hartopp of Dalby Hall, Leicestershire and had thirteen children, died in 1892, the same year as Gertrude. In 1901 Catherine and Agnes were living together in Haywards Heath. Catherine, who survived all her brothers and sisters, had moved to St Leonards by 1911 and died in 1916, aged eighty-three.

---

[1] H. Beauchamp Yerburgh *Leaves from a Hunting Diary* 1900 Vinton & Co Ltd. 9 New Bridge, St Ludgate Circus, London.

Caldwell Family Tree

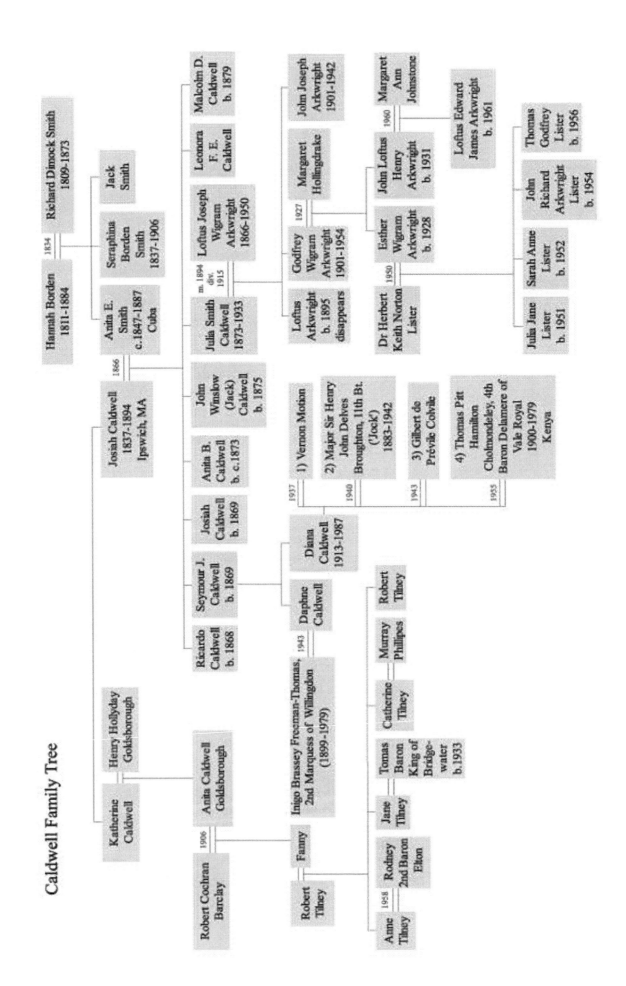

16
The Caldwell Family
Tenants at Mark Hall 1892-1894

The first tenant of Mark Hall after the departure of the Misses Arkwright was Josiah Caldwell, by then a widower, whom Loftus Joseph may have met at Easton Lodge. Mrs Anita Caldwell had died in 1887, leaving Josiah with five sons: Ricardo, Seymour, Josiah, John and Malcolm and three daughters: Julia, Anita and Leonora. On the 1891 Census Seymour is absent but the rest of the family, ranging in age from twenty-three to twelve, are all at Mark Hall, together with their German governess, Miss E. Von Ender, aged twenty-eight. The Caldwells' stay at Mark Hall was very brief but tales about their exploits descended in the Arkwright family because Josiah's eldest daughter Julia married Loftus Joseph. Many years later Dr Lister, Julia's 'grandson-in-law', described Josiah as *'a flamboyant entrepreneur who was either very rich or penniless.'* He made his money on the Baltic Exchange and had sugar-planting connections with Cuba. These sugar plantations belonged to Mrs Caldwell's family. Anita's brother, Jack Smith, is alleged to have been largely responsible for starting the Spanish American war in 1898. A despatch he sent to the New York Tribune resulted in the arrival of the USS *Maine* in Cuban waters where it was blown up by a Spanish mine and hostilities began. Another family legend maintained that one of Josiah's sons was invited to become president of Cuba, an offer he apparently declined.

Anita Caldwell

Julia Caldwell was born in Boston and the family spent their time travelling back and forth across the Atlantic in pursuit of both business and pleasure. While in England they rented a succession of different houses. Dr Lister remembered that during his brief tenancy Josiah *'began to refront the exterior of Mark Hall with pilasters but fortunately ran out of money'*. In 1894 Josiah moved on to The Firs, Kelvedon Hatch, Brentwood and Mark Hall was re-let to Newman Gilbey.

At this stage, Loftus Joseph decided the time had come to marry Julia and move

Seymour Caldwell

Josiah Caldwell

back into Parndon Hall. The wedding took place in June 1894 and during the first years of their marriage they continued to hunt together. Their first son, another Loftus, was born in 1895 and the twins, John and Godfrey arrived six years later. In that same year, 1901, Julia's sister, Anita Caldwell, appears on the Census as a boarder at Dorrington's farm, Little Parndon. Seymour Caldwell, then aged thirty-two, was also a boarder, living at Gardener's Farm, Theydon Garnon where he is described as *'Stockbroker / Agent own a/c'*.

Like his father, Loftus Joseph Arkwright had a severe accident while hunting and was no longer able to ride. This was probably in 1899 when he gave up his position of Joint Master of the Essex Hounds. From then on he concentrated on planting pine trees, breeding pheasants and shooting.

Gilbey Family Tree

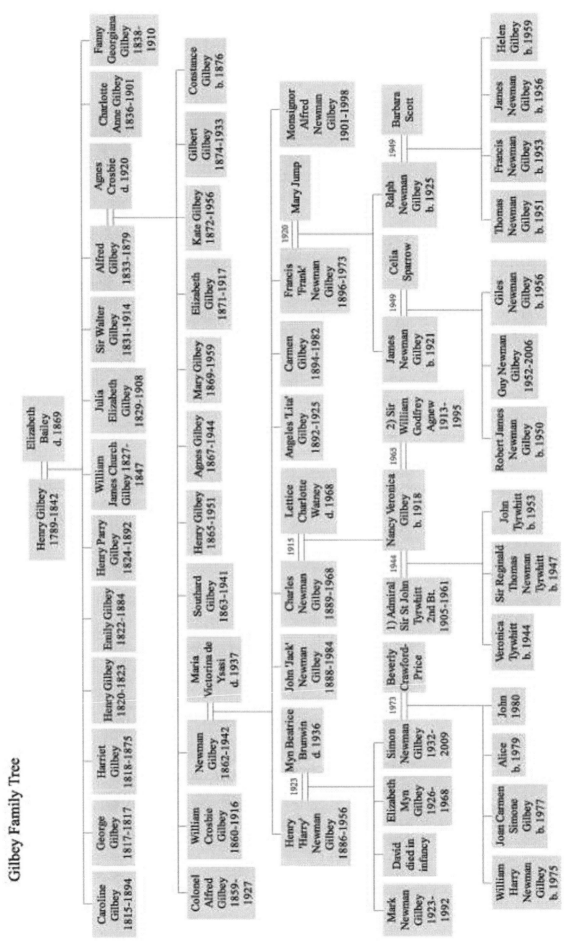

17

The Gilbey Family
Tenants at Mark Hall 1894-1943

1894 Loftus Joseph Arkwright leases Mark Hall to Newman Gilbey. 1942 Newman Gilbey dies.	1943 The Gilbeys leave Mark Hall. Women's Land Army at Mark Hall.

Henry Gilbey, described on his tombstone as a 'coach proprietor', was well known in this area, long before the name of Gilbey became associated with wines and spirits. Before the railway ruined his business Henry prospered as his stage coaches picked up Harlow passengers at the Crown Inn on their frequent journeys between Bishop's Stortford and London, but after his death in 1842 his three sons, Henry Parry, Walter and Alfred had to seek their fortunes elsewhere. The family already had connections in the wine trade. Walter and Alfred were both employed by an uncle in that trade and Henry Parry set up his own wine business in 1851. At first their interest was mostly in importing wine from the developing vineyards of South Africa.

In 1854 Walter and Alfred both volunteered to go to the Crimea as clerks in the Army Pay Department. There they met up with a cousin, Henry Grinling, who was working for the War Office under Dr E.A. Parkes. The idea of exploiting the obvious demand for inexpensive wine among soldiers and officers appealed to all three young men and, as soon as they returned to England, Walter and Alfred set up their own company. With no financial backing whatever, they imported wine directly and sold it by mail order, thus eliminating middlemen and making use of the new fast steamships and railways. Henry Parry joined them in 1860 and in that year they became the third largest British importers of wine from all over the world. Their customers included *'upwards of 80 of the chief Hospitals, Military Messes and Public Institutions'*, but their real breakthrough was made possible by Gladstone and the free trade movement. The Free Trade Treaty of 1860 greatly reduced the duties on French wine, and the 'Single Bottle Act' allowed grocers and other small retailers to sell single bottles of alcoholic liquor. Gilbeys set up over 2,000 agencies enabling shopkeepers to stock any number of bottles at a fixed price, plus help with advertising and license charges, on condition they never dealt with competitors. By this time the Gilbey range included over 200 varieties of drink.

In spite of the vociferous Temperance movement, the Gilbey enterprise was greatly encouraged by the Liberal Establishment. In 1880 Mr Gladstone declared: *'Since the wine duties were altered fundamentally in 1860, great progress has been made in facilitating the consumption of wine, cheap wine, and of sound wine throughout the country. The character of the Trade has been fundamentally changed – adulteration is greatly diminished, and the consumption of sound wine and cheap wine has been very greatly increased'*.

In the last decade of the nineteenth century the firm acquired several distilleries and Gilbey's Gin became a household name. From the outset it was an exclusively family business. Henry Grinling had joined the firm in the mid sixties and by recruiting 'in-laws' as well as direct descendants the Gilbeys kept total control for over a century.

Of the three brothers who started the enterprise it was Walter Gilbey who became the most well known and who lived the longest (1831-1914). His interests were by no means confined to wine. Horses were his passion – an enthusiasm he shared with his friend Edward VII. It was Walter who insisted on importing English shire horses to replace some of the oxen used on the Chateau Loudenne vineyard near Bordeaux, bought by the family in 1875. His collection of pictures included twenty-eight by Stubbs.

Walter was knighted in 1893 for his services to horse breeding and agriculture and the family lived in considerable luxury at Elsenham Hall near Bishop's Stortford where they grew fruit and started a jam factory. Alfred, his brother and partner (1833-1879) lived at Wooburn House, Buckinghamshire with his wife Agnes and their seven children. The firm owned many stores and bonded warehouses, including a huge bottling plant in Camden, but their central showplace, first leased then bought, was the Pantheon in Oxford Street. This impressive building, originally intended as *'a place of evening entertainment for the Nobility and Gentry'*, was transformed to provide suitable accommodation for storage, offices and a splendid board-room. There were also suites where members of the family could stay while visiting London. This edifice was retained by the Gilbeys until 1937 when it was sold to Marks & Spencer.

Alfred's eldest son, Newman (1862-1942) preserved the family tradition by marrying into the wine trade and becoming a partner in the Gilbey firm. In order to obtain the hand of Victorina Ysasi, a niece of Manolo Gonzalez, Marquis of Torre Soto, a great friend of the Gilbeys, Newman had to become a Roman Catholic. This he did in 1886 and their first son, Harry, was born in that same year. By the time Newman and Victorina decided to rent Mark Hall they had three more children, Jack, Charlie and Lita (Angeles), and Carmen was born shortly before the move. A fourth son, Frank, arrived in 1896 and in 1901 Alfred, the last and eventually the most well known son, completed the family. While Newman Gilbey was working in his office at the Pantheon as a partner and managing director he kept in touch with his five sons while they were away at boarding school by dictating circular letters to them – a collection that was later bound and treasured by Alfred.

The Gilbey family by the summer house, Mark Hall

Newman Gilbey and his brother's family at Elsenham Hall belonged to the same hunting and shooting set as Lady Warwick, the Caldwells and the Arkwrights. Newman and his nephews Guy and Tresham are frequently mentioned in H.B. Yerburgh's *Leaves from a Hunting Diary* (1900). The book includes an ecstatic description of a hockey game played on thick ice at Elsenham on a day when hunting was impossible.

'No more charming place within the confines either of Essex or Herts could be found for the exhilarating pastime of skating than the beautiful lake some nine acres in extent lying in the grounds of Elsenham Hall. No pains had been spared to ensure the ice being in capital order, every vestige of snow had been swept off, and all the cracks carefully filled up – it must have involved a great deal of work. Sir Walter and the late Lady Gilbey, however, it is needless to add, never considered trouble

and expense when the comfort and pleasure of their guests and friends were concerned. A hot luncheon for at least sixty was served in a marquee on the ice, and two huge coke fires gave a cheery look to the wintry scene of bare trees and snow-clad fields.'

The hunt usually met three times a week in the season and formed an important part of the social life of the land-owning classes. The hunting field was one of the few places where women could equal men and both Elizabeth Arkwright and her daughter-in-law Julia made use of the opportunity. Victorina Gilbey came from a very different tradition and never accompanied Newman, though she was occasionally driven to watch point-to-point races at which Frank Gilbey excelled.

Ever since the death of the Revd Joseph Arkwright and his son the Revd Julius, Mark Hall and St Mary's church had ceased to be the centre of parish life in Latton.

Tresham and Guy Gilbey

With the arrival of a Catholic family, the gulf between the Hall and the parishioners widened further, though Newman Gilbey and Victorina took on many of the duties of lord and lady of the manor. Newman became chairman of the local magistrates, and allowed his grounds to be used for county and village functions. Rosemary Wellings' collection of old picture postcards includes one of Harlow Flower Show in 1908 and another of the Essex Show, both in the grounds of Mark Hall. Local men were employed as gamekeepers, gardeners and stablemen and the vicar of St Mary-at-Latton dined with the Gilbeys every Sunday but his congregation gradually diminished.

Mrs Julia Arkwright

Influenced by their devout mother and educated at Beaumont College or Stonyhurst, the Gilbey sons all became convinced Catholics. As soon as Newman and Victorina arrived in Mark Hall, they had converted one room into a chapel – the first local centre for Catholic worship in Harlow since the Reformation. With the cooperation of all the family, but especially of Jack, Harry and Alfred, the centre was dedicated to the Apostolate of the Sacred Heart and, although there were very few Catholics in Harlow at that time, Sunday mass was attended by increasing numbers from further afield.

When war broke out in 1914, Mark Hall, Parndon Hall, Moor Hall and Down Hall were all designated as collecting points for livestock in the event of an invasion. Jack aged twenty-six, Charlie aged twenty-five and Frank aged only eighteen became officers and served abroad. They all survived but both Charlie and Jack were seriously wounded. After the war Jack came back to Mark Hall and Charlie, who had married Lettice Charlotte Watney in 1915, returned with his wife and their two-year-old daughter Nancy to the Red House at Sawbridgeworth, rented from a

Newman Gilbey

doctor. From then on Nancy was a frequent visitor at Mark Hall and it is to her that we owe most of our information about life at the manor house between the wars.

Sir Walter Gilbey had died in 1914 but the wine business continued to flourish, providing employment for Harry and most of the family, some of whom set up their own independent ventures.

Hunting revived and the first Hunt Ball after the Great War was held at Mark Hall in 1919. Small dogs and horses named Electron, Tally Ho, Blanco and Farnley, the last two belonging to Aunts Carmen and Lita, remained in their niece's memory. *'The huntsman lived down the drive, across the London Road, down to the kennels, horses and knacker's yard.'* Lita was keen on photography and had her own dark room upstairs.

In 1919 Mrs Newman Gilbey agreed to become President of the newly formed Women's Institute, a branch that included Latton, Netteswell and Harlow. Their first meeting place was the old Laundry building, once occupied by the Lanagan sisters, until the numbers exceeded the space and the Institute moved, first to the Drill Hall in Harlow, and then to their own hall. The Laundry was on Bromleys Farm and the children used to pass it on their way to swim in the river near Latton Mill. In April 1920 the local paper described a gymkhana held at Mark Hall on a Friday afternoon. Mrs Newman Gilbey had done most of the preparation but was unable to present the prizes, owing to an indisposition, and the event was *'somewhat inconvenienced by heavy rain'*.

Victorina Gilbey was a great friend of Dr Doubleday, the Bishop of Brentwood, who ordained Alfred in the drawing room of Mark Hall in 1929 and employed him as his secretary for the next three years. Then from 1932 until 1965 Alfred held the post of Catholic Chaplain to Cambridge University. In 1950 he was chosen as domestic prelate to the Pope and was honoured with the title of Monsignor. Independent and uncompromising, he disapproved of modern egalitarian trends and was a staunch

Monsignor Alfred Gilbey

supporter of traditional Catholicism. In 1995 he visited the USA to promote his book *'We Believe'* and was invited to appear on Mother Angelica's coast to coast chat show in Alabama. He died in 1998 aged ninety-seven.

Jack shared his mother's and brothers' devotion to religion which he often expressed in poetry. Memories of the gardens at Mark Hall often appeared in his publications. In 1945 one slim volume of poetry begins: *'Had you walked past the stables at Mark Hall and on through the orchard you would have come to a little railed garden. It was here that in the early months of the year there was to be found a profusion of snowdrops. In later years these had overrun the garden and had wandered into the shrubbery and into the wood itself, so that they spread a delicate carpet for nearly a quarter of an acre. It was here that my mother used to walk and admire the snow-like loveliness of the scene, and to pluck the tender blooms with which she loved to adorn Our Lady's statue in the chapel.'*[1]

Gravestone of Lita Gilbey carved by Eric Gill

Newman and Victorina's eldest son Harry lost his first wife Myn (née Brunwin) in 1936, four years after the birth of Simon, their fourth child. David had died as a baby so Harry was left with three children in need of care: Mark aged thirteen, Elizabeth aged ten and four-year-old Simon. Their grandparents welcomed them at Mark Hall which became their new home. Their aunt Lita had died in 1925 and Mrs Victorina Gilbey lived only a year after their arrival so, especially for small Simon, it was Carmen Gilbey, the only surviving daughter, who took the place of their mother.

In June 2008 Jenny Handley visited Simon Gilbey and his wife at their home in Guernsey where they had lived for over thirty years. Simon had always been interested in agriculture and details concerning the farm and gardens at Mark Hall remained vivid in his memory. He described the sheep and the red bullocks in the park and a building, known to some as 'stockman's cottage,' where the loft was divided into four grain storage sections – a haunt of warring rats and stray tom cats. His memories of a happy childhood included pigs, chickens, a white pet goat called Daisy and blackberrying in Tye Green. Ploughing was done by steam and a big cable linked one engine to another. *'The walled garden was a lovely area. Adjacent to the back was another walled garden, smaller but substantial, and beyond that another. It ran behind the stables. It was private for the family and grew all the produce.'*

---

[1] Jack Gilbey *Snowdrops at Dusk and other poems*. Burns, Oates & Washbourne Ltd. 1945.

Both Carmen and Alfred had shared their father's love of hunting, though, after he was ordained, Alfred had decided that beagling was more suitable than pursuing foxes. Simon remembered the hounds rushing into the yard (now the car park) on one occasion when the hunt met at Mark Hall.

Another enthusiastic huntsman was the Revd Oliver, vicar of St Mary-at-Latton, who would take a service before hunting with his spurs on. *'They used to poke out of his cassock'*.

Among the twenty-five people who worked on the estate and in the house, Simon Gilbey recollected first the head gardener, George Cordell, who lived at the Lodge where the key to the fruit store was kept. *'We used to visit the Head Gardener. We would creep in for the key and say 'Hello Mr Cordell! The store had apples, peaches and greengages.'* Nancy recalled Mr Cordell's predecessor, Mr Mackett, a shorter man who

Trees in Mark Hall Park 1937

'used to wear a bowler hat, ruled the garden with a rod, and frequently exclaimed 'Oh my bleeding corns!'.

Mr Savage, an intimidating figure to the children, was a gamekeeper who *'used to creep about'* and was rewarded with five shillings by their grandfather if he found a pheasant's nest. He had a house in the woods.

An old lady with a cap on her head, who seems to have worked as a housekeeper, was also remembered as frightening.

The Round House near New Hall

Mr William Banham was the butler who lived in Bury Road, Harlow with his wife and family and came up to the house every day. He had joined the household before the First World War in which his two eldest sons were killed. Mr Banham's domain was near the locked entrance to the extensive cellars and he was in charge of the keys. Nancy remembered two rooms under the butler's pantry entirely full of corks. Mr Banham was the unfortunate servant who was sometimes required to act as caddy when the young people of the house decided to play golf on the nine-hole course at the front of the house. On one occasion it was not only clubs that filled his cart but weights from the kitchen surreptitiously added by one of the uncles. It could well have been the same uncle who persuaded an elderly German visitor connected with the wine trade, who was just about to leave, to climb a ladder and lean over to peer into one of the walled gardens at some unusual spectacle. The ladder was then removed and the visitor missed his train.

Clement Lincoln, who lived on the London road near one entrance to Mark Hall, worked on the farm and used to collect the eggs for the house and Miss Adie used to cycle over from near Latton Common to arrange the flowers and do all kinds of jobs in the house and in the garden under Mr Cordell's direction.

The laundress was Mrs Cantley who wore tight curlers. She was stone deaf. Simon Gilbey remembers visits to her home where there were rows of flat irons all lined up. She lived in the Round House.

Some rooms in Mark Hall were recalled particularly clearly and the Guernsey house contained various pictures, ornaments and pieces of furniture from the old home. To Simon as a boy the entrance hall seemed large, almost square and very grand. The staircase was on the left and along the back wall was a row of large blue and white Wedgwood plaques. *'The butler used to stand in front of them.'* Nancy recalled an alcove at the back of the hall, filled with flowers.

One decorative object from Mark Hall, preserved in Guernsey, was a piece of a carved marble chimney piece, probably salvaged for Joseph Arkwright, after the demolition of Parndon House in

Harlow Station

1832. In his memoirs Francis Kerril Amherst described the chimney piece in the drawing room at Parndon as a *'magnificent piece of sculpture in white marble supported on Ionic columns. The subject was cattle, horses and sheep in high relief, and I believe it is now at Mark Hall, near Harlow, the seat of Loftus Arkwright Esq whose father bought also the pillars of the portico when the dear old house was subsequently pulled down.'*[1]

Another link with Parndon House was the cupola on the stable building. The story went that Joseph Arkwright had taken it from Parndon House stables and used the clock mechanism on the farm building in Purford Green known as the Clock House. Sixty years later Nancy, now Lady Agnew still recalled the sweet little chime of the stable clock.

The Gilbey family had several cars. Charles possessed a bull-nose Morris and

E. Salvin Bowlby

Newman had a Vauxhall with running boards, driven by another Mr Gilbey who lived *'over the*

Gilston Park c. 1900

stables with his wife and child'. Long journeys such as summer trips to Cromer were taken by train. Sir Walter Gilbey had owned a carriage that would be linked to the train, enabling him to carry on board meetings on the way to London.

Pointing to a rug on the sofa, Jenny's host recalled that, when his father Harry Gilbey travelled by train, the butler used to bring him out a stone hot water bottle wrapped in that same rug. More memories were preserved in shooting books that recorded the many birds of every description that had been shot by his uncles when they were boys at Mark Hall. A note states *'The birds were put in a pudding on Easter Sunday'*. His grandfather's loss of his left thumb was the result of a shooting accident.

When four-year-old Simon arrived he was taught first by a governess and then at a private school at Sheering before being sent to the Oratory School near Reading. Social visits he recalled included Dorrington House, the home of Sir Harry Goschen, Moor Hall to see the Balfours, and

---

[1] *Memoirs of Francis Kerril Amherst, D.D. Lord Bishop of Northampton* by Dame Mary Frances Roskell O.S.B.

Hubbards Hall, then occupied by the Swires. Accompanied by his Aunt Carmen and driven by Gilbey the chauffeur, Simon went to dancing lessons at Gilston Hall, the home of the Bowlby family.

His older cousin remembered earlier visits to Moor Hall, to Campions and to Seymour Gosling, an eccentric bachelor who lived in Harlow and collected everything to do with the hunt. *'He hung his pheasants for a long time and when you were invited to dinner there was always a smell of pheasant cooking. He had a great party trick – standing on his head outside the dining room.'*

Another eccentric recalled by Simon was the hermit who had his home under a bridge. The man (whose name was Charlie Haddock) had hollowed out his cave under the railway line, near the station that is now Harlow Mill, and used to hang his washing outside.

After explaining the layout of every room on the ground and first floor of Mark Hall [see plan overleaf] Nancy, Lady Agnew, recalled several other places of interest within the grounds. The east wing was built on a steep slope and you went out of the back door into the dairy at the bottom of the hill.

In the largest of the walled gardens there was a summer house opposite the greenhouses and in the shrubbery to the north of the stables, near an eighteenth century shell house, the dogs' cemetery was marked with their tombstones. The churchyard attracted the children's attention because of the plentiful birds' nests among the thick bushes that surrounded it, and the story that a black servant had once been buried there.

The Gilbey family thought it likely that the reason Mark Hall was destroyed so rapidly by fire in 1947 was that there were old beams in the main chimneys which were liable to smoulder and burn if the chimneys were not regularly swept.

Glimpses of life at Mark Hall viewed from different angles can be gathered from the reminiscences of two Harlow residents who once worked or visited there and remained in this area.

Mrs Betty Wiltshire, looking back in 2007, the year before she died, recalled that to be a Catholic in Harlow in the thirties was to be a *'person apart'*. She wrote: *'There were few Catholics in Harlow in the early 30s. The nearest Church was St Joseph's in Bishop's Stortford. We were fortunate to be able to attend Mass on Sunday mornings in the Gilbey private chapel at Mark Hall.'*

Betty described how she and a friend would make their way from

Latton Church 1938

(Old) Harlow through the entrance to the park by the East Lodge (which is still there), over the cattle grid and through the woodland behind the stables (now the Museum) to the basement entrance into the servants' block. A wide stone-flagged passage led to a door into the hall. They went through another passage on the right to reach the chapel. When the door to the dining room opposite the chapel was open they could see a big sideboard with chafing dishes to keep the food warm.

'The chapel was a beautiful room at the heart of the house set between the family part and the servants' quarters. There was a floor-to-ceiling window on each side of the altar looking out over the park, and on each side-wall there were large gilt framed mirrors which reflected each other. A large religious picture hung behind the altar. Mr Gilbey's chauffeur fetched the priest from Brentwood, also the two Sisters who came (not every week) to give instruction to the children after Mass. There were often 30 or 40 people in the congregation and more at Christmas and Easter. On these special occasions Father Gilbey would conduct the service and I enjoyed that because he was so dramatic in his colourful vestments'.

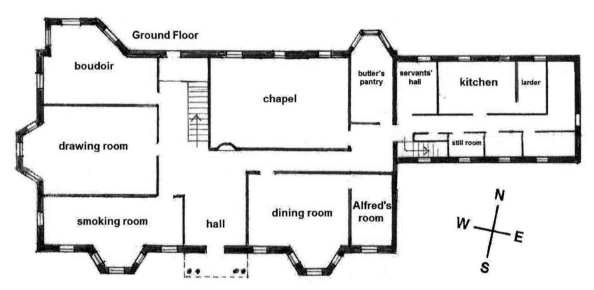

Plan of Mark Hall before 1943 based on oral evidence

In the later 1930s, as people moved out of London, the congregation grew too large for Mark Hall and Mass was said each Sunday in the Drill Hall in Old Road. While the number of Catholics in Harlow increased, the attendance at St Mary-at-Latton steadily dwindled. Newman Gilbey made sure that the graveyard was kept in good order but the church was empty. Monsignor Alfred Gilbey used to describe Latton in his boyhood as *'the perfect parish with virtually no parishioners, save for the head gardener of Mark Hall and his wife who walked up to church on Sundays from North Lodge.'*[1]

In his *History of Latton* Jonathan Edmunds confirms Alfred Gilbey's description of the state of St Mary's at this time, but from a rather different angle.

'The vicar for the greater part of the early twentieth century was the Revd Austin Oliver. He was an old-fashioned hunting parson and kept three horses for the purpose... The annual vestry meetings deteriorated into conversations between Oliver and Mackett, a gardener at Mark Hall. In 1924 and from 1926 to 1941 these two were the only attenders while in 1925 Oliver held the meeting on his own. W.C. Mackett was the vicar's churchwarden from 1923 to 1941'...'Austin Oliver was an old man by the time he died in 1942 and the parish had been allowed to decay with him.'

---

[1] From *Alfred Gilbey, a Memoir by some Friends.* Ed. David Watkin.

Subsequently the church almost fell out of use but, with the coming of the New Town, it took on a completely new lease of life.

Mr Jack Baker, still resident in Harlow in 2010, recalled a brief period when he worked at Mark Hall just before the Second World War.

My Memories of Mark Hall Estate
by Jack Baker.

'In March 1938 I thought it was time I had a change of employment as being a gamekeeper I was very restricted to time off. I applied for a gardener's job at Mark Hall, the home of Mr Newman Gilbey. He gave me the job and I expect it may have been a shilling or two more than I was getting at Gilston Park. No youngster would get man's pay until they were twenty-one.

The working day started at seven o'clock. On Saturday we had to work until one o'clock. However, working in the walled garden at Mark Hall seemed very shut in to what I had been used to and I missed the open fields and woods. I used to refer to it as 'prison'!

I worked on the vegetable side of the garden under George Cordell; two other people did the flower garden and lawns. Also adjoining the garden was a small farm which was run by another man. Two or three cows were kept to supply milk for the house. On the park land sheep and bullocks were kept and sold to the local butcher for slaughter.

As the months went past I soon found that quite a lot of overtime was expected, working until eight o'clock four evenings a week, after which I had to cycle home to Gilston. This made quite a long day and my mother was not too pleased having to get me a cooked meal at that time.

At least Saturday afternoons were free and we were able to go to the cinema at Sawbridgeworth or Bishop's Stortford. We went on our bicycles to Sawbridgeworth and left them at 'The Gate' public house in a cycle shed at the back. We had to pay two pence for each bike! The cinema was small and had a corrugated tin roof. The entrance fee was nine pence. A bar of chocolate was twopence.

The cinema at Bishop's Stortford was more up to date, quite luxurious compared to the one in Sawbridgeworth. When we went to Stortford we had to go by train from Burnt Mill station. The trains ran at about two hourly intervals and we had half an hour's walk to the station. We sometimes could not wait to see the end of the film as we had to catch the train home. All in all it took seven hours to go to the pictures on a Saturday! What a difference today with most people having their own cars and much more money to spend.

The level crossing at Burnt Mill Station

During my first summer working at Mark Hall estate, the 1938 Essex Agricultural Show was held in the park there, Mr Newman Gilbey being President. In those days the show was held in a different location each year. Later on it had a permanent site at Great Leighs.[1] The area where the show was held at Mark Hall is now where East Park, Mark Hall School and Fesants Croft are situated. The workers at Mark Hall were given a day off to visit the show. I think it was the only day I had ever had off with pay since starting work – and we were given a free entrance ticket, but this did not matter too much as I knew certain places where the boundary fence was weak.

During the summer we gardeners had to help with the hay making and sheep dipping and anything else where extra hands were needed. The hay making was quite hard work as we did not have any up-to-date equipment. The chauffeur would sweep the hay up to the stack with a small sweep attached to the front of his Sunbeam car, and George Cordell and myself would fork it up to the two men on top of the stack. During the haymaking time we used to work until eight o'clock in the

---

[1] The Essex County Show lost its site at Great Leighs and was discontinued in 2001.

evening. This meant that my mother had to pack up three lots of sandwiches – breakfast, dinner and tea. We made our own tea on the shed fire where we had our meals.

Another job which happened twice during my two years at Mark Hall would be to help drive about twenty-five Devon bullocks from Harlow station (now Harlow Mill) to Mark Hall park. It would take all six of us to help with this job as all side roads, gateways, paths etc. had to be blocked as we drove them up the station road. They were full of life, having been shut in a railway wagon for a day or so. One of us would take a bicycle so that we could ride in front of them. Cattle were always driven on the roads in those days. Our Devon bullocks would graze on the park at Mark Hall and when fat enough would be sold two or three at a time to the local butcher.

In the summer months Mr Gilbey used to pay the gardeners overtime to cut the grass in St Mary's-at-Latton churchyard although he was Roman Catholic and they had their own chapel in the house.

Towards the end of 1938 and into 1939 it looked as though another war with Germany was getting nearer and the Government had decided to introduce military training for all young men between the ages of twenty and twenty-one. That was my age at this time. They were going to call us up in batches at two monthly intervals beginning in July 1939 with six months training and two years on the reserve.

As that summer passed by I wondered how soon I would have to go. Anyway, the haymaking came and went at Mark Hall and the build up to war was taking place. At the end of August I think I had three days holiday from work and I went to Clacton to join the rest of the family who were there for a week. When we arrived back on the Saturday evening my call-up papers had arrived. I had to report to the Gibraltar Barracks at Bury St Edmunds on the 15th September 1939.

On 3rd September 1939 war was declared with Germany, just a week after we got back from our Clacton holiday. I now had a fortnight to go before I was on my way. I think I carried on work for at least another week or so. On my last day at work Mr Newman Gilbey, came to wish me well and gave me ten shillings to help me on my way. This does not seem much of a tip today, but it was almost half a week's pay in those days.'

Newman Gilbey died on 12 June 1942 and was buried next to his wife in the graveyard of St Mary-at-Latton. The Gilbeys decided to leave Mark Hall in the following year.

In David Watkin's memoir of Alfred Gilbey[1] Jack Gold, Newman's cousin, describes the auction sale that was held after the family had removed their more treasured possessions.

'I attended the view day when the usual crowd of inquisitive neighbours filled the house but few of the family attended. An exception was Frank Gilbey, the third son, who was something of a connoisseur. He was also exceptionally handsome in a Spanish way, with manners to match his looks. I happened to witness his meeting with Loftus Arkwright, who arrived at the front door just as Frank was leaving. Frank's greeting of the owner of the house was so elegant and self assured that any witness would have thought their roles were reversed.'

By this time Loftus Arkwright was living as a near recluse at Parndon Hall with his housekeeper, Mrs Martin. Julia had divorced him in 1915, and moved to Worthy Manor, Porlock in Somerset where she ran the church choir and took an active part in village life. She had sailed to America in 1913, visited Cuba in 1926

Julia Caldwell

[1] Jack Gold in *Alfred Gilbey. A Memoir by Some Friends.* Ed. David Watkin 2001 Michael Russell (publishing) Ltd.

and America again in 1930. She died in 1933.

Jack Gilbey at Glan Avon

Loftus, their eldest son, had disappeared and John, one of the twins who had both become naval officers, was killed on HMS Avenger in November 1942.

Soon after the sale, Mark Hall was requisitioned for the use of the Women's Land Army.

Jack Gilbey took on a lease of Hastingwood House and he and his sister Carmen moved there with Harry's children Mark, Elizabeth and Simon for a few years. When the owner returned, Jack rented then bought Glan Avon in Potter Street where he spent the rest of his life. He died in 1984 aged ninety-six. Carmen, who moved with Simon when he took up his first farming post at Chief's Farm, Great Bardfield, died in 1982. Elizabeth, Simon's sister, had died in 1968 at the age of forty-four.

Newman Gilbey left sufficient money to build a Catholic church in the small field near Mulberry Green that he had bought for this purpose some time before his death. No building took place for several years after the Second World War and the congregation continued to use the Drill Hall. Then in 1951 the present church, which was intended to be the hall of a future larger building, was erected. Dedicated to Our Lady of the Assumption, this simple building is still Old Harlow's Catholic church though the New Town now possesses four larger Catholic churches. The fourteen Stations of the Cross and the silver door of the Tabernacle, which came from Mark Hall chapel, are still there. The tall picture of the Nativity behind the altar was donated by Lord Petre. On 18 August 1951 Monsignor Gilbey visited the church and unveiled a tablet in memory of his parents.

Simon Gilbey 2009

Eight members of the Gilbey family are buried in the churchyard of St Mary-at-Latton and two of their servants, Mary Ryan and Antonia Ruiz. Antonia's inscription, dated 1959, reads: *'Greatly loved for over 60 years in the service of Newman Gilbey and Maria Victorina'*. Simon Gilbey, who died in March 2009, asked that his name should be added on one of the stones.

18

The Women's Land Army at Mark Hall 1943-1947 (& 1948-9)

The Gazette & Citizen Sept 1943:

OPENING OF NEW W.L.A. HOSTEL AT HARLOW

"Dear Mother, I have arrived here safely," were the words of some of the 120 members of the Women's Land Army when writing home, after they had arrived on Monday at their new hostel, Mark Hall, Harlow, the Georgian mansion, previously owned by the late Mr. Newman Gilbey.

The girls marched from Harlow station and were cheered by the small crowd that gathered at Station Road. There were no flags or bands to greet them, but they marched happily along.

Mrs Solly-Flood, the organising secretary for Essex, addressed the girls on their arrival at Mark Hall, when she told them that a hostel is not a prison but a place where everyone gives and takes, considering the community.

Mrs Solly-Flood was accompanied by Miss Evans, the assistant welfare officer, and Mrs Tom Howard, who were introduced to the head girl, Miss Ann Spendlove.

Now the largest in Essex, the hostel has three recreation rooms, a reading and writing room, large dining halls, and a room for the sick.

Mrs Warren Foster, who is the warden, told a Gazette reporter that the first thought of the hostel staff was the health and welfare of the girls.

BISHOP VISITS W.L.A. HOSTEL

The Bishop of Chelmsford visited the Women's Land Army Hostel, Mark Hall, Harlow, when he held a short service and gave an address. The Bishop said that he had enjoyed his visit and would like to come again when asked. Among those present were: Miss O Tritton, County chairman of the Essex W.L.A.; Mrs Solly-Flood, County organising secretary; Mrs T Howard, Mrs James Elwell, Miss G Evans, County organiser W.L.A.; Mrs Warren Foster, warden of the hostel; and the hostel Staff. The Bishop was thanked by the head girl, Miss Ann Spendlove.

The experiences of the girls who lived at Mark Hall and worked on the local farms during and after the Second World War are best described in their own letters and memories. Some of the extracts included here were published at the time in the local papers and others were collected later from Harlow residents. News of the arrival of the girls was described in newspaper articles that convey the protective, 'boarding school' attitude of those in authority at the time. The reporter, in common with many local people, assumes that the Gilbeys, not the Arkwrights, were the owners of Mark Hall. Fifty-seven years later, Ivy Cox, one of those first volunteers, remembered arriving at Mark Hall on the day the Land Army hostel opened. *'I lived in north London - Stoke Newington - and when we were all called up and got our papers we had to meet at Liverpool Street Station. We came from all over London, from all walks of life. We came down to what's now Harlow Mill station, got off there and walked to Mark Hall straight up Station Road. I always remember there was a huge great field of carrots in Soper's field. We walked up past some shops and there was this cattle grid by Mr. Cordell's cottage. You walked up this long, long drive – it was a park then – and then there was another cattle grid and you came to a private drive. There was a huge pond on one side[1] and bushes on the other. Up this drive and round the corner and you went in there at a back entrance. Some of the rooms were huge with great marble fireplaces. It was a gorgeous place'.[2]*

---

[1] The pond was in what is now Fesants Croft, near The Lawns tower block.
[2] Quoted in *The Life and Death of Burnt Mill Village. Ed.* H. Lake

Most of the girls remembered their farm work and their encounters with future husbands more clearly than the mansion itself, but some indoor details were described. Mrs Jean Levesque, writing from America, recalled that they were always well chaperoned and had to be in their bunk beds by ten o'clock at night, sleeping usually fourteen to a room. Mrs Joan Dale (née Bruce) described a comfortable

top bunk in a room at the front, on the left side of the main entrance, and an uncomfortable bottom one in a room at the back. She also recalled what she thought were beautiful marble fireplaces, almost invisible behind sheets of asbestos. *'The floor of the entrance hall was tiled with stone black and white tiles and a wide staircase rose from it which made you feel grand when you went up it'*. Several contributors mentioned an enormous dining room, a 'Chapel Room' full of bunks, and *'mirrors on all the walls, stretching from the floor to the ceiling'*.

Supervised by a Mr Gilbey, a few of the girls worked in the walled gardens, *'designed like 3 rooms surrounded by hedges'*, growing vegetables to help with the catering.

Mrs Jean Hudspeth (née Brett) who was still living in Potter Street in 2010, contributed interesting recollections from the point of view of a local resident.

'At the age of about 13 in 1945, I was asked by a Mrs Sargent, who was a member of the St John's Ambulance, and also lived in Hillside, Potter Street, if I would like to help her and other ladies to prepare tea for the Land Girls at Mark Hall, on as many afternoons after school as my parents would let me go'.

'We lived in Brook Cottage, Potter Street, next door to a tiny shop run by Mrs Browning and her son Archie, who sold and delivered newspapers in the surrounding areas. To get to Mark Hall, I walked or cycled down Latton Street until we reached a five bar gate, which we went through into parkland which had a foot or cycle path to Mark Hall and the Latton Church.'

'Mark Hall had a Lodge House in Old Harlow (opposite where the old Post Office is now). There was a large gate and small gate leading onto the big drive to Mark Hall, where carriages and cars could drive'.

'We worked in the kitchen in the Victorian wing at a large scrubbed wooden table. Mrs Sargent and I would butter (or marg) a large number of loaves. They were cut when I buttered them but I don't know if 'sliced bread' was invented then or if they had been cut by hand before we got there. It was still whilst food rationing was in force and I remember being told not be too heavy-handed with the spread, then there might be an ounce or two to take home to Mother! We did not go into any other rooms on the ground floor, but I did go upstairs quite often. As far as I can remember the stairs were marble as we had to be careful not to slip when carrying food. If any of the girls were off work and confined to bed we would take their supper up to them and they would enjoy a chat as they came from far and wide and did not know very much about Harlow. They used to smoke upstairs but had to be very careful as they were supervised and watched.'

Mark Hall kitchen provided packed lunches for some of the girls but Audrey Clarke remembered that after a morning grafting in the fields, the girls would trek over to Victoria Hall in Old Harlow for a hot main meal, a pudding, and a cup of tea, all for five old shillings. *'Vegetables, vegetables and more vegetables were the fare of the day'*. If they were lucky the occasional sausage or scraps of meat graced their plate. Audrey added: *'It's funny – we ate really stodgy, bulky food and we always had a suet or sponge pudding, yet we never gained weight.'*

The Land Girls worked on the Arkwright estate, for Mr Soper at New Hall, for Mr J. Foulds on Dorrington Farm, Rye Hill and on a potato farm on Nazeing Hill, plus several more farms locally. Some of the girls drove tractors and also worked in the dairies.

The discomfort and the piercing cold in the early mornings remained in most girls' recollections. Audrey Clarke wrote, *'The foreman had his favourites – I wasn't one of them, so I got lumbered doing some of the worst jobs. Breaking the ice to scrub carrots is one of the lasting memories of the war – it was freezing cold and my hands were numb!'*

Ivy Cox explained how the jobs were divided up. *'We worked in what they called gangs. If a farmer wanted extra help a gang of six or maybe ten girls would go out on a lorry and do whatever was needed. Bean picking – that was nice – or lifting sugar beet. On frosty mornings you'd pull them up. They'd been ploughed up so they were loose. We used to bang them together and they were often wet. Horrible! And ditching. I liked ditching. That was a nice job. You could see what you'd done. On wet days we were often paddling in water. Sometimes it could be falling down with rain at seven o'clock in the morning but we had to go out till eleven. If it was still raining hard then we could go home.'*

They were paid £1 per week but board and lodging was deducted from their pay. For picking peas they were paid 2/6 [12½p] a bag but it was a hard day's work to fill two bags.

Not all the stories were of hard work and early nights. There was a room at Mark Hall where they could relax, a piano in the hall and at least one visit from a party from ENSA. When asked about amusements in the evenings, Mrs Dale described how she made slippers from rabbit skins which they bought for 6d each, but most of the girls, including Mrs Jean Levesque and Ivy Cox, soon found partners to accompany them to the Crown in Harlow or to the cinema in Sawbridgeworth.

'I met my husband in Harlow, he was stationed at Bishop's Stortford, with the United States Air Force. We used to go to one of the two Pubs and the owners would give us a lovely meal. They got to know us quite well, as we used to go there for our evening each week'.

'I met my husband while I was at Mark Hall. There was nothing to do in Harlow then and we used to go out for walks and this particular night we went to the Crown public house. We sat in the little lounge sort of outside and I saw this chap and thought "He's rather nice." He'd got a raincoat on with lapels and he really did look nice. Well, I kept going down to the toilet so we got talking and he walked me home. You couldn't walk back to Mark Hall alone at night. It was so creepy. There were no lights along the drive. A bunch of boys used always to wait at the station on Sunday nights when we came back from our weekends at home just to walk us back to the Hall. On my twenty-first birthday my parents gave me a bicycle and my fiancé and I used to go for rides round and about. He had come back from Japan where he had been a prisoner of war for four years. He got captured very soon after he got out there. He was on that rail-road but he would never talk about it. He was all right but he used to get sudden attacks of malaria. He never complained but he would never touch a piece of rice'.

Prisoners of the war in Europe were sometimes mentioned in the girls' recollections. *'Once or twice we worked with prisoners of war. One of the German prisoners had a piece of a log and drew a picture on it. I had that for years. He was a nice chap. We were allowed to be friendly with them but not too friendly.'*

'I remember one Italian prisoner called Mario – he had the loveliest voice. I can still hear it now – it was beautiful'

The reality of the war was never very far away and the work itself sometimes proved dangerous for girls unused to farming. *'One of our land girls was riding on a horse and cart – she was sitting on the shaft – and it went through a gate and she fell off and got killed. The land girls bought this book in memory of her and put it in Latton Church. I wonder if it's still there'.*

Presented to Latton Church by the Girls and Hostel Staff of Mark Hall, Harlow,

in memory of

Jean Lakin

aged 18 years,

who died on 27.9.1944

as the result of an accident

at her work.

The Book of Common Prayer with its memorial inscription is still preserved in the vestry of

Latton church.

> *'I can't quite remember how I felt when I heard my first Doodlebug – I suppose I was frightened, probably excited. We were always told to take cover, but I doubt whether we'd have escaped if a Doodlebug had dropped on our field!'*

> *'When we were working near Harlow Common we saw a doodle-bug come down. It landed on a cottage and burst into fire'.*

The Land Girls would arrive back from work in lorries, having been transported by the various farmers who employed them, and have a bath or shower in the Ablution Block downstairs in the old building or the bathrooms upstairs.

Not all the girls were collected in trucks. If the fields where they were working were near Mark Hall they used their bikes which were usually kept in the stables. *'The man who lived at the lodge on London Road used to come and service the bikes in the evenings'*. It was always dark when they set out in the morning and they had to make sure the headlights were in good working order.

Ivy Cox recalled her last night at Mark Hall very clearly.

> *'We were still at Mark Hall when the war ended. Then one evening when we were in our bedroom a lot of us could hear a strange noise. You put your head to the wall and you'd hear a noise like silver paper when you crumple it. You know how it crinkles and crackles? But of course no one realised. And then in the night the fire broke out. "Get out! Get out! Just get out!" But I said, "My engagement ring's in my box!" We all had padlocked kit boxes at the bottom of our beds and I hadn't time to find the key. I just picked up the box and took it out. And then of course when we were standing outside I remembered my bike. There was a rack for bicycles out at the back but I had hidden my new bike inside under the stairs where I was sure it would be safe. I shouted, "My bike's in there!" But the firemen wouldn't let me go back in and get it.'*

> *'I remember everybody running across the field. All the soldiers and the Yanks. We stood there and watched the house burn.'*

The blaze was visible from Potter Street. Mrs Hudspeth, who was still helping at Mark Hall in 1947, wrote: *'I can remember it was late evening when the fire started and the voluntary Fire Brigade from Old Harlow was on the site first. Lots of people went to watch the flames as soon as they saw the smoke and flames arising. I understand the girls were evacuated to hostels in Roydon and Brentwood that night or went to local houses whose owners offered a bed or two. It was all very frightening.'*

The Gazette of November 1947 reported the event.

MARK HALL DESTROYED BY FIRE
100 Land Girls Escape

Mark Hall, Harlow, the fine old 52-roomed manor house designed in the 18th century by the famous Adam brothers, was completely gutted by fire late on Tuesday night. To-day all that remains is the blackened shell of a graceful residence that stood in 200 acres of parkland.

There were 100 Land Army girls in occupation of the building under their Warden, Miss Dorothy Baker, when the alarm was raised and though some of them were in night attire, all safely got out into the grounds where they had to stand watching the place that had been their home burn furiously and finally collapse into ruins. The girls were able to save little of their personal belongings. Three dogs in the building were unharmed.

The alarm was raised at about 11.30 p.m. by 18-years-old Miss Betty Belton, whose home is at Chelmsford. On being awakened by thick smoke pouring into her bedroom, she immediately aroused Miss Baker and together they ran from room to room warning the girls of their danger.

Girls Nearly Overcome by Smoke

Two of the girls who were sleeping on the first floor, Miss Hope Bartlett, who is 23, and Miss Barbara Erskine, 27, told a Gazette representative that they were nearly overcome by smoke – there was no time to dress and they had to be helped downstairs by another girl.

As they trooped out onto the lawns, the girls saw that the upper part of the building was a blazing mass – shortly after, the roof collapsed into the inferno which blazed until only parts of the walls and chimney stacks remained. The masonry over the impressive portico entrance crashed to the ground.

The girls were later marshalled together and taken to St Margaret's Hospital, Epping, for accommodation until the morning. Then they were allowed to go to their homes until other billets could be arranged.

The only casualty so far reported was that of a member of the Hoddesdon Brigade, who was taken to the hospital at 4.20 a.m., but was allowed to leave later in the day.

It was like a Furnace

Mr W Churchman, officer in charge of the Harlow N.F.S., said that when he arrived, he could only see from the ground a small amount of flames licking around the roof, but when a ladder was run up the top of the building, and before the firemen could investigate the extent of the flames, the top of the ladder was destroyed as flames suddenly belched upwards. "It was like a furnace in a few minutes," he said.

A Grand Old Mansion

Mark Hall is the property of Mr L J W Arkwright, of Parndon Hall, Great Parndon, but for 53 years, up to his death in June, 1942, it was the home of Mr Newman Gilbey and his family. Mr Gilbey was the son of the founder of Messrs. W & A Gilbey the famous wine and spirit merchants; and was a member of the Harlow Bench and its one time chairman, and a keen and active supporter of the Essex Hunt and the Essex Agricultural Society.

One of his five sons, Capt. Jack N Gilbey, lives at Hastingwood. He told a *Gazette* representative that he went to Mark Hall first as a boy of six years when his father rented the manor from Mr Arkwright. "The house was a fine example of Adam's work and I feel very sad to think that the beautiful old place has gone" he said.

Officers of the N.F.S. are investigating the cause of the fire.

ONCE SO STATELY The stark ruins of Mark Hall, Harlow after the fire (as reported in last week's *Gazette*) had destroyed the Adams building.

No alternate accommodation has been found for members of the Women's Land Army who escaped from their burning hostel at Mark Hall. They are still at home waiting for news as to where they will be directed. Meantime, farms where they were engaged are without labour. Firemen pumped water on the gutted building until Thursday afternoon, and since then dangerous walls and chimney stacks have been pulled down. Under the bricks and charred timber lie the personal belongings of the girls.

Several hundred people travelled to the estate over the weekend to see the ruins.

In spite of the cold and the hard work, most of the contributors remembered their Land Army years and the friends they had made with pleasure. Sixty years later Joan Dale recalled 'Rene', 'Edie', Betty Evans and Pat Dempsey as members of her gangs.

Jean Hudspeth concluded: *'The Land Girls were accepted into the area and appeared a jolly lot who added a bit of colour to the local community'*.

Another local resident with memories of Mark Hall at this time is Mr Leslie Lewis of Old Harlow. In 1943 his grandmother, mother and four small brothers were evacuated from London very early one morning and dumped on the London Road, somewhere near Mark Hall. Told to wait until it was light to find their way to their new home, Mrs Lewis let her hungry baby suck dried milk off the teat of his bottle until the dawn appeared. Their accommodation, when they eventually found it and climbed the stone stairs, consisted of the upper part of 'the stockman's cottage' (later used by the Boy Scouts) which was to be their home for eight years. The boys attended Fawbert and Barnard school and revelled in the freedom they enjoyed in the grounds of Mark Hall. The primitive living conditions were not resented but the family still remember their delight when they first moved into a proper house where the water came, not from a pump in the yard, but from taps in the kitchen. After the arrival of Leslie, her fifth son, Mrs Ethel Lewis worked on Soper's farm for the next twenty-five years.

A debate on agriculture in the House of Commons on 23 February 1948 provides an interesting postscript to the Land Girls' accounts of life at Mark Hall.

Mr Solley to the Minister of Agriculture (1) 'Is he aware that the Women's Land Army hostel at Orsett, Grays, Essex, was formerly a prisoner-of-war camp, and does he know what alterations have been made in the sanitary, cooking, heating and sleeping arrangements of the camp since its use as a hostel?' (2) 'Is he aware that last week three members of the Women's Land Army walked out of the hostel as a protest against the bad conditions there; and what steps does he propose to take to remedy this state of affairs?'

Mr T. Williams 'I am aware that three new recruits to the W.L.A. recently left Orsett hostel after complaining of the conditions. This hostel is an ex-Army camp and it is in sound order structurally. It was called into use last November in an emergency to house 108 members of the Land Army from Mark Hall, Harlow, which was destroyed by fire. Alterations were necessary to bring the hostel up to proper standard and arrangements were made for these works to be done.'

The Minister listed the alterations but Mr Solley was not satisfied. 'Can my right hon. Friend confirm that there are no baths for these girls, that there are eight shower baths among 120 girls and 24 sinks which have to be used not merely for cleaning hands and faces, but for clothes? Further, may I ask whether or not it is the fact that a recreation room is completely unheated, and that this hostel has not even a radio? In response to the Minister's comment that the missing things were being replaced 'as speedily as possible', Mr Solley enquired whether the Minister agreed that three or four months was an ample period in which to obtain a wireless set for the girls and other elementary amenities.

The remains of Mark Hall
Winter 1947

19
Harlow New Town

Chronology pages 166-67

St Mary-at-Latton after 1950

When the New Town was being planned in 1947 it was intended to use Mark Hall as a centre for the staff of the Corporation. *'At that time it was occupied by the Women's Land Army who were reluctant to give up possession. However fate intervened. A short circuit during a storm set fire to the building and, save for one wing, it was destroyed'.*[1] The Corporation staff established themselves over the river at Terlings, the ruins of the old house were flattened and the Victorian wing was sealed off with a new west wall.

For a brief period, while there was still an acute shortage of labour on the farms, some Land Army girls returned and continued their work from the undamaged wing of the old house. Mrs Lily Cook, still resident in Harlow in 2009, remembers returning as a ganger from Brentwood and

Terlings in 1940

appreciating a proper bed after a narrow bunk. She left to get married and by 1950 the Corporation had managed to buy the building and the whole Mark Hall area from Loftus Joseph Arkwright who was still living at Parndon Hall. He died in that year and Godfrey Arkwright, the only remaining son, succeeded him and lived at Parndon Hall until 1953.

With the coming of the New Town, Mark Hall and St Mary-at-Latton ceased to be isolated units separated by wide areas of park land from other dwellings. Muskham Road was constructed, dividing the stables (now the Museum) from what was left of the house, but a green area has been preserved sweeping down to the north from the site of the old mansion. The corner of one of

---

[1] *Harlow. The Story of a New Town* p.29.

the walled gardens by the stables presented a planning problem in the construction of Muskham Road. This was solved by rounding the corner off and rebuilding the wall with the original bricks as far as possible.

The Schools at Mark Hall 1951-60

During the final years of what remained of Mark Hall the Victorian wing was used as a school. In 1949 and 1950 house building began at Chippingfield in what became known as Old Harlow and then moved west into Latton. 'Harlow North' was soon completed, families moved in and schools were needed but the first primary and secondary schools, Tany's Dell and Mark Hall, were not completed until 1952 and 1953. As a temporary measure the old building was hastily equipped with a row of toilets in the basement and the basic essentials of classrooms

Mr Dunn's class 1951

on the ground and first floors. A Sunday School was also held there.

The area where the eighteenth century house had stood, to the west of the remaining building, was covered with asphalt and surrounded by an iron railing to serve as a playground.

The first school was opened in May 1951 and was known as Mark Hall County Primary school. Several of the earliest residents in the New Town have contributed memories of their schooldays in the old building which later became an annexe to Tany's Dell school.[1]

Approaching the building from the direction of the church you crossed the playground and were confronted with a roughly plastered wall. A black

Family Group by Henry Moore

metal fire escape had been added, vividly remembered by one unfortunate child who hit her head on it. The hard but uneven asphalt playground caused a fall and a broken tooth on another occasion and the area soon needed resurfacing. One boy remembered looking down into the excavation when the Church Hall was being built and seeing bits of brick walls. When told of the death of George VI in 1952 the children had to stop playing and stand still for two interminable minutes. Happier memories included watching the squirrels, walking in woods that were full of

A path through Mark Hall park

[1] Ex-pupils of the schools in Mark Hall who contributed to this chapter include: Mrs Margaret Beensen (née Dunn), Mrs Phyllis Bellward, Bridget McAlpine, Mrs Brenda Thompson (née Alderson) Barbara and Margaret Prindiville, Jean Mann (née Culverhouse) Mrs Shirley Harrison, Mrs Avron Cooper-Gray (née Hartshorn) Evelyn Silk, Vivienne Hannibal.

snowdrops and climbing onto Henry Moore's Family Group (now in the Civic Centre) which was originally sited on the edge of the playground. Playing marbles, tag and swapping cigarette cards occupied the boys while the girls skipped and played hop-scotch.

A steep path, nicknamed 'Breakneck Hill', ran down the south side of the block, passing the upper entrance that was rarely used. Mr Dunn's offspring, who lived nearby, used to career down this slope on trolleys equipped with pram wheels. The door at the bottom on the east side led into the basement – a creepy, dingy storage area. The toilets were on the left and a wide stone staircase led up to the ground floor. A window had been left in the reconstructed west wall so that as the children climbed the stairs they could look out onto the playground. The kitchen, with a hatch through to the room where school dinners were consumed, was on the north side of a corridor on the ground floor with a view out over the park. One child helped count the dinner money – three threepenny bits in a pile made the required nine pence. Smaller rooms, some of them locked, were on the other side of the passage. Monitors wearing red sashes used to control the children as they filed up and down.

The stairs led on up to the top floor where there were more classrooms, the library and the needlework room. Black iron stoves provided the heating.

Once Tany's Dell school was completed, the groups in the old building would walk to the main school for some functions but it was not until July 1960 that new school building managed to keep pace

1955 class, Tany's Dell Annexe

with the influx of children and the last remnant of Mark Hall was left to disintegrate. Before it was completely flattened, several contributors remember playing in the cellars. The local paper reported extensive vandalism, fires were started and the building became dangerously littered with twisted metal and broken glass.

The Victorian wing of Mark Hall in 1960

118

Exploring the Cellars 1960

Rumours of tunnels running from Mark Hall to St Mary's church, to Latton Priory and various other destinations were widely believed by local people before the coming of the New Town and would have been supported by at least two of the Land Girls. Writing from America in November 1988 Mrs Jean Levesque still remembered the size and extent of the underground passages she saw as a girl of sixteen.

'Mark Hall also had a cellar, where one early evening a friend of mine and I decided to investigate. On arriving there, we saw huge tunnels going in all directions. We were too scared to go into any as you can imagine. But I did notice how thick and solid the bricks and beams were made to form a very, very strong foundation for a lovely mansion.'

The fire of 1947 exposed a cavity in the area soon covered by the school playground and the rumours persisted. Then, shortly before the last remnant of the old house was finally demolished, a local group of enthusiasts, led by Mr Fred Smith, set about excavating the area where the asphalt playground had subsided.

By this time a church hall had been built to the east of St Mary's and evidence of brickwork had been revealed below the new foundations. Traces possibly dating back to the Altham's buildings were found in the garden of the present vicarage.

The local press became very excited.

Harlow Gazette. September 1960.

TUNNELERS ENTER ANCIENT CELLARS

A few hours after excavations started, the Harlow Tunnel Group broke through to one of the cellars of Mark Hall on Saturday.

Already the first finds have been reported, pottery and glass possibly hundreds of years old, an ancient coin and bones.

The Group is looking for the secret tunnel believed to run for three miles under Harlow. Most of the stories centre round the cellars of Mark Hall although it is thought the tunnel was bricked up many years ago.

Most of Mark Hall was destroyed by fire in 1947, and a playground was built over the rubble. Early on Saturday morning work began on the strip of land between the playground and the Church Hall of Mary-at-Latton.

As the top layer of earth was removed, a labyrinth of brick-work was revealed. Careful measurements were taken, and within hours a hole had been cut into the roof of the cellar.

A ladder was brought and the first men to set foot there since the New Town was built went down.

The air was thick and heavy, and it was impossible to stay there for long but a first examination by torchlight showed that the work would be long and detailed.

TWO ARCHWAYS

On one side were two archways filled with rubble and completely impassable. They led underneath the playground.

At each end were alcoves and recesses and through one arch a narrow five-sided well, apparently full of broken bottles.

The floor was tiled with red brick but mysteriously subsiding down in the centre. Along one side was a row of brick wine bins, obviously more recently built, and there were two bricked up arches.

The first work has shown that nothing can be taken for granted. A hole was knocked through one of the arches and loose gravel trickled through. A second hole failed to penetrate a massive thickness of brick.

Outside in the same place a hole was being dug and this brought to light a mysterious brick shaft. Bucket after bucket of the excavated gravel was put through the sieve. Stained glass was found almost obliterated by age; there was pottery too and delicate glasswork.

LIGHT CABLE

By now an electric light cable had been run into the cellar from the church hall. Two naked lights swung grotesque shadows round the walls as bricks and masonry were cleared from the floor.

From the well the first layers of broken glass were removed handful by handful, the workers stooping over the narrow entrance. At first the glass seemed to be 19th century wine bottles thrown in between layers of gravel.

A few feet down the glass changed. Older glass appeared, and pottery and broken clay pipes. One of the bottles was labelled 1728, and many of the necks were corked.

By Tuesday evening the workers were eight feet down, working with buckets and long handled tools. Water had to be pumped out continuously.

But the first major finds were being made. One jug came out whole.

It showed a complicated badge on one side and a gross portrait of a face. Other pottery showed similar designs but none identical.

No one can say how far the well goes down or even what the next layer will produce. But it does seem apparent that material was dumped there at greatly different periods.

OLD COIN

In one corner under the brick floor the coin was discovered. Its age has not yet been determined, but it has been crudely stamped out and bears the fleur-de-lys of France.

A discovery on Monday was a circular drain underneath the centre of the floor. Its bottom has not yet been dragged but it is proving valuable to the Tunnel Group.

Water can be pumped there from the well and sievesful of glass and pottery washed in the murky waters.

Work was continuing almost every evening this week. A barricade round the cellar entrance keeps out trespassers.

An iron grill is lowered over the hole to prevent accidents, and is padlocked at night. Hour after hour the work goes on below.

Late on Tuesday another clue was found - a narrow shute[?] behind one of the sealed off arches. First theory was that it could be an ancient form of speaking tube. Now it is believed to be a drain, but where and from what is not yet known.

Tomorrow (Saturday) more of the important outside work can continue, with trenches sunk for detailed examination of the cellar walls.

At present there seems no end to the directions in which the investigation could continue.

With possibly months of work stretching before them, members are jubilant at the discoveries already made.

Within two or three weeks the Mark Hall School annexe is to be demolished. This is not expected to interfere with the Tunnel Group, and Harlow Development Corporation have given permission for an investigation there.

ROOF CAVES IN DURING TUNNEL EXCAVATIONS
Group's narrow escape from death

The roof of a 'secret room' in the labyrinth of cellars at Mark Hall, Harlow collapsed on Sunday, nearly burying three of the Tunnel Group under an avalanche of debris.

They had entered the room after breaking through a bricked-up archway from the main cellar which they have been investigating since the end of September.

As they were working there, small pieces of rubble began falling from the roof. Mr Frederick Smith, leader of the Group, looked up and saw a number of cracks appearing. "It seemed to be snowing," he said. "Recognizing the signs we made a quick exit."

They were hardly back in the main cellar when there was a crash as tons of debris, loosely packed under the surface of the playground above, came down.

Clouds of choking dust filled the cellar and Mr Smith with Mr William Howard and another member of the Group climbed out until it had cleared.

Meanwhile, Mr Smith's son Malcolm returned from lunch. He saw three coats hanging up and a pile of rubble where he knew they had been working.

"I thought they were all buried there," he said. "No one was around".

Malcolm hurried round to the other side and found them working in the Mark Hall annexe, now being demolished.

IMPORTANT NEW DISCOVERY IN THE CELLARS

Another passageway has been discovered in the cellars at the site of Mark Hall, Harlow.

It runs for 25 feet underground and almost certainly one end links up with the first cellar discovered at the site. The other end was sealed off some time in the past but probably continues on the other side.

The extent of the new discovery will not be known until the week-end when the western end is unblocked. It appears to branch off to the right – underneath Mark Hall Moors and towards Old Harlow.

The discovery was made by Mr Frederick Smith, leader of the Harlow Tunnel Group. For months past the Group has been investigating the foundations and cellars of Mark Hall.

Two weeks ago a mysterious shaft was discovered towards the front of the building, and it was even thought that it might be the tunnel itself, a tunnel believed to run underneath Harlow.

It wasn't. It ran up towards the front of the former mansion.

But an iron grid gave Mr Smith the clue he needed to the building line of an even earlier Mark Hall. One building or another has stood on the site for at least a thousand years.

MORE TO BE FOUND

As yet several cellars have still to be found, but careful calculations showed the tunnellers where to dig. Three feet down they knocked a hole in the side of the new passage-way.

Mr Smith was the first through, scrambling over the rubble on his stomach. He took a torch, a steel helmet and a pick-axe in case the roof collapsed.

In the pitch blackness he walked for 20 feet, but bricks and rubble blocked the end. The passageway is solidly built of brick, with an earth floor. No one knows its age although parts of it seem to have been

reinforced within the last few hundred years. This may have been to take a building above it.

C.D. EXERCISE

This week-end the Harlow Civil Defence Corps has promised to hold an 'exercise' down there. Casualties will be removed but members will also help to clear the blocked end.

The new excavation has also brought to light another cellar loosely filled with rubble, but several more remain to be found.

And Mr Smith, whose predictions so far have been astonishingly accurate, says that he has 'a funny feeling' that something big is about to be found.

"No one knows exactly what cellars there are". He said "We have records of the sale of the house – a 52-room mansion it was – but there are no records of any cellars".

MYSTERY PASSAGE IS ONLY A FEW FEET IN LENGTH

The mysterious passageway leading from the cellars of Mark Hall and pointing towards the church of St Mary-at-Latton has been cleared.

But it is NOT a tunnel. It slopes up towards the surface.

Members of the Harlow Tunnel Group broke down the bricked-up entrance on Sunday and cleared away the rubble.

But the passage which leads from a secret room in the cellars was only 15 feet long.

More bottles and stained glass were found inside, clearly indicating that it was sealed off some time during the 17th century.

It seems to be a ventilating shaft – much too big for the present set of cellars. It could be a link with the supposition that there was once an underground meeting place there, quite possibly with religious significance.

SMALL ARCHWAY

Immediately opposite the entrance, and high above the floor of the secret room, is another small archway, still filled with rubble from the fire and demolition of 1947. That has yet to be investigated.

On Sunday, while the wall was being knocked down, the Tunnel Group suffered a minor casualty – to Gazette chief reporter Robert Weyers. High winds blew down a board marked "DANGER" and it struck him on the forehead, severing a small artery. Members of the Group performed first-aid and a doctor later inserted three stitches.

He was able to return to the cellars during the afternoon – to find that the hoped-for 'discovery' was not what it seemed.

Bellarmine jugs

At this stage Fred Smith still had ambitious plans for throwing the cellars open for public inspection. The Gazette reported that *'A proper and convenient entrance is being built with concrete steps. The Harlow Antiquarian Society – which will become the parent body of the Tunnel Group – is to be formed in January. Other projects may be started later, with talks, discussions and lectures over a wide field'*. Whether this scheme ever developed beyond the planning stage is not recorded. The excavations were eventually refilled and an empty green space now stretches between the church hall and the trees beside Muskham Road.

Mark Hall manor house has gone but we are fortunate in having enough documentary and physical evidence to be able to describe its position and some of its history. The expanding urban area once called Harlow New Town already includes the sites of at least fourteen ancient Halls and will probably include more in the future. Some had disappeared long before 1947. Beneath the border between Orchard Croft and Cook's Spinney the cellars of successive Latton Halls must lie, buried more than two centuries ago. Harlowbury House and Chapel still stand in the old parish of Harlow, and Moor Hall is still remembered by a few local residents. Thanks to Jon and William Moen, grandsons of William Soper of New Hall farm, the old manor of Brend Hall or New Hall is now becoming another carefully designed 'town in the country' between Churchgate Street and the old London road. Beyond its eastern boundary Hubbards Hall appears almost unchanged beside its cottages and barns and Kitchen Hall has been undisturbed by the construction of Church Langley. The fine barn near St Andrew's church indicates where the Hall of Netteswellbury once stood, until it was finally demolished in 1820. A fragment of a gateway on Great Parndon's golf course is all that remains of the splendid mansion of Canons, a name that recalls the brief sojourn of the 'White Canons' 900 years ago. Elsewhere in Great Parndon, Passmores, Katherines, Sumners, Stewards and Taylifers (Little Canons) still stand on their old foundations, though many times rebuilt. In Little Parndon the last in a succession of manor houses survives, encircled by Princess Alexandra Hospital. Its predecessor lies beneath a car park opposite Hare Street and a still earlier Hall has a protected site opposite Little Parndon church.

At Mark Hall it was a fire that destroyed the relatively modern house and made it possible to explore the older cellars. Now it is more likely to be major excavations, required by changes in town-planning, which may briefly uncover valuable traces of lost buildings. If these could be recognised and accurately recorded the long history of Harlow would be enriched.

The Cycle Museum and the Walled Gardens

The fire at Mark Hall prevented the house from being used as offices but Harlow Development Corporation used the walled gardens for holding and raising thousands of roses, shrubs and trees that became part of the landscaping of the New Town. The buildings provided a base for the Corporation's Landscape Maintenance Department, and by the mid 1970s the Muskham Road Depot housed eighty mowing machines, eighty tractors and an assortment of landscape materials. Early New Town residents remember visiting the nursery to buy plants for their new gardens.

By April 1978 the Landscape Maintenance Department had been moved elsewhere. The walled gardens and the stables were transferred from the Corporation to Harlow District Council and later that year it was decided to convert the stables into a museum to house John Collins' unique collection of veteran bicycles.

The Collins family

In the first years of the nineteenth century, when Montagu Burgoyne had completed the new mansion that William Lushington had left unfinished, Harvey Collins was setting up his wheelwright's workshop in Harlow High Street. It may well have been Collins' workshop that serviced Burgoyne's and Arkwright's numerous carts and farm machinery. The business prospered and in 1896 William Collins, Harvey's grandson, opened his own works in the front room of his house in Fore Street, Harlow. The new store, which eventually filled the house and pushed the family next door, sold petrol and serviced the first automobiles but William's main interest was the new craze for cycling. Not only did he stock a variety of different models but he designed one of his own, christened 'the Harlowite'. William's son Reginald, who inherited the business, was joined by his son John in 1948.

John Collins combined an interest in architecture and history with a passionate enthusiasm for all cycling activities and an unrivalled knowledge of the development of the bicycle. Starting with the frame of a 'penny farthing' which required many hours of patient reconstruction, John gradually amassed over seventy machines and accessories connected with cycling. This was the collection that the Harlow District Council bought in 1978 as the nucleus of the Cycle Museum. The new buildings were designed to provide adequate galleries to exhibit these machines and any future purchases.

John Collins sold his shop in Fore Street and became the museum's curator.

Adapting the stables

Before the conversion, the eighteenth century stable block had consisted of living quarters for the grooms above store-rooms which later became accommodation for the chauffeur's family, facing west towards the main house. The coach-house was on the north side of this and the wing that housed the tack room and the horses formed a right angle on the south side. This wing was, and still is, topped by a cupola. The bell that hung beneath it is preserved in the Museum, but the clock faces, which probably dated from Joseph Arkwright's time, have disappeared.

The stables before 1978

Retaining the original tiled roof and the basic structure, Ray Hooper of A.D. Architects, Hertford designed the museum with two small galleries and three large ones to illustrate the history of

Mark Hall, the story of the Collins family and the evolution of the bicycle. John Collins co-operated in the work and it was he who pointed out the value of high ceilings so that some of the machines could be hung and viewed from all angles. Before the paralysis that limited him to a wheelchair, John would sometimes enliven the proceedings by demonstrating his skill on the penny-farthing.

The long glass-fronted gallery to the right of the original entrance still houses several machines from the original Collins collection and the rest can be seen by request.

On completion, the Cycle Museum conversion won a Civic Trust Award and both the building and the walled gardens were listed with Grade II status. The architect arrived at the award ceremony with a colleague, both suitably mounted on bicycles.

The Walled Gardens

As the conversion of the stables developed, attention turned to the walled gardens which had become overgrown and neglected. In order to provide an attractive setting for the Museum, it was decided to replan and replant them before opening them to the public. Ambitious designs illustrating sixteenth, seventeenth and eighteenth century gardens were discussed and modified. Crumbling sheds, a pig pen, ruined glasshouses and other outbuildings were removed and the work began.

The walled garden in 1978

The Museum archives hold a complete list of every plant and tree that was ordered to carry out the new schemes and many of these can still be identified in the beds and borders. The three walled gardens were retained: the largest, with a gated entrance from First Avenue, being named the Peace Garden and divided into four sections which remain much the same today. The roses in the quarter to the right of the entrance have been replaced as they aged but the plan is the same. The original lawn remains in the north east quarter and though grass has now replaced the island beds in the section inside the curved wall, the basic scheme of wide borders, trees and climbing plants clothing the old walls has been preserved. The fourth quarter, by the side of the museum, was divided into two parts. One represented a cottage garden and the other became an early demonstration of what could be achieved in an 'organic' allotment. The adjoining enclosure, the 'Seventeenth Century Garden', was sponsored by Marks & Spencer who added the raised viewing platform and six teak seats where visitors can still relax and enjoy the scents of lavender and box. Its centrepiece, a sundial contrived by Nathan David with a simplified metal sculpture of a penny-farthing, combines the themes of past and present.

The sundial

Finally, an 'Unusual Fruits Garden' was planned, which has now become the entrance to the museum from the enlarged car park. Several of the 1980s trees, including a medlar, still flourish there

near a group of fig trees, possibly dating back to Joseph Arkwright's time.

After the gardens were opened to the public, a local amateur theatrical company was given permission by the council to stage outdoor productions for a paying audience. The classic plays produced by Centre Stage over several years included Shaw's 'Pygmalion', Wilde's 'The Importance of Being Earnest', Sheridan's 'The Rivals', and Goldsmith's 'She Stoops to Conquer' as well as twentieth century musical revues.

A stage was erected from scaffolding and plastic sheeting, and the cast and crew, together with costumes, furniture, bits of portable scenery and props were all housed in

The seventeenth century garden

a large marquee in full view of the audience. As there was no night time security for the first of these productions, the cast and crew camped out in the tent all night with a camping-gaz stove, several tins of baked beans and various brands of liquid refreshment. For later productions it was possible to hire a private security officer. Unfortunately he could not guard against the weather and one night, during the run of 'The Rivals,' there was a horrendous thunderstorm which turned the lawn into a marsh and the stage and tent almost floated away. The heavy eighteenth century costumes were soaked – people were staggering about with armfuls of dripping fabric desperately seeking tumble dryers and steam irons. But by the time the evening audience turned up everything was back to normal.

A production of Pygmalion in the walled gardens

The Museum of Harlow 2002-

See Chronology page 167

In 1998 Harlow Council decided to combine the Cycle Museum with Harlow Museum (established in 1972 at Passmores House). The new creation became the Museum of Harlow at Mark Hall. During the transition period, the archives, which had been stored in St Andrew's church as part of the Study Centre, were moved first to Passmores House and then to Mark Hall. This process took four years. The new Museum opened on 23 March 2002.

Opening night of the Museum of Harlow

Since the closure of the Cycle Museum, Ray Hooper's original plan has been changed considerably to accommodate different demands, though the building looks much the same from the old Muskham Road entrance. Two wings still project westward from the old stable building and the one on the right still displays bicycles but on the left the toilets have been improved and the tall brick wall hides valuable new storage capacity. The room directly inside the old west door is now the reception area and visitors enter from the opposite side, through the old Unusual Fruits garden and down a ramp to the new door. A gateway has been constructed through the old garden wall to provide direct access from the enlarged car park east of the Museum. Walkers can also come in through the double gates off First Avenue.

The Gilbey still

New developments in the gardens include a pergola for outdoor activities and a growing collection of sculptures and objects connected with some significant local event. The largest of these arrived in June 2003 and was deposited with difficulty in the old organic garden. Because of the long-standing connection of the Gilbey family with Harlow, and particularly with Mark Hall, Chris Lydamore, the Museum manager, agreed to provide a resting place for the still which once stood inside Gilbey's huge display window in the Little Parndon distillery. A more recent sculpture commemorates the last day of Brays Grove School.

Inside the building the old reception area now contains information on the prehistoric era, then comes the Roman Gallery, and the display leads on chronologically through the medieval, Tudor and Stuart periods. A full length photograph of the 1616 map of the Altham estate hangs on one wall near Mary Altham's initialled altar cloth and the eighteenth and nineteenth centuries are conveyed by portraits, toys and costumes.

In the Roman Gallery

The twentieth century is represented in Gallery 4 by a number of household objects familiar to older visitors but a source of astonishment to the young. This area also contains a collection of views of pre-New Town scenes, contrasted with photographs of the same spot today. The final part of this Gallery covers the planning, building and growth of Harlow New Town, with objects complemented by the first-hand experiences of Harlow residents.

The history of the bicycle is displayed in Gallery 5 with examples of several machines, including those made and used in the town.

Beyond Gallery 4 and beside the bicycle display is the Community room, constantly used by visiting children in the daytime and by many different groups in the evenings and on Saturdays. An important function of the Museum is the continuous collection of oral as well as written and photographic local history.

At the end of the bicycle gallery is the study area with its large collection of photographs, slides, video and audio tapes, archives, maps, local newspapers and books. The Museum of Harlow has been an Access Point for the Essex Record Office since 2002.

Besides four salaried staff, the Museum relies on a large number of dedicated volunteers who share their considerable knowledge of local history, photography, coins, pottery and other crafts and help with accessing new acquisitions, identifying and cataloguing the objects, producing fact sheets and answering enquiries.

One of the most important of these activities has been reconstructing the Metropolitan ware that was once Harlow's most famous product. Some of the best examples were excavated around

Restoring pottery

Mark Hall and are well displayed in the Museum. In 2009, after many years of work with other volunteers, first at Passmores and then at Mark Hall, Wally Davey, a local teacher and archaeologist, at last completed his definitive study of *The Harlow Pottery Industries* which he has been able to publish with a grant from English Heritage. It is now on sale in the Museum with other aspects of local history.

In June 2007 the Museum received its full Accreditation from the Museums, Libraries and Archives Council. In 2009 it gained additional awards under the Visitor Attraction Quality Assurance Scheme and the Council for Learning outside the Classroom in recognition of the high quality of the services it provides.

During its first eight years more than 100,000 people have visited the Museum of Harlow or made use of its resources in local schools and other institutions. Groups visiting from schools with their teachers are catered for, activities for children are offered in the school holidays and family events are organised. Reminiscence sessions take place and research into the collections is undertaken.

The manor house has gone but more evidence of the remarkable history of Mark Hall manor is still being discovered.

20
Latton Priory

c.1200-1534

c.1190 A small Priory is built near the south boundary of Latton.	1348 The le Waleys of Mark Hall and Latton Hall hold the advowson of the Priory directly from the Crown.
1247 The Prior of Latton is pardoned for a forest offence.	
1250 A deed from Richard Gernon[1] gives the Priory 12d rents from Sawbridgeworth, witnessed by three de Taneys: Richard, Peter and Walter.	Sometime in the fourteenth century the Priory is enlarged.
	1364 The advowson of the Priory is held by Mary de St Pol.
1250 Geoffrey, Prior of Latton, witnesses an agreement between the Abbey of Waltham Holy Cross and Netteswell.	1534 John Taylor, the last Prior, leaves the Priory.
After 1280, when the de Taneys leave Latton, the advowson of the parish church comes entirely into the hands of the Priory.	1534 An inquisition into the state of Latton Priory finds the foundation rules have been broken.
1346 Part of Latton Hall manor now belongs to Latton Priory.	Sir Henry Parker is granted the Priory by the Crown.

Most Harlow residents have never heard of Latton Priory and very few have visited Priory Farm, where the ruins of the church of St John the Baptist still stand, deserted since before the Reformation. Separated from the New Town by many acres of unchanged farmland east of Rye Hill, the remains of the nave now serve as an unusually lofty barn. Only once, in the 1950s, when the Essex

Priory Farm 2009

County Show was held on Priory land, did the noise and activity recall the August celebrations of the Festival of St John the Baptist, held on that same land since the fourteenth century.

There is some confusion about the largest manor in Latton, previously owned by Thurgot, a free man, and, according to Domesday, presented to St Edmund's Benedictine Abbey by 1086. This has been generally assumed to refer to the southernmost part of Latton where the Priory was later erected, less than half a mile to the right of the present road from Harlow to Epping. This theory seems unlikely for two reasons. St Edmund's archives hold no record of it and the Benedictine abbot would not have accepted an Augustinian priory on his land. It seems probable that Thurgot's land lay elsewhere and may later have been added to Harlowbury which had belonged to the Abbot of St Edmund's since 1041. As the building of the Priory is usually credited to the de Merk family it seems that some of the wooded uplands in the south of the parish must have belonged to that family in the medieval period.

The earliest document that mentions Latton Priory, a request from the nuns of Hedingham Priory for prayers to be said for the soul of Lucy, their late prioress, dates from about 1200. Latton Priory was one of more than a hundred religious houses that responded to the nuns' request. It was at this Hedingham convent, founded by Aubrey de Vere, that a chantry for Sir John Hawkwood was to be established in the time of Henry V.

Two deeds of about 1250 include the name of Geoffrey, the prior of Latton at that date.

Another of the rare documents that mention Latton Priory is a Latin cartulary housed in Kings' College, Cambridge. This consists of nine charters relating to property and rents settled on

---

.[1] Richard Gernon was a descendant of one of the knights rewarded by William I after the Conquest. A Robert Gernon received ten manors in Cambridgeshire, thirteen in Hertfordshire including Stansted Mountfitchet and more than forty in Essex including Matching in the Harlow Hundred. By 1135 the Gernons had been replaced by the Mountfitchet family.

Emma, who is also referred to variously as Emma Estenoire and as the wife of William Balstede. Emma was the sister of Robert de la Hyde who was born in 1225 in Eglinton, Herefordshire, married Cicely Walerand and had two daughters, Alice and Joan. One of the charters dated AD 1276 confirms a grant by brother Geoffrey (Galfridus) Prior of the church of St John the Baptist of Latton and the religious house (conventus) there to Robert de la Hyde and Emma his sister of an annual rent of one mark 'from the gift of Hugh de Nevile' charged on property in the 'villa of Warvisend'. In the final charter, in which all property mentioned in the other charters is apparently granted by Robert to his sister, there is a second reference to the 'rent of one mark from the gift and feoffment of the Prior and Convent of Latton.'

The fact that only these thirteenth century documents have survived does not necessarily prove that no earlier religious foundation existed on that site. Three ancient trackways converge nearby: one leading over Rye Hill Common to Waltham Abbey, a second from Epping to Harlow and a third running north. Travellers would certainly have valued hospitality at the crossroads and it seems unlikely that there was nothing there before 1200. Excavations, connected with a new pipeline laid by Thames Water, revealed evidence of small round dwellings of the third or fourth century a quarter of a mile from the Priory, but the actual site of the existing ruins has not been investigated.

Augustinian or 'Black Canons', who follow the rule of St Augustine of Hippo (354-430), first established themselves in Britain in the eleventh century. After the reforming Lateran Council of 1059, which exhorted clergy to live in community, holding all things in common, the 'Black Canons' quickly spread across Europe and over the Channel. In Britain their first priory, St Botolph's, was founded in Colchester between 1095 and 1105, closely followed by Holy Trinity, Aldgate, founded by Matilda the wife of Henry I. Before 1300 the Augustinians had over 250 priories and abbeys in Britain. In Wales they frequently established priories on sites where Celtic Christians had previously gathered. The Catholic Encyclopaedic Dictionary (1931) defines them as *'priests bound by the vows of religion and living in community under a rule. Though they sing the Divine Office in choir and normally live the life of monks, canons regular are at all times prepared to undertake the works of the active apostolate.'* Their black cloaks distinguished the Augustinians from the white-clad Premonstratensians and the Cistercians. In London both St Bartholomew's and St Thomas's Hospitals owe their origins to Augustinian foundations.

The number of canons in each Augustinian priory was usually very small but they would probably have formed the nucleus of a much larger group of lay brothers and farm workers. For some families Latton Priory would have been nearer than their parish church for Sunday worship and their lives would have revolved around its festivals and holy days.

At times one of the Black Canons probably conducted the service at St Mary-at-Latton and the Prior would have appointed the priest or priests in the periods when he, rather than the lord of Mark Hall or Latton Hall, held the advowson of the parish church. In 1291 the Priory was valued in the Taxation of that year at £4 yearly. This sum was based on rent from 'temporalities' (land) in Moreton, Chelmsford, Moulsham, Matching, North Weald, Ongar, High Laver, Roydon, Stortford and Gilston as well as Latton itself which yielded £2 11s.6d.

In about 1327 a document indicates that the prior and his canons *'used to take tithes of bread, beer, flesh, wax candles and other provisions within the manor of Ongar by grant of Maud de Lucy, whose son changed these tithes into a rent of 40 shillings until the manor came into the king's hands'.*

The tomb of Aymer de Valence in Westminster Abbey

Mary de St Pol[1], who held the advowson of the Priory from 1364 until her death in 1377, was a wealthy widow who outlived her husband, Aymer de Valence, Earl of Pembroke, by over fifty years and spent that period in setting up and supervising several religious and educational establishments. It was she who founded Pembroke College, Cambridge, in 1347 and in 1356 she tried to set up a college

---

[1] Mary de St Pol had a remote connection with the Valognes family. Sir John Comyn, (died 1306), a descendant of David and Isabel Comyn (née Valognes), married Joan de Valence, daughter of William de Valence, Earl of Pembroke. Their son was Aymer de Valence (died 1324). His second wife was Mary de St Pol.

in the University of Paris but was prevented by the Hundred Years War. Finally she turned her attention to Denny Abbey where she apparently joined a group of Franciscan nuns known as Poor Clares and where she lies buried.

Denny Abbey 2009

Latton Priory may first have been planned as a small building but the ruins show that it was later extended, possibly during the time of Mary de St Pol, and became a lofty and impressive church, surrounded by cloisters and outbuildings. Such a grand building must have been a centre for worship, medical treatment, poor relief and hospitality over a wide area, but little has been recorded in detail of its history. It seems that its numbers gradually declined and, as Canon Fisher observed in his *Deanery of Harlow,* there were frequent vacancies among the canons and as there were then too few to elect a Prior, the right to appoint often lapsed to the Bishop of London.

The desertion of John Taylor, the last Prior, before 1534 and the 'inquisition' concerning the Priory that followed have been more fully documented than its previous history. Besides declaring that the Priory had become 'a profane place' by neglecting many divine services, the inquisitors linked the origin of the Priory with the Shaa family, then in possession of Mark Hall – a link that has never been substantiated.

1534-2010

After the last 'Black Canon' left, Latton Priory was granted to Sir Henry Parker, soon to be the owner of Mark Hall. On February 1 1541 Sir Henry Parker had licence to grant it to William Morris and by 1556 it was owned by John Hethe. With the coming of the Althams the Priory again became part of the Mark Hall estate and remained so until 1778 when it was bought by the new squire's father, the Revd Henry Lushington. A farmhouse, cow-sheds and other farm buildings were erected and, like so many ancient buildings, the Priory was forgotten except in a name. The appearance of human bones during ploughing occasionally provided evidence of the position of the canons' graveyard. In 1824 Priory Farm was owned by Revd Clayton Glyn and by 1839 it had been bought by the Arkwrights. In recent times the farm has belonged to the Brown family.

The ruins crumbled very slowly and even today the occupants of Priory Farm still work beside ancient walls and under massive archways. Bit by bit the old cloisters were demolished and the valuable masonry used elsewhere until only the part that is useful as a huge barn remains.

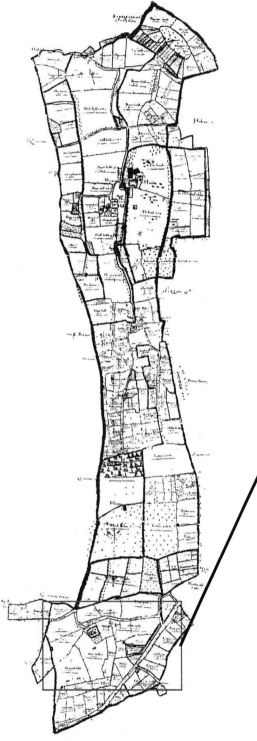

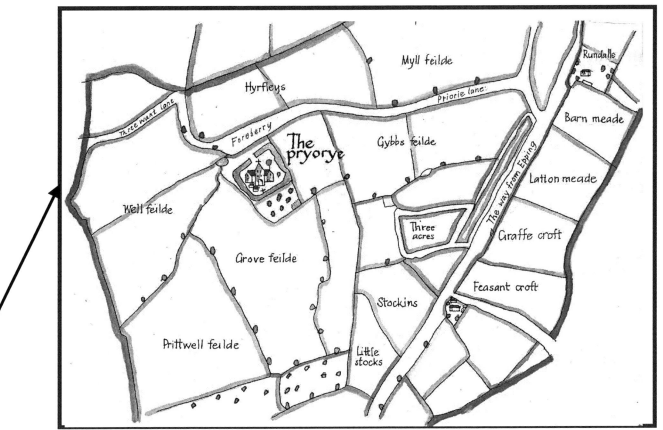

Altham estate map 1616

Writing in 1893 in his *Essex: Highways, Byways and Waterways* C.R.B. Barrett gives a description of Latton Priory which is still accurate today.

> *'From Netteswell I made my way to Latton Priory, of which there is not much to see. Still it is rather a surprise when on entering a cruciform barn, I find myself standing within the four fine tower arches of a church. The columns are massive, being in clusters of three with a beading, and the arches singularly bold. Such however is the case at Latton, and beyond these four arches and a few feet of wall projecting from their faces, in which traces of windows and a piscina are found, there is nothing more. One of these windows, an elegant little cinquefoil, will be found on the north wall of the north transept, and in the south-west corner of the church there are the remains of an external staircase.'*

Barrett then describes three sides of a moat which in his day was filled with water. He concludes, quoting Revd Holman, [1630-1765] *'Holman states that in his time most of the priory church was standing; would that it were still so, for the tower arches are really noble.'* Today only one side of the moat is still visible and the old farm buildings have been replaced by aluminium structures, but the listed Priory is unchanged.

Eighteenth century drawing of Latton Priory

In the year 2006 Mr Ian Brown, the present owner of Priory Farm, picked up a small object in his garden which turned out to be the lead seal of a papal bull. It was first sent to Harlow Museum for identification and then, as the Priory is no longer in Latton, to the Epping Forest Museum, before being eventually returned to the estate where it had lain for seven hundred years.

Lead seal of a papal bull sent by Pope Alexander V 1307

134

Bibliography

Altham, 'A descendant', *Some Althams of Mark Hall in the seventeenth century,* The Essex Review Vol, XVIII, 1909

Andrews, H.C., *The Chronicles of Hertford Castle.* Hertford, Stephen Austin & Sons Ltd., 1947, reprinted 1997

Axton, M. & Carley J.P. (Eds.), *'Triumphs of English' Henry Parker, Lord Morley,* The British Library, 2000

Bartlett, R., *Harlow Temple Excavations,* 1985-6, An Interim Report, 1987

Bateman, L., *History of Harlow,* Harlow Development Corporation, 1969

Bell, A. R. Brooks, C., Dryburgh, P.R., *The English Wool Market 1230-1327,* Cambridge Un. Press, 2007

Bott, A. and Dunn, M., *The Priory and Parish Church of St Mary Beddgelert,* Friends of St Mary's, Beddgelert, 2004

Briggs, N., *John Johnson 1732-1814: Georgian Architect & County Surveyor of Essex,* Essex Record Office, 1991

Brown, A.F.J., *Prosperity and Poverty. Rural Essex, 1700-1815,* Essex Record Office, 1996

Casey, P.J., *Carausius and Allectus,* University of Durham, Yale University Press, 1995

Cheetham, A., *Richard II,* Weidenfield & Nicolson, 1972

Cocks, M.E.M., *The Great House of Hallingbury,* Gt. Hallingbury Local History Soc., 1988

Colthorpe, M. & Bateman, L.H., *Queen Elizabeth I & Harlow,* Harlow Development Corporation, 1977

Cuttyhunk Historical Society, Monograph: *Bartholomew Gosnold (1571-1607) New World Adventurer*

Domesday Book, Williams, A. & Martin, G.H. (Eds.), Alecto Historical Edition, Penguin Classics, 2003

Edmunds, J., *A History of Latton,* St Mary-at-Latton, 1980

Eiden, H., *The Peasants' Revolt in Essex and Norfolk.* The Journal of the Historical Association. Vol. 83, 1998

Fisher, J.L., *The Deanery of Harlow,* Colchester, Benham & Co., 1922

Fitton, R.S., *The Arkwrights. Spinners of Fortune,* Manchester University Press, 1989

Feiling, K., *A History of England,* Book Club Associates, 1950

Green, J., *Chasing the Sun,* Jonathan Cape, 1996

Handley, J. & Lake, H., *Progress by Persuasion. The Life of William Smith,* 2007

Harlow Museum Education Service, *Mark Hall* (pre 1983)

Ibbetson, D., *Sir James Altham (c.1555-1617) Judge,* Oxford D. N. B., Oxford University Press, 2004-7

Jones, J., *The secret history of Harlow's Roman Temple,* Harlow Museum, 2001

Jones, I., *Domesday Book and Harlow,* Harlow District Council, 1988

Lake, H., *The Arkwrights and Harlow,* 1995

Murray, C., *Elizabeth Arkwright. The Huntress who lived in a Painting*, unpublished notes, Museum of Harlow

Musset L., *The Bayeux Tapestry,* translated by Richard Rex, The Boydell Press, 2002

Neville, D., *Lost Castles of Essex,* Ian Henry Publications, 2003

Norrington, R., *In the Shadow of a Saint. Lady Alice More,* The Kylin Press, 1983

Outhwaite, R.B., *Scandal in the Church. Dr Edward Drax Free 1764-184,* Hambledon Co., 1997

Pewsey, Stephen & Brooks, *East Saxon Heritage,* Alan Sutton Publishing Ltd, 1993

Richards, J.D., *Viking Age England,* Tempus, 1991

Rickword, G., Borough Librarian, *Bailiffs & Mayors of Colchester*, Colchester Library, c.1902

Roskell, Clark & Rowcliffe, *The Commons 1386-1421,* Stroud, 1992

Rothwell, W., *Walter de Bibbesworth. Le Tretiz,* Anglo-Norman Text Soc., Birkbeck College, London, 1990

Searle, A. (Ed.), *Barrington Family Letters 1628-1632,* Camden Fourth Series, Vol 28, London Offices of the Royal Historical Society, University College London, 1983

Strong, R., *The Story of Britain,* Pimlico, 1998

Shilleto,W., *The Parochial History of Latton,* (lecture notes 1865) Manuscript in Harlow Museum.

Starr, C., *Medieval Mercenary: Sir John Hawkwood of Essex,* Essex Record Office, 2007

Stenton, D.M., *English Society in the early Middle Ages,* Penguin Books, 4th Ed., 1965

Thrupp S. L., *The Merchant Class of Mediaeval London,* University of Chicago Press, 1948

Tyrell, J.H., *A Chronological History of the Tyrells,* Phillimore & Co. Ltd, 1980

University of London Institute of Historical Research, *Victoria History of the County of Essex*, Vol. VIII, and the County of Hertfordshire, Oxford University Press

Varley, B., *The History of Stockport Grammar School,* Manchester University Press, 1957

Vere-Hodge, H.S., *Sir Andrew Judde,* Tonbridge School Shop, 1953

W.E.A.G. *The Romano-British Temple at Harlow,* 1985

Ward, J., *English Noblewomen in the Later Middle Ages,* Longman, 1992

Watkin, D., *Alfred Gilbey. A Memoir by some Friends,* Michael Russell (Publishing) Ltd, 2001

Watson, J.N.P., *Lionel Edwards. Master of the Sporting Scene.* The Sportsman's Press London 1986

W.E., *Notes on Latton Priory,* unpublished manuscript, Harlow Museum

Williams, H., *Chronology of World History,* Wiedenfeld & Nicolson, 2005

Williams, J., *Maud Rothing c.1290-1355: A Woman of Means and Ways,* Transactions of the London and Middlesex Archaeological Society, vol. 52, 2002

Williamson, J.A., *The Evolution of England,* Oxford, 1944

Wood, M., *In Search of the Dark Ages,* BBC, 1981

Yerburgh, H.B., *Leaves from a Hunting Diary,* Vinton & Co Ltd., 1900

Illustrations

CHRONOLOGY

Chronology

Invaders, rulers and rebellions	Religious events
From at least 1000 BC successive waves of tribes, some originating from lands around the upper Danube, invade Britain. From 200 BC Germanic tribes push westward into Gaul. Some flee from the Roman legions into Britain.	Worship of the spirits present in nature in all its forms is conducted by priests.
By 100 BC the river Stort divides the area occupied by the Belgic Catuvellauni tribe (Hertfordshire) and the Trinovantes (Essex).	
Colchester becomes the capital city of the Trinovantes.	
57 BC General Julius Caesar defeats the Belgic tribes in Gaul.	
55 BC First Roman attempt at invasion of Britain.	By 50 BC some form of sacred site has been established on the summit of Stanegrove Hill by the river (the Stort). Settlements develop nearby to the south of the hill.
54 BC Second Roman invasion, both led by Julius Caesar, successful but brief. Annual tribute agreed to by some British kings of invaded territories.	
Before the next Roman invasion more Belgic tribes invade Britain from Gaul bringing closer contact with Roman culture.	
49 BC **Julius Caesar** becomes ruler of Rome.	
44 BC Julius Caesar is assassinated.	
31 BC **Mark Anthony** is defeated by Octavius at the battle of Actium. Octavius adopts the name **Augustus** and becomes the first Roman Emperor.	c.4 BC Birth of Jesus Christ.
10 BC Death of Tasciovanus, king of the Trinovantes.	Roman Emperors are included among the gods.
AD 5 Cunobelinus (Cymbeline) becomes king of the Catuvellauni. He defeats the Trinovantes and sets up his capital at Colchester.	
AD 41-54 **Claudius**, Emperor of Rome.	
AD 43 Death of Cunobelinus, an ally of Rome.	
AD 43 Third Roman invasion of Britain led by Aulus Plautius. By 47 AD the Romans control an area south of a line from the Bristol Channel to the Humber estuary. Fosse Way constructed (A46). Thousands of traders & merchants arrive. Camulodunum (Colchester) becomes first Roman capital.	Slow spread of Christianity, persecuted by Roman authorities.
AD 50 Londinium is founded – the main trading centre.	
54 AD Claudius is poisoned. **Nero** succeeds him.	
AD 61-62 Rebellion of Boudicca, queen of the Iceni (Norfolk & Suffolk).	
AD 64 Fire consumes Rome.	St Peter, first Bishop of Rome, is crucified under Nero.
The London Wall is built with six gates.	
	AD c.80 A Roman temple is superimposed on the earlier sacred site on Stanegrove Hill.
AD 117-138 **Hadrian**.	AD c.100 The temple is extended and surrounded by a wooden palisade.
AD 122 Hadrian's Wall is begun.	
AD 138-161 **Antoninus Pius**. Antonine Wall is built.	
AD 193 **Septimus Severus**. He dies in York in 211.	AD c.200 The wooden palisade of Stanegrove temple is replaced with a stone and rubble wall and an arched entrance is constructed.
	AD 208/9 Death by decapitation of St Alban – the first British Christian martyr.
AD 259-274 Britain is part of the Gallic Empire with Gaul and Spain.	AD 275 St Anthony begins a hermit life in the Egyptian desert. The origin of Christian monasticism.
AD 284 **Diocletian**. He divides Britain into four provinces.	
AD 286-296 Rebellion of **Carausius** followed by **Allectus**	The persecution of Christians intensifies under

Invaders, rulers and rebellions	Religious events
in Britain. By developing sea power they establish an independent British kingdom for a decade.	Diocletian.
307-337 **Constantine the Great** is first proclaimed emperor of Britain in York, then of the whole Roman Empire. He moves his capital from Rome to Byzantium – renamed Constantinople (Istanbul).	312 Constantine I is converted to Christianity. He builds St Peter's Basilica over Peter's tomb and the Holy Sepulchre in Jerusalem.
	313 The persecution of Christians by the Romans ends.
	354-430 The teachings of St Augustine of Hippo become the basis of the Augustinian Order.
	356 All Roman temples are ordered to close.
364-375 **Valentinian** becomes Emperor in the West.	Some Romano-British households have become Christian.
367 Major attacks on Britain by Picts, Scots & Saxons.	
393-423 **Honorius**, Emperor in the West is crowned in Milan.	After c. AD 400 the Stanegrove temple is apparently deserted.
393 Withdrawal of Roman troops from Britain begins.	Christianity is made the established religion of the Empire.
395 **Arcadius** Emperor in the East.	
408 Death of Arcadius.	At an unknown date the head of Minerva (found in the remains of the Stanegrove temple) is deliberately disfigured.
410 Revolt in Britain by Constantine III who joins Alaric the Goth in his attack on Rome. From c.400 the Roman Empire in the West disintegrates.	Remnants of Christianity fade after the breakdown of the Roman occupation.

Events concerning the owners of Mark Hall manor printed in bold type

National events	Religious matters	Local events
End of 4th century. Increasingly dangerous raids on Britain from N.W. Europe by Picts, Frisians, Franks, Angles, Saxons and Jutes (esp. in Kent)	The Germanic invaders worship a variety of gods including Woden and Seaxnent, both gods of war. Every Saxon king claims one of the gods of war as his ancestor.	
c.443-6 Outbreak of plague hits Britain.	427 & 429 St Germanus visits Britain. His biography suggests that the country was still Romanized, Christian and wealthy as late as 480.	
448-449 *'The coming of the Saxons took place.'* Bede. Beginning of period covered by his *Anglo-Saxon Chronicle*.		
450 Anglo-Saxon mercenaries invited possibly by 'Vortigern' overlord of southern Britain to fight off other invaders or rival British kings. The mercenaries revolt and are strengthened by new Anglo-Saxon arrivals.	Christianity is carried westwards into Wales and Ireland by Celtic refugees from the pagan invaders. 432 St Patrick (373-461) begins his mission in Ireland.	
490 British victory over the Saxons at 'Badon Mount' described by Gildas. Basis of Arthurian legends.		
The newcomers form hundreds of small warring statelets, each with its own chief or king.		Possibly by AD 500 several small Saxon settlements are established along the river to the west of Harlow.
Gradually the small states merge into seven warring kingdoms – Northumbria, Mercia, Kent, Sussex, Wessex, East Anglia and Essex (East Saxons including Middlesex and London).	525 St Benedict of Norsia's 'Rule of Monks', issued from his monastery in Monte Cassino, becomes widely adopted across Europe 563 St Columba takes Christianity to Iona.	
By 600 Kent is the most powerful kingdom.	597 Pope Gregory I sends Augustine to Kent to convert Ethelbert. He	One group of farms is named Laectum (late place? kitchen

National events	Religious matters	Local events
c.560-616 **Ethelbert**, King of Kent, with his capital at Canterbury, marries Bertha, the Christian daughter of a Frankish king. Before 616 Sebert rules in Essex.	baptises the king and founds the Benedictine monastery of Christ Church, Canterbury. 602 St Augustine becomes Archbishop of Canterbury. He sends Melitus to lead a mission to convert Sebert, King of the East Saxons. 610 Muhammad (c.570-632) begins preaching in Mecca. 616, 617 Ethelbert and Sebert die. The mission ends with a return to paganism. 638 Islamic forces capture Jerusalem. 653 Celtic Christianity arrives in Essex from Lindisfarne. St Cedd is made bishop of the East Saxons. Roving missionaries visit the villages. St Cedd dies of plague.	garden?). **The farm nearest the river includes the hill crowned by the crumbling Roman temple**. Another Saxon free man, probably a close relative, establishes his farm nearby.
Wessex and Mercia vie for power. 731 Bede is writing his *Ecclesiastical History of the English People* at Jarrow, Northumbria.	664 Synod of Whitby. The Bishops agree that the Roman form of Christianity shall prevail in England. 672 Council of the whole Church in England creates many more sees and minster churches which become centres of learning, baptism and burials.	
c.800 The power of Mercia declines. Wessex becomes dominant. 835-6 Extended Viking raids. 866/7 Danish Great Army destroys the kingdom of Northumbria. 869 **Edmund**, King of the East Angles, is defeated and killed by Inguar, King of the Danes. 871 King **Ethelred I** of Wessex is killed fighting the Danes. His brother **Alfred the Great** succeeds. 878 Alfred defeats the Danes. 886 Alfred expels the Vikings from London. A treaty defines the area of the Danelaw. *The Anglo-Saxon Chronicle* is supervised by Alfred. 894 The Danes sail up the river Lea to Ware and Hertford. Alfred cuts off their retreat by flooding the Waltham marshes.	By 800 the majority of East Saxons are Christians. Edmund is regarded as a martyr and becomes Saint Edmund.	
899 Alfred is succeeded by **Edward the Elder**. 911 Viking invaders settle in Normandy. Viking King		Little evidence of Danelaw in Harlow area.

National events	Religious matters	Local events
Rollo agrees to baptism in a pact with French King Charles the Simple who grants him land.	Normandy becomes famed for monasteries and church life.	
924 Edward dies. **Athelstan** claims the crown of a united England.		
England is divided into shires and 'hundreds' or 'wapentakes'.		The 'Half-hundred' of Harlow includes Harlow, Latton, Netteswell, Roydon, Great and Little Parndon, Matching, Sheering, Hatfield Broad Oak, Great and Little Hallingbury.
939 Athelstan dies. Succeeded by **Edmund I**.		
942 Edmund I reconquers the Danelaw.	945 Edmund I grants the land around Bury St Edmunds for the maintenance of St Edmund's shrine.	
946 Edmund I is murdered. Succeeded by **Edred**.		
955 Edred dies. Succeeded by **Eadwig**.		
959 Eadwig dies. Succeeded by **Edgar**.		
975 Edgar dies. Succeeded by **Edward** aged 12.	Most villages now have a wooden church near the home of the thegn or head man. The area around each thegn's land becomes his manor. Parish boundaries are established, sometimes including several manors.	
978 Edward (the Martyr) is murdered. His half-brother **Ethelred** succeeds him.	**By 950 Latton's first church has been built on or near the present site of St Mary-at-Latton, near the home of the Saxon free man whose manor contains the old Roman temple.**	
991 At the battle of Maldon the Saxon governor is defeated by the Danes.		
1002 Emma of Normandy becomes Ethelred's second wife.		
1004 More Vikings are welcomed in Normandy.		
1010 Thurkill the Dane lands at Ipswich.	1009 Ailmar is consecrated bishop of the South Saxons. (See 1200 – de Merk).	
1013 Ethelred is defeated by **Svein**, who becomes king. Ethelred flees to Normandy.	1012 The Vikings murder Alphege, Archbishop of Canterbury.	
1014 Svein dies. **Ethelred** returns and displaces Svein's son Cnut.		
1015 Cnut invades England.		
1016 Ethelred dies. **Edmund II** (Ironside) succeeds. He agrees to share England with Cnut. Edmund dies. **Cnut** claims all England.		
By 1025 Viking Normandy has become French speaking.	1030 Discovery of the Holy Cross at Montecute, Somerset on land owned by Tovi, Cnut's standard bearer.	
1035 William, the illegitimate		

National events	Religious matters	Local events
son of Robert, Duke of Normandy, succeeds him as duke. Cnut dies.	Cross transported to Waltham where Tovi builds a church.	
1037 **Harold Harefoot** is recognized as king of England.	Before the Conquest the manor of Eppinga is given to the abbots of Waltham Abbey.	
1040 **Harthacnut** succeeds Harold Harefoot.		
1042 Harthacnut is succeeded by **Edward the Confessor.** Harold, son of Godwin, Earl of Wessex, is made Earl of East Anglia.	1045 The lordship of Harlowbury is donated in his will by Thurstan to St Edmund's Abbey.	
Duke William of Normandy meets Edward the Confessor and possibly gains a promise of the English throne.	Edward the Confessor appoints Norman priests and bishops including Robert, Bishop of Jumiege, Archbishop of Canterbury.	
1054 & 7 William of Normandy repels French attacks.	1059 Earl Harold erects a Norman church on the site of Tovi's church at Waltham Holy Cross.	
	1059 Lateran Council encourages clergy to live in communities like the Apostles. Augustinian priories spread across Europe.	
1061 Normans invade Sicily.	1062 Harold founds a college of secular canons at Waltham Holy Cross supported by seventeen manors including Netteswell.	
1064 Harold is shipwrecked and taken to William's court. Alleged to have sworn to accept William as next king of England.		Latton in the time of Edward the Confessor:
		1) **The smallest manor near Stanegrove Hill is owned by Ernulf. (Later Mark Hall manor).**
1066 Edward the Confessor dies. Next day **Harold** is crowned king.	1065 Westminster Abbey is consecrated.	2) The neighbouring manor is owned by an unnamed free man. (Later Latton Hall manor.)
Harald III of Norway invades Northumberland and is killed by King Harold of England at Stamford Bridge.		3) The remaining land in Latton is owned by Thurgot, a free man.
Sept 28 William of Normandy lands at Pevensey. King Harold marches south and is killed at the battle of Hastings.		
1066 December 25 **William I** is crowned in Westminster Abbey.	King Harold's body is reburied at Waltham Abbey.	
William begins to share out English land among his barons.		
1067 Eustace of Boulogne assists the Kentish men in a failed attempt to seize Dover Castle.		
1069 William I defeats rebellions in the Midlands and the north.	1070 William I replaces the English Archbishop Stigard with Norman Lanfranc.	

National events	Religious matters	Local events
c.1077 the Bayeux Tapestry is completed.		
1078 William I begins building the Tower of London.		
1082 'The Great Famine' (Anglo-Saxon Chronicle).		Six shillings per hide is demanded in tax.
Normans impose strict laws within the King's Forest of Essex, reserved for royal hunting.		
1083 'A great and heavy tax' is levied all across England by William I.		
1085 William commissions the Domesday Book.		
1086 Domesday book is completed.	1086 A large unidentified area in Latton, previously owned by Thurgot, is given to St Edmund's Abbey.	**1086 Mark Hall manor** **Overlord – Count Eustace de Boulogne.** **Tenant – Adelolf de Merk.**
1087 William I dies, succeeded by **William II** (William Rufus).	1088 Revolt by Odo, Bishop of Bayeux and Rochester.	Latton Hall manor Overlord – Peter de Valognes Tenant – Turgis.
	Between 1095 and 1105 St Botolph's, the first Augustinian Priory in Britain, is founded in Colchester.	Population of Latton – twenty-five households.
	1095 Anselm quarrels with William II over papal authority.	Peter de Valognes' heir Roger marries Agnes Fitz John. Seven children. Property divided.
	First Crusade. Pope Urban II	
	1097 Anselm is exiled.	
	1097 Abbot Baldwin builds a new church over St Edmund's shrine.	
	1099 Jerusalem is taken. End of first Crusade.	c.1100 Latton Hall manor Overlord – Roger de Valognes
1100 William II dies in a hunting 'accident'. **Henry I** succeeds him and recalls Anselm.	1103 Anselm refuses to accept bishops consecrated by the king and is exiled again.	1103 Eudo the Steward founds a leper hospital in Colchester.
1100 Norman Tower of London completed.	1107 Henry I and Anselm are reconciled.	Roger Valognes' eldest son Peter (2) marries Gundred de Varenne. No children.
	1107 Augustinian Priory established at Aldgate by Henry I's wife Matilda.	
	1109 Anselm dies (Canonised in 1720).	
1120 Death of Henry I's son on the White Ship. Matilda, Henry's daughter is chosen to be queen.	1118 Rival Popes are elected – John V and Gregory VIII.	
1131 English barons pledge allegiance to Matilda as their future queen.		
1135 Death of Henry I. His nephew **Stephen** seizes power.		
1138 Robert, Earl of Gloucester, illegitimate son of Henry I, Matilda's half-brother, rebels against Stephen.		Roger de Valognes, overlord of Latton Hall, also a rebel against Stephen, enlarges his castle, Benington Lordship.
1141 Robert defeats Stephen. **Matilda** is proclaimed Queen of England.	1145-6 Second Crusade. Pope Eugenius III.	1141 Roger de Valognes dies His second son Robert Valognes inherits Benington Lordship

National events	Religious matters	Local events
1148 Matilda is forced out by cousin **Stephen**.		One daughter Gunnor de Valognes. She marries 1) Durand de Ostilli.
1152 Eleanor of Aquitaine marries Henry of Anjou.		
1153 Henry of Anjou lands in England and takes up his mother Matilda's campaign.	c.1153 The Premonstratensians (the Order of Premontre) or 'White Canons' establish an abbey in Perhendune (Parndon). The area is still known as Canons in Great Parndon.	
1154 Stephen dies. **Henry II** succeeds. First Plantagenet. He controls a large part of France as well as England. The *Anglo Saxon Chronicle* is completed covering 449-1149.		
1155 Henry II appoints Thomas Becket as chancellor. During the 12th century the system of 'franc pledge' or 'tithing' becomes established in most shires.	1159 Pope Hadrian dies. Two popes again: Alexander III and Victor IV.	1158 Peter de Valognes (2) dies.
1166 Henry II's reforms become the basis of the English legal system.	1162 Thomas Becket is consecrated as Archbishop of Canterbury. He asserts the rights of the church and refuses Henry's demands for secular rights. 1170 Dec 29 Becket is murdered in Canterbury Cathedral. 1174 Henry II does public penance for Becket's murder and extends the Waltham Cross church. An Augustinian Priory replaces Harold's college. 1180 After thirty years the White Canons move from Parndon to Maldon. Their Maldon house becomes known as Beeleigh Abbey. 1182 Samson is chosen as Abbot of St Edmunds. Harlowbury House and chapel are built by Abbot Samson c.1180 for his own use on journeys to London. Arnold de Latton is 'keeper of Harlowbury'.	1177 Henry II has Roger de Valogne's castle at Benington Lordship destroyed. By this time both the first Norman manor houses, **Mark Hall** and Latton Hall have probably been built.
1183 Henry II's eldest son Henry dies.	1184 Waltham Priory becomes Waltham Abbey. Netteswell ponds provide fish. 1187 Third Crusade. Defeated. Constantinople falls into Muslim hands for the first time since 1099. 1188 Henry II and Philip of France combine on a fresh Crusade.	1184 Ralph de Latton is first mentioned as 'tenant in demesne of Latton Hall, holding a knight's fee'.
1189 Office of Lord Mayor of the City of London is created. Henry II dies in France.	The wooden Saxon church is rebuilt in	

National events	Religious matters	Local events
Richard I (Coeur de Lion) crowned.	flint and stone near Mark Hall manor house.	
	1191 Richard & Philip capture Acre and massacre the inhabitants.	
1192 On his way home Richard I is captured by Leopold of Austria. John claims the English throne. Philip of France seizes Richard's lands in Normandy.	c.1190 The first small Priory is built near the southern tip of Latton. It is of the same Augustinian order of 'Black Canons' as Waltham Abbey. Probably under the control of the Bishop of London, not the Abbot of Waltham.	
1194 Richard returns to England and defeats John. Heavy taxation imposed to pay his ransom. Richard I is crowned again.	The Priory estate at this time includes 200 acres of farmland, 200 acres of pasture, thirty acres of meadow and ten acres of woodland. Geoffrey possibly the first Prior.	1194 Gunnor de Valognes' first husband dies. She marries (2) Robert Fitzwalter.
1195 Measure of a foot is filed in the royal treasury. Common weights and measures are established across England.	1195 and 1198 Fr. Roger and Fr. Anfred are named as priests of Latton.	
	1198 Fourth Crusade proclaimed by Pope Innocent III.	**Peter de Merk succeeds his father Alewin at Mark Hall.**
1199 Richard I is killed besieging the Castle of Chalun in France. Succeeded by brother **John.**	1198 A portion of the advowson of the living of Latton is taken from de Merk for the Priory.	
	1200 Fr. Ralph, the priest, 'residing at Mark Hall'. Eutropius de Merk gives the Preceptory of the Knights Hospitallers at Little Maplestead one acre of land 'viz that acre over which Ailmar, the bishop, passed'. *(See 1009 AD)*	**Eutropius de Merk possibly residing at Mark Hall.**
1205 The English barons refuse to fight for John in France.	1204 Constantinople is captured by the Crusaders. Chaos. End of Fourth Crusade.	1204 The 'men of Essex' offer King John 500 marks and five palfreys for the disafforestation of the forest of Essex 'which is beyond the causeway (Roman road) between Colchester and Bishop's Stortford'.
	1206 Stephen Langton is chosen as Archbishop of Canterbury against John's wishes.	
	1209 St Francis of Assisi begins to preach a new version of Christianity based on poverty and respect for all created life.	**c.1210 Henry de Merk (1) is demesne tenant of Mark Hall. He marries Rose 2 sons, Ralph and Henry.**
	1212 'The Children's Crusade' ends in shipwreck off Sardinia. Some are captured by Arabs.	
	1212 Death of the Abbot Samson of Bury St Edmunds.	
1215 The Barons rebel against John. Magna Carta is signed	1213 King John submits to papal authority.	Robert Fitzwalter of Roydon, husband of Gunnor de Valognes,

National events	Religious matters	Local events
at Runnymede. Charter allows freemen of the City of London to elect the Lord Mayor. Civil war resumes. 1216 King John dies. Infant son **Henry III** is crowned at Gloucester. 1217 Forest Charter granted by Henry provides some redress of grievances caused by forest laws.	Pope annuls Magna Carta. Fifth Crusade.	is among the barons who force John to sign Magna Carta.
1220 Henry III is crowned again in Westminster Abbey. 1224 Louis VIII of France declares war on Henry III.	1227 Sixth Crusade. Pope Gregory IX 1229 Sixth Crusade ends. Jerusalem is divided between Christians and Muslims.	1218 The Abbot of St Edmunds obtains grant of a Monday market and a fair in Harlow. 1220-25 Harlowbury House is built. (Timbers dated c.1221) 1222 Ralph the potter is mentioned in an assizes roll.
1236 Henry III marries Eleanor of Provence.	1234 Evidence of a tower on Latton church. The priest Fr. Ernoldus 'falls' off it and is hastily buried without an enquiry. The villagers are fined.	**By 1234 Henry de Merk (1) has died. Rose, his widow, disputes the tenancy of Mark Hall with her son Ralph de Merk.** 1235 Valognes estates are divided. Overlordship of Latton Hall falls to Isabel Comyn, daughter of David and Elizabeth Comyn, descendant of Peter de Valognes. 1236 Latton Hall is tenanted by 'William, son of Richard'. **1240 Mark Hall is conveyed to Henry de Merk (2), Ralph's brother.**
Historian Roger of Wendover dies; his *Chronicle* is continued by Matthew Paris.	Abbot Hugh follows Samson at St Edmund's Abbey. c.1245 William Fitzgerald – priest.	1246 Latton Hall is inherited by William's daughter Margaret, married to Sir Richard de Taney.
Henry III repudiates Magna Carta and reafforests large areas of his kingdom. Gascons revolt against Henry III's deputy, Simon de Montfort.	1247 The Prior of Latton is pardoned for a forest offence. 1248 Seventh Crusade. 1250 A deed from Richard Gernon giving the Priory 12d rents from Sawbridgeworth is witnessed by three de Taneys: Richard, Peter and Walter.	Harlow Hundred is included in the King's Royal Forest again. 1249 St Edmund's Abbey is granted a Friday market in Harlow.
1251 Simon de Montfort suppresses Gascon revolt. 1253 He returns to England and leads the barons' revolt against	1250 Geoffrey, Prior of Latton witnesses an agreement between the house of Waltham Holy Cross and Netteswell.	1253 Isabel Comyn dies. 1253 The Earl of Gloucester's men seize Kitchen Hall in the barons' revolt. Richard Gernon is one of

National events	Religious matters	Local events
Henry III. 'Barons War'.	Seventh Crusade ends. Crusaders still hold Acre.	the leaders.
1254 Civil war among the Crusader States.		1253 Richard de Taney is licensed to cut timber in his own woods.
1258 Henry III accepts the barons' demands. Provisions of Oxford. A committee of twenty-two barons is formed. Peace treaty with France.	1260 Fr. Simon – priest.	**c. 1258 Henry de Merk (2) dies leaving a son Henry (3).** **1268 Henry de Merk (3) comes of age. No children.**
1264 Civil war in England.	Pope Clement IV excommunicates the rebellious barons.	**1270 Henry de Merk (3) dies. Niece Aubrey inherits, daughter of Henry's sister Rose who had married Sir Geoffrey Dynant after rape in Marks Tey church during the 'Barons' War'.**
1265 An English Parliament is summoned by Simon de Montfort including burgesses and knights of the shires. Henry III's son Edward defeats de Montfort who is killed.	1270 Eighth Crusade. Prince Edward sets out for Acre. Walter Bibbesworth (later of Latton Hall) joins the Crusade.	1270 William Comyn is overlord of Latton Hall. 1270 Richard de Taney dies. Son Richard succeeds at Latton Hall.
1272 Henry III dies. **Edward I** succeeds.		
	1274 General Council of Lyons meets to end Church schism. 1276 Geoffrey, Prior of the church of St John the Baptist of Latton, is mentioned in a charter as owing rent to Emma, sister of Robert de la Hyde.	**1276 Aubrey Dynant dies. Her great uncle Andrew de Merk inherits Mark Hall. His son Thomas later claims Mark Hall but it passes to Henry de Merk (4) who marries Juliana.**
		c.1277 Latton Hall passes to Walter Bibbesworth.
		Isabel Comyn's son William holds overlordship of Latton Hall.
	After 1280 when the de Taneys leave Latton the advowson of the church comes entirely into the hands of the Priory. From then on the Prior probably appoints all the priests of St Mary's until the Dissolution. 1280 Robert de la Hyde and his sister Emma are named in a Priory document.	c.1280 The de Taney estates are all sold to Hugh de Bibbesworth. Latton Hall is held by the Bibbesworths for over 200 years.
	1281 The attempt to reconcile the East and West Church is abandoned. 1286 Edward I lists the issues which can be dealt with by ecclesiastical courts.	1283 William Comyn dies.
1290 Queen Eleanor dies. Her body rests at Waltham Abbey for one night.	1291 Eleanor of Castile's funeral crosses are erected at Charing Cross and eight other places. 1291 Rents due to the Priory are listed. Taxation is paid to Pope Nicholas IV for a Crusade. 1291 Mamluks conquer the kingdom of Jerusalem.	**1291 Henry de Merk (4) dies. The Mark Hall estate is divided.** 1296 Elias of Colchester becomes an MP.
	1297 Edward I, supported by the Pope,	1301 Harlow Hundred is excluded

National events	Religious matters	Local events
	outlaws the English clergy when they refuse to pay taxes.	from the royal forest of Essex.
		1302 Ralph de Ardern owns Moor Hall.
The Inns of Court are established. 1307 Edward I dies leading his army in Scotland. **Edward II** succeeds.	By 1303 Latton Hall is divided between the Priory and Hugh Bibbesworth. Edward I's body rests for three months near Harold's tomb at Waltham.	**By 1303 Juliana, widow of Henry (4) has married Elias of Colchester and disputes Thomas de Merk's claim to Mark Hall.**
c.1300 A mini ice-age begins. 1308 Edward II marries Isabella, daughter of Philip IV of France.	1307-14 Suppression of Knights Templars. Knights Hospitallers occupy Rhodes.	**1309 part of Mark Hall passes to Henry de Seagrave.** 1315 William de Ardern follows Ralph at Moor Hall.
1315-17 Torrential rain. Famine across western Europe. Population falls.	1317 Fr. Walter – 'late rector' A new Pope is chosen after a two year interval. The advowson of the Priory is passed to Augustine le Waleys.	**1317 Juliana (de Merk) and Elias of Colchester convey Mark Hall to Augustine le Waleys and his wife Maud of Roding.**
1326 Stapleton, Bishop of Exeter, is murdered in a popular rebellion. Edward II flees, is captured at Neath Abbey and deposed. 1327 **Edward III** aged fourteen succeeds. Edward II abdicates and is murdered at Berkeley Castle, Gloucestershire. His widow Isabella and her lover Roger Mortimer rule until Edward III is of age. 1328 Edward III (aged 16) marries Philippa, daughter of the anti-French Count of Holland & Hainault. 1330 Edward III captures Mortimer and takes him to London to be tried. Isabella retires.	Sometime in the 14th century the Priory is greatly extended. The existing remnants date from this period. 1327 A Priory petition mentions a grant from Ongar and Maud de Lucy. Fr. Roger de Overe – priest.	**1332 A charter for an annual Fair is granted by Edward III to Augustine le Waleys of Mark Hall on the Feast of John the Baptist (29 August till 5 Sept).**
1337 100 Years War with France begins. Gascony is confiscated from the English. Edward III claims the French throne through his mother Isabella. The French burn Portsmouth and declare England's claim null and void. 1340 Edward III declares himself king of France. Edward's son, John of Gaunt, is born. 1340 The English defeat the French navy and attack	1346 Part of Latton Hall manor still belongs to Latton Priory.	1346 John de Bibbesworth is at Latton Hall.

National events	Religious matters	Local events
France.		
1346 Battle of Crecy. French defeated. Siege of Calais. Bubonic plague – the 'Black Death' – spreads from the Crimea across Europe.		
1347 Calais falls to the English who hold it for 211 years.		
1348-1351 Plague reaches England and spreads across the whole country. At least one third of the population dies.		
1351 Statute of Labourers. Attempt to freeze wages and keep up labour supply.	1350 Waltham Abbey acquires Copped Hall.	
		1353 Augustine le Waleys dies, survived by widow Maud.
1354 100 Years War resumes.	1357 John, Prior of Latton.	**1355 Maud le Waleys dies. Mark Hall is divided between two daughters: Margery marries John Malmayne; Margaret marries 1) William Carlton, 2) John de Ludwick, 3) John de Foxcote.**
	1358 Fr. Robert de Latton – priest. 1361 Fr. William de Gatesdon – priest.	1361 John de Bibbesworth dies at Latton Hall. Succeeded by his son Hugh.
1362 English is recognised as the official language of the kingdom. The English Parliament suspends tribute to the Papacy.	1364 The advowson of the Priory is held by Mary de St Pol – a distant connection of the de Valognes.	**By 1363 the whole Mark Hall estate is held by Margaret and John de Foxcote.**
1377 Edward III dies. Grandson, **Richard II** succeeds aged 10, son of the Black Prince. Richard struggles with his uncles John of Gaunt and the Duke of Gloucester for power. A poll tax is levied.		**1374 John Bishopton (clerk) quitclaims Mark Hall to Sir William Berland of Lincolnshire and Christian.**
1381 The 'Peasants Revolt' is led by John Ball & Wat Tyler. Wat Tyler is killed by the Lord Mayor.	1378 Rival popes are elected – French and Italian in Avignon and Rome. The 'Great Schism'.	**1375 All Mark Hall property and rights pass to Sir William Berland.** 1381 In Harlow, records are burned at Harlowbury and Kitchen Hall. Sir William Berland is urged to join the rebels in Prittlewell.
1385 Richard II tries to govern without parliament.	1382 Courtenay, the new Archbishop, attacks the Lollards, Wyclif's followers. An English translation of the Bible is completed.	**After 1383 Elizabeth Berland marries John Baud who inherits Mark Hall.**
1397 Murder of Gloucester in prison.	1393 John, Prior of Latton.	After 1394 Thomas Proudfoot holds an estate in Latton (Possible origin of name Purfotts/

National events	Religious matters	Local events
1398 Richard II loses control of England. He exiles Henry Bolingbroke, son of John of Gaunt.		Purford/Puffers Green).
1399 John of Gaunt dies. Richard II seizes his estates. Henry Bolingbroke captures Richard and becomes **Henry IV**, the first Lancastrian king.		
1400 Richard II dies at Pontefract Castle.	1402-9 Fr. John Selirir – priest.	1402 Edmund and Goditha de Bibbesworth at Latton Hall.
1413 Henry IV dies. His son **Henry V** succeeds him.		
	1414 A Lollard revolt in London is repressed.	
1415 Henry V invades France. English longbows succeed in the battle of Agincourt. Slaughter of prisoners.	1415 Fr. Thomas Bardolf – priest. 1417 William Tallebury, Prior of Latton. Wyclif's teachings are condemned. Huss is burnt at the stake.	
1420 Treaty of Troyes with Charles VI. Henry V marries Charles' daughter Catherine.	1421-2 Fr. R. Munk – priest.	**1422 John Baud, the owner of Mark Hall dies.**
1422 Henry V dies in France. His son, **Henry VI** is nine months old. John, Duke of Bedford, who is fighting in France, and Humphrey, Duke of Gloucester act as regents for baby Henry VI.		**1422 Mark Hall, in a ruinous state, is inherited by Elizabeth Berland, widow of John Baud whose son William Baud grants it to William Rokesburgh.** John Bibbesworth – son of Edmund and Goditha – of Latton Hall marries Joan.
1428 Siege of Orleans 1429 Joan of Arc joins Charles VII of France against the English and liberates Orleans. Philip the Good replaces Bedford as regent for Henry VI in France.		**1426 William Roxburgh conveys Mark Hall to John Tyrell.** 1428 Fewer than ten households in Latton.
1430 Joan is captured by the English.	1430 Fr. John Fowke – priest.	
1431 Joan of Arc is burnt at Rouen. Nine-year-old **Henry VI** is crowned in Paris as King of France.	1431 Fr. William Matthew – priest. 1432 Fr. Thomas Laverok/Loverdale.	
1435 Death of Bedford. Richard, Duke of York is made Regent.	1434 William Tallebury/Tilberg resigns as Prior of Latton, succeeded by William Cotyngham. 1439 Fr. Hugh David – priest.	**1437 Sir John Tyrell dies. His trustees name his brother Edward Tyrell his successor. 1442 Edward Tyrell dies.**
1445 The first French standing army is established. War with England continues. Marriage of Henry VI and Margaret of Anjou.	1440 Fr. George Sutton – priest. Fr. George Akyrs – priest. 1440 William Cotyngham resigns as Prior. He moves to Berden (near Bishop's Stortford) Priory of St John the Evangelist, succeeded by Thomas Wapelode, previously Prior of Berden.	**Thomas, John Tyrell's son succeeds.** **1445 Robert Rolleston is named at Mark Hall.**
1446 Richard Duke of York		**1446 Sir Thomas Tyrell**

National events	Religious matters	Local events
begins building Hunsdon House.		**quitclaims Mark Hall to Sir Peter Arderne.**
	Fr. Henry Overdo resigned 1446 1446 Fr. John Straugman – priest	**1446 Gregory Wery releases the rights over Mark Hall to Sir Peter Arderne.** **Arderne daughters: Elizabeth marries 1) John Skrene (the King's escheater).** **2) Richard Harper.** **Anne marries John Bohun.**
1448 Sir Peter Arderne becomes Chief Baron of the Exchequer. 1450 The French regain Normandy. Jack Cade leads a rebellion in Kent and Suffolk against war taxes. The rebellion fails. Cade is executed. The English are routed near Bordeaux. England loses all French lands except Calais. End of 'Hundred Years War' (from 1337). 1454 January. Henry VI becomes mentally ill. Richard Duke of York acts as regent. 1454 First moveable type used in Mainz. December. **Henry VI** recovers from insanity and banishes the regent, Richard Duke of York. 1455 Richard leads a successful army against Henry VI October. Henry VI's illness returns at Hertford. Richard of York becomes Protector again. 'Wars of the Roses' begin. 1459 Battle of Blackheath. 1460 Henry VI is taken prisoner by Richard who claims the English throne but is killed at Wakefield by the forces of Margaret of Anjou (Henry VI's wife). Richard's son Edward declares Henry deposed and claims the throne himself. **1461 Edward IV** is crowned and drives Henry VI into Scotland. 1464 Edward IV marries Elizabeth Woodville.	1453 Fr. John Barlowe – priest 1453 The Ottoman Turks enter Constantinople. Greek scholars flee to the west. 1456 Fr. Robert Belamy – priest. Fr. Nicholas Sylvester – priest. 1460 Fr. John Warkeworth – priest. 1465 Fr. Thomas Hathon – priest.	1449 John de Bibbesworth of Latton Hall dies leaving son Thomas aged three. Inquisition at Ware into Bibbesworth inheritance led by John Skrene. **1465 Sir Peter Arderne becomes Justice of the Common pleas.**
	1466 Edward IV grants Sir Peter Arderne and his wife Katherine licence to found two chantries for two priests to say mass.	1466 Goditha Bibbesworth dies.

National events	Religious matters	Local events
1468 Charles the Bold of Burgundy marries Edward IV's daughter Margaret, uniting England and Burgundy against France. 1470 Richard Neville ('the Kingmaker') Earl of Warwick & Salisbury changes sides to Henry VI from Edward IV. Edward's younger brother then defeats Warwick at Stamford. 1471 Warwick is killed at Barnet, Herts. Henry VI is murdered. **Edward IV** regains throne. 1476 Caxton establishes a printing press in Westminster. 1477 Edward IV bans cricket – a rival to archery practice. 1482 Edmund Shaa becomes Lord Mayor of London. 1483 Edward IV dies – his son **Edward V** (aged 12) is his heir. Richard, Duke of Gloucester is named Protector. Richard, helped by Ralph Shaa, declares both Edward's sons illegitimate and proclaims himself king. 1483 **Richard III crowned** Edward V and his brother disappear from the Tower. 1485 Henry Tudor, a descendant of the Lancastrians, defeats Richard III at the battle of Bosworth. **Henry VII** is crowned king. First Tudor monarch. End of 'Wars of the Roses'. 1487 Lambert Simnel is defeated by Henry VII at East Stoke, Notts. Henry VII invades France. In return for payment Henry VII abandons all claims on French lands and Perkin Warbeck is expelled from France. 1493 Pope Alexander VI divides the New World between Spain and Portugal. 1495 Perkin Warbeck fails to land at Deal. 1497 War taxes provoke Cornish rebellion led by Perkin Warbeck. 15,000 men	1472 John Hurst resigns as Prior, succeeded by William Chase. 1476 Sir Brian Rouclyffe, a Baron of the Exchequer, leaves the rent of property in Latton and Gilston as a stipend for the chantry priest. 1479 Fr. Geoffrey Sampor – priest. 1483 Sir John Bohun and Anne of Mark Hall appoint a priest to serve in the chantry. 1485 William Chase resigns as Prior succeeded by Christopher Brown. 1486 John Stafford becomes Prior. 1491 John Cradok – Prior.	**1467 Sir Peter Arderne dies. He leaves Mark Hall to his widow Katharine Arderne and daughters Anne Bohun and Elizabeth Harper.** By 1485 Latton Hall is in a ruinous state. 1485 Thomas Bibbesworth dies with no direct heirs. Cousins: Joan Barley wife of Thomas Barley of Bibbesworth manor & John Cotes, inherit Latton Hall. 1486 Latton Hall is conveyed to Richard Harper and others. 1489 William Harper and others at Latton Hall. 1492 Richard Harper dies. Latton Hall passes to his son Richard.

National events	Religious matters	Local events
defeated on their march to London. Perkin Warbeck is executed.		**By 1500 Anne Bohun owns Mark Hall.**
1501 Sir John Shaa becomes Lord Mayor of London.		**1501 Sir John Shaa buys Mark Hall with 220 acres.**
1501 Henry VII's eldest son Arthur marries Catherine of Aragon.	1503 Fr. James Hauden – priest.	**1503 John Shaa dies. Edmund Shaa (John's son) inherits Mark Hall.**
1502 Arthur dies.		1507 Richard Harper dies. Grandson Sir George Harper inherits Latton Hall.
1509 Henry VII dies. **HENRY VIII,** married to Catherine of Aragon, is crowned.		
1515 Cardinal Wolsey, Lord Chancellor.	1517 Martin Luther attacks corruption in Catholic Church.	
	1518 William Taylor, Prior of Latton, dies, succeeded by John Taylor.	
	1521 Henry VIII's book denouncing Luther is published. He becomes *'Defender of the* [Catholic] *Faith'.* Luther's books are burned in St Paul's.	**1521 Henry Parker (Lord Morley) leases Mark Hall from Edmund Shaa for ninety-nine years.**
1525 Henry VIII acquires and extends Hunsdon House.		**1523 Henry Parker's son Henry marries Grace, daughter and heiress of John Newport of Furneux Pelham.**
1529 Thomas More becomes Lord Chancellor.	Latton church tower is badly rebuilt early in the 16th century. Thin walls owing to lack of local stone.	**1525 Edmund Shaa is declared insane. Custody of Mark Hall passes to Edmund's brother Thomas or Sir Thomas More.**
1530 Wolsey dies in disgrace. 1532 Thomas Cromwell becomes Henry VIII's chief minister.		**1525 Jane Parker, Lord Morley's daughter marries George Boleyn, brother of Anne Boleyn.**
1533 Henry VIII's marriage to Catherine of Aragon is annulled. He marries Anne Boleyn.	1533 Fr. Edward Clifton presumably presented by the only remaining canon at the Priory. 1534 John Taylor leaves the Priory. 1534 An Inquisition into the state of Latton Priory finds the foundation rules have been broken. 1534 **Sir Henry Parker** is granted the Priory by the Crown. 1534 Act of Supremacy. Henry VIII proclaims himself head of the English Church. 1535 Execution of Thomas More and John Fisher.	**1530 Margaret Parker, Morley's younger daughter, marries John Shelton, cousin of Anne Boleyn.** Eastwick is presented to Anne Boleyn as a wedding present by Henry VIII. **George Boleyn inherits the title of Viscount Rochford.** 1535 William Harper passes Latton Hall on to his son George but his title is disputed by Joan Bibbesworth's grandson.
1536 Death of Catherine of Aragon. 1536 Execution of Anne Boleyn Henry VIII marries Jane Seymour.	1535 The moated vicarage is valued at £7. The chantry of Latton Church is valued at £7 11s 8d. Dissolution of the Monasteries.	**1536 Rochford is convicted of incest with his sister Anne Boleyn and executed. Jane, his widow, remains at Court.**
1538 Birth of Edward, Prince of		**1538 Thomas Shaa receives a**

National events	Religious matters	Local events
Wales. Death of Jane Seymour.	1539 Cranmer's 'Great Bible' in English is published.	**'license to alienate' Mark Hall to Henry Parker (Lord Morley) which then descends with Great Hallingbury till 1562.** **Henry Parker's grandson possibly resident at Mark Hall.**
1540 (Jan) Henry VIII marries and (July) divorces Anne of Cleves. 1540 Thomas Cromwell is beheaded. 1540 Henry VIII marries Catherine Howard.	1540 The Augustinian canons are expelled from Waltham Abbey.	
1541 Henry VIII is proclaimed King of Ireland. 1542 Queen Catherine Howard is beheaded. 1543 HenryVIII marries Catherine Parr. 1544 Part of Waltham Abbey is demolished.	1541 Sir Henry Parker conveys the Priory to William Morris.	**1542 Jane Rochford is beheaded with Queen Catherine.**
1547 Death of Henry VIII. **EDWARD VI** is crowned aged 9. Somerset made Protector.	1547 Suppression of the chantries. 1549 First English language Book of Common Prayer prescribed. Act of Uniformity. 1549 Sir John Peryent is granted the chantry and the chantry house.	1548 Sir George Harper conveys Latton Hall to John Hethe, cooper of London.
1550 Somerset replaced by Northumberland. 1550s 'Sweating sickness' (virulent malaria) spreads widely. Series of bad harvests.	1552 Second Book of Common Prayer imposed.	
1553 Edward VI dies of T.B. 1553 Lady Jane Grey is proclaimed queen by Northumberland (her father-in-law). Mary Tudor at Hunsdon House also proclaimed queen. **1553 MARY I** 1554 Lady Jane Grey is beheaded. 1554 Mary I marries Philip of Spain.		
1558 War with France. Loss of Calais. **1558 ELIZABETH I**	1555 Heresy laws revived – c.300 'heretics' burned. By 1556 John Hethe owns the Priory estate.	By 1556 John Hethe owns Latton Hall. He conveys them both to John Titley. **1556 Henry Parker (10th Lord Morley) dies. His grandson inherits Hallingbury and Mark Hall** 1556 Thomas Stallon (alias Butler) mapmaker dies.
	1559 Act of Supremacy. Elizabeth I becomes Governor of the English	

National events	Religious matters	Local events
1559-60 Enquiry into the state of the churches.	church. Church attendance made compulsory. 1559 Church enquiry in Latton. Revd William Fletcher (presented by John Titley) *'resident keepeth hospitality, not able to preach'*. 1561 Revd John Bendall presented by John Titley. Chantry house (north of churchyard) is added to the Mark Hall estate.	I561 James Altham becomes an MP. His second wife is Dame Mary Judd. **1562 James Altham, London 'ironmonger', buys Mark Hall from 11th Lord Morley.** **James Altham buys Latton Hall from John Titley.** **The Althams hold Mark Hall till c.1776.**
1564 Birth of Shakespeare.	James Altham buys the Priory estate. 1566 Revd Thomas White presented by James Altham. 1569 Revd Hugh Weston presented by James Altham.	1566 Latton Hall is a 'small but elaborate 16th century building', probably rented from the Althams by Emanuel Wollaye, Lady Judd's son.
1577 Drake sets out to sail round the world.		**1570 James Altham becomes Sheriff of Essex.** **1571 Elizabeth I's first visit to Mark Hall.** **1576 Elizabeth I's second visit to Mark Hall.** **1578 Elizabeth I and her Privy Council meet at Mark Hall.**
1585 English intervention in the Spanish/Dutch war.	1579 One new tenor bell is hung in Latton church. 1580 Revd Esdras Blande MA presented by James Altham.	**1583 James Altham dies.** **Edward Altham (second son) succeeds. He marries Elizabeth Barne, Dame Mary Judd's granddaughter.**
1587 Execution of Mary Queen of Scots. 1588 Spanish Armada fails to attack England. 1600 East India Co. founded by George Clifford, Earl of Cumberland. 216 merchants. 1601 Rebellion and execution of the Earl of Essex. September. Spanish force lands at Kinsale, Cork, Ireland and is defeated. 1597 & 1601 Elizabethan Poor Law. 'Poor rate' to be imposed. 1603 March. Death of Elizabeth.	1593 Revd Joseph Birde MA presented by Dame Mary Judd. 1600 Revd Thomas Denne presented by Dame Mary Judd. 1602 Silver cup and paten given to church probably by Wollaye family. 1602, 1611, 1612, 1627 Four new	By 1600 the road from Epping to Newmarket through Harlow has been opened. **1602 Dame Mary Judd dies.** Denne sets up a private school in Latton.

National events	Religious matters	Local events
James VI of Scotland becomes **JAMES I** of England. Union of England and Scotland proclaimed. 1603 Plague outbreak.	bells hung in Latton church.	1603 four deaths from plague in Latton, nine in Great Parndon.
1604 Parliament opposes union of Scotland and England. 1605 Gunpowder Plot. Guy Fawkes bought gunpowder from Waltham factory.	1604 Shields for Emmanuel & Margaret Wollaye placed in church.	**1605 Edward Altham of Mark Hall dies. Succeeded by Sir James Altham who marries Elizabeth of Barrington Hall, Hatfield Broad Oak.**
Parliament again opposes union with Scotland. Dec. London Virginia Co. sends three ships with 120 colonists to Virginia. 1607 Virginia colonised. Adventurers led by Captain John Smith. James I prorogues Parliament – still refusing to accept union. 1608 French fur trading settlement at Quebec. 1609 Henry Hudson, English navigator, explores Hudson river.	1606 Anti Catholic legislation.	**1607 Death of Thomas Altham – Catholic eldest son of James.** **1609 James Altham is knighted.**
1610 Conflict between English and Dutch in India increases.		**1610 Sir James Altham dies. Only child Joan marries Oliver St John, solicitor general in Cromwell's Parliament. James' brother Sir Edward Altham inherits Mark Hall. Edward marries 1) Mary North 2) Joan Leventhorpe of Shingle Hall, Sawbridgeworth.**
1612 Death of Henry, James I's eldest son.	1611 Authorised version of the Bible published. 'King James' Bible.' 1611 & 1612 New bells hung in Latton belfry. 1612 Legate and Wightman burned for heresy.	
1613 English colonists in Virginia destroy French settlement in Nova Scotia. James I's daughter Elizabeth marries Frederick V Elector Palatine of the Rhine. Basis of later Hanoverian monarchy. 1614 James I dissolves obstinate Parliament and imprisons four Members.	Before 1616 Church Acres in Broadmead is donated for the benefit of two poor inhabitants chosen annually. Chosen two had to pay wardens 3s 4d and strew the church with bean straw at Whitsun.	**1613 Edward Altham is knighted by James I. 1613-20 Sir Edward Altham is joint captain with Sir Henry Lee of Harlow Half-Hundred muster (territorial army).**
1616 Death of Shakespeare.	1616 Edict of inquisition against	By 1616 Latton Hall is rebuilt.

158

National events	Religious matters	Local events
	Galileo's sun-centred astronomy.	**1616 Map made by Jeremiah Bailey of the Mark Hall estate for Sir Edward Altham.**
	Priory estate is 259 acres	**1616 Nineteen constables elected at the court of Mark Hall.**
		Two men elected to supervise cutting of furze from Mark Bushes for use by tenants for repairs.
1617 James I makes Villiers Earl of Buckingham.		**1617 Emanuel Wollaye's gift to the poor of Latton** *'to be paid for ever'* **by the owner of Mark Hall.**
Francis Bacon becomes Lord Chancellor.		
Sir Walter Raleigh, released from the Tower, sets off for Guiana.		
1618 Walter Raleigh returns and is executed.	1618 Puritans object to James I's *Book of Sports*.	
1619 William Harvey (ancestor of Elizabeth Burgoyne, later of Mark Hall) announces his discovery of the circulation of the blood.	1620 Pilgrim Fathers settle in New England.	
Thirty Years War begins.		
1625 CHARLES I	1627 Another bell is hung in Latton belfry.	
1625 Charles I marries (Catholic) Henrietta of France.	Archbishop Laud's anti-Puritan reforms.	
1629 Charles I begins to govern without Parliament.	1630 Revd Thomas Denne resigns the living of Latton.	
	1632 Revd Thomas Denne, son of former vicar, presented by Edward Altham.	**1632 Sir Edward Altham dies. James Altham inherits Mark Hall.**
1635 John Hampden refuses to pay 'ship money'. Supported by Oliver St John.		1635 Margaret Wollaye dies leaving thirty shillings to the poor of Netteswell parish.
		1635 Emmanuel Altham dies in Goa.
1638 Charles I tries to extend royal forest boundaries.		**1638 Sir William Martin of Netteswell and James Altham ordered to compensate the king for disafforestation since 1301.**
'Long Parliament' begins.		
	1641 Drunk bell-ringers smash new altar rails in St Mary's church	1639 Copped Hall hit by a great hurricane.
1642 Attempted arrest of the 'Five Members'. Civil War begins.	1643 Puritan Council of Divines includes Sir Thomas Barrington, of Hatfield Broad Oak and Sir William Cecil, Lord of Roydon manor.	
	In Great Parndon the Royalist rector is deprived of his living, accused of reading the *Book of Sports* in church on the Lord's Day and other transgressions.	
	1644 Cross on steeple and sanctus belfry removed from Latton church.	
1645 Cromwell's 'Model Army' organised.	Archbishop Laud executed.	
1648-52 Second stage of Civil War. Siege of Colchester.		

National events	Religious matters	Local events
1649 CHARLES I executed. Commonwealth established. The Levellers cause disturbances in the army.	1650 Vicarage valued at £50.	
1653 OLIVER CROMWELL dismisses Parliament and is made Lord Protector. 1658 Death of Oliver Cromwell. **Richard**, his son, chosen by Oliver to succeed him. 1659 Richard Cromwell resigns.		1650-1694 Edward Altham, a Catholic, is living in Rome.
1660 April **RESTORATION of CHARLES II.** Sept. James, Duke of York, Charles's brother, marries 1) Anne Hyde (Protestant).	Sundial placed on south side of Latton church. 1660s John Bunyan writes *Pilgrim's Progress* in prison. James Altham restores the rectorial tithes to St Mary-at-Latton.	**Sir James Altham is knighted for his services to Charles II.**
1662 Charles II marries Catherine of Braganza. 1662 Birth of Mary daughter of Duke of York and Anne Hyde. 1665 Birth of Anne, Mary's sister. 1665 May-Sept. Outbreak of plague. 1666 Sept. Great Fire of London.	1662 New Act of Uniformity. New Prayer Book published.	1670 Forty-three houses in Latton. 1672 Water wheel of Latton Mill replaced.
1673 James Duke of York marries 2) Mary of Modena. (Catholic). 1677 Mary, James' eldest daughter, marries William of Orange, grandson of Charles I. 1678 Act requiring all corpses to be buried in woollen shrouds. 1683 Rye House Plot to murder King Charles and James. Marriage of Anne and Prince George of Denmark. Death of Charles II. No legitimate children.	1680 Revd Thomas Denne dies. 1680 Revd Michael Altham MA presented by Leventhorpe Altham, his cousin.	**1675 Sir James Altham dies. Leventhorpe Altham inherits Mark Hall.**
1685 JAMES II, brother of Charles II. Monmouth's rebellion crushed. 1688 Birth of James, son of James II and Mary of Modena. 'Glorious Revolution' James II flees to France. **1689 WILLIAM III and MARY** (daughter of James II) 1689 Bill of Rights. 1694 Bank of England founded. Queen Mary dies.		**1681 Leventhorpe Altham dies. James Altham inherits Mark Hall.**
1701 William III dies. **QUEEN ANNE** crowned. Seventeen children. None survive		**1697 James Altham dies. Peyton Altham holds Mark Hall for forty-five years.**

National events	Religious matters	Local events
infancy.		
1701 War of Spanish Succession.	1705 Revd Roger Altham DD presented by Peyton Altham. Son of previous vicar.	
1713 Treaty of Utrecht.		
1714 **GEORGE I**		
1715 First Jacobite rising led by James, the 'Old Pretender'.		**1717 Peyton Altham comes of age and takes charge of Mark Hall estate.**
1720 South Sea Bubble.	1720 Priory Farm is described as 'a mean farmhouse' on the site of 'the old house'. Priory used as a barn.	
1721 Robert Walpole. First Prime Minister.		
1727 **GEORGE II**	1728 Little bell hung in Latton belfry.	
1773 John Kay's flying shuttle invented.	1730 Revd James Altham presented by Peyton Altham. Revd Stephen Lushington is his curate.	
1740 War of Austrian Succession.		**1740 A black servant of Peyton Altham is baptised 'Mark Hall' and the servant of Richard Nicholl is baptised 'Kent Latton'.**
1743 Battle of Dettingen. George II leads English troops.		**1741 Peyton Altham of Mark Hall is succeeded by his widow Mary and two eldest sons who die young.**
1745 Second Jacobite rising led by 'Bonny Prince Charlie'.		1748 James Altham dies, probably in Calcutta.
1746 Battle of Culloden.		
1750 London earthquake.	1751 Revd Stephen Lushington dies.	
1752 September. Calendar revised, eleven days removed.	1753 Hardwick's Marriage Act.	**1752 Date of Bush Fair changed to 9th and 10th September. Big cattle, hiring and pleasure fair.**
1757 Seven Years War begins.	1758 Revd Thomas Altham MA, husband of Jane Lushington presented by William Altham.	**1765 William Altham inherits Mark Hall.**
1760 **GEORGE III**		In William's time the thatched 'Round Houses' in Latton Street, near New Hall and the 'Glass House' near Maypole Corner may have been built.
	1764 Bricks and foundations first noted on Temple site.	1768 Latton Mill, described as demolished 'many years before' is rebuilt by 1778.
1766-1769 River Stort Navigation built joining Bishop's Stortford to the Lea.		Latton loses three fields north of the river because of construction of the Stort Navigation. Epping & Ongar Highways Trust take over Epping road. By 1769 Latton lock has been constructed.
1769 'Water frame' invented by Richard Arkwright. Mass production of strong cotton thread begins.		
1770 'Spinning jenny' is invented by Hargreaves.		
1772 Mansfield's judgement – slavery in Britain not		1772 Court rolls of Latton Hall signed for the last time by

National events	Religious matters	Local events
sanctioned by English law. 1775-1783 American War of Independence. 1777 Surrender of General John Burgoyne (cousin of Burgoyne, later of Mark Hall).		William Altham. 1777 Latton Hall court rolls signed by William Lushington. **By 1777 William Lushington has bought and begun to rebuild Mark Hall. Latton Street is moved further west and Latton Hall is demolished.**
1778 War with France. 1779 War with Spain.	1778 Dr Henry Lushington, husband of 1) Mary Altham 2) Mary Gilbert, buys Latton Priory. In the late 18th century the chancel and nave of Latton Priory disappear. Part of a circular window and arches survive. 1780 Anti-Catholic Gordon Riots in London. 1782 Death of Revd Thomas Altham and Jane (Lushington) his wife. 1782 Revd James Stephen Lushington MA vicar of Latton presented by William Lushington.	1778 Revd Henry Lushington buys houses and land near Thornwood Common and Rye Hill from William Altham, Esq. By 1778 Assembly Rooms have been built on Bush Fair Common. Originated as a 'tea booth'.
1789 French Revolution begins. 1793 Louis XVI beheaded. Napoleonic Wars begin.	By 1790 Burgoyne is supporting a Sunday School in Latton.	**1786 Montagu Burgoyne buys Mark Hall and Kitchen Hall.** 1792 Union Archery Society. 1793 Essex Society for the Encouragement of Agriculture partly Burgoyne's inspiration. **1793-1815 212 volunteers enrolled by Burgoyne. Loyal Essex Light Dragoons drilled in Mark Hall park.**
1796 War with Spain. 1798 Battle of the Nile. 1800 Union of Gt. Britain and Ireland. 1802 Peace of Amiens. 1803 War with France again. Fear of invasion. 1805 Battle of Trafalgar. Death of Nelson. 1806 William Pitt (PM) and Charles James Fox (Whig leader) both die. 1807 Slave trade abolished in British Empire. 1808-1814 Peninsular War. **1811–1820 Regency period.**	1801 Revd Charles Sanderson Miller, also vicar of Harlow. Deputised for by vicar of Amwell and later by curate of Netteswell.	1801 Population of Latton 279. **By 1802 Montagu Burgoyne, now Colonel, commanding cavalry troops.** **1803 John Batt sells New Hall and Kitchen Hall to Montagu Burgoyne of Mark Hall.** Sun and Whalebone Inn becomes headquarters of London fox-hunting club. **1810 & 12 Burgoyne stands for Parliament as a Whig.**

National events	Religious matters	Local events
1812-1815 War between Britain and USA. 1812 Spencer Percival PM assassinated in House of Commons. 1815 Spa Fields riots over corn prices. 1815 Battle of Waterloo. Final defeat of Napoleon.		Defeated. 1818 Burgoyne's daughter Frances Elizabeth Campbell dies in childbirth in Florence.
1819 'Peterloo' massacre.	1819 More foundations found on Stanegrove Hill.	**1819 Richard Arkwright of Willersley Castle, Derbyshire buys Mark Hall, New Hall and Kitchen Hall for his youngest son Revd Joseph Arkwright.**
1820 **GEORGE IV**	1820 Revd Joseph Arkwright succeeds Revd Charles Miller as vicar of Latton. 1821 John Barnard reports 'very strong walls' in 'a field called Standing Groves'. 1824 Revd Clayton Glyn owns Priory Farm.	1820s Assembly Rooms enlarged by Joseph Arkwright. Annual Essex Hunt Ball held there and West Essex Archery.
1825 Stockton to Darlington railway.		**1826 Horse races held in Mark Hall park.**
1830 **WILLIAM IV** 1832 Cholera epidemic in London. 1832 First Reform Bill.	1829 Catholic Emancipation Act.	1831 Population of Latton 378. Two Amherst children die of cholera in London. The Amhersts leave Little Parndon and Parndon House is demolished.
1834 Tolpuddle martyrs. 1834 Palace of Westminster destroyed by fire. 1835 Poor Law Amendment Act. Epping 'Union'. 1835 Tithe Commutation Act. 1836 Chartists' first petition. 1837 **VICTORIA** 1837 Civil Registration Act. 1839 Anti Corn Law League.	1835-7 Further excavations by Hill & Coterill reveal the southern court of the Roman Temple. By 1839 Arkwrights had bought the Priory.	1836 Montagu Burgoyne dies.
1840 Penny post. 1840 Victoria marries Albert Saxe-Coburg.	While the railway is being constructed six Roman coffins are discovered on the south side of Stanegrove Hill, part of Bromleys farm. Reinterred under new station forecourt. (Now Harlow Mill).	**1841 Railway line opens passing through Arkwright land.**
		1843 Richard Arkwright dies. Revd Joseph Arkwright inherits Mark Hall and Normanton Turville in Leicestershire where he holds a second living at All Saints church, Thurlaston.
	1845 Revd Joseph Arkwright gives up	**New wing added to Mark Hall.**

National events	Religious matters	Local events
1848 'Year of Revolutions'.	the Thurlaston living. By 1848 St Mary-at-Latton has been restored by Revd Joseph Arkwright. 1850 Revd Julius Arkwright MA. Joseph Arkwright resigns the Latton living which he presents to his son, Julius. He builds a new rectory (now Moot House).	1848 Railway opens for passengers. **Joseph Arkwright buys Little Parndon and makes his fourth son Loftus Wigram manager, aged 21.**
1851 Great Exhibition. Window Tax abolished. 1854-56 Crimean War. 1857-58 'Indian Mutiny'.		1853 Henry John Conyers of Copped Hall dies. He had been Master of the Essex Foxhounds. **1857 Joseph Arkwright becomes Master of the Essex Foxhounds.** **1860s Joseph Arkwright builds a small school and the Clock House on Latton Street.**
1861 Prince Albert dies of typhoid fever. 1861-65 American Civil War.		1861 Population of Latton 196. **Loftus Wigram Arkwright marries Elizabeth Reynolds. One son – Loftus Joseph.** Population never above 270 until after 1947.
	1864 March. Revd Julius Arkwright dies of 'a wasting disease'. Revd William Shilleto comes as locum tenens after Julius Arkwright's death. 1865 Shilleto lectures on the history of Latton at Latton School. Revd William Pitt Wigram presented by Loftus Wigram Arkwright.	**1864 Feb. Joseph Arkwright dies. Loftus Wigram Arkwright (fourth son) inherits Mark Hall manor and all Joseph's property.**
1867 Second Reform Bill.		**1867 Mark Hall is still occupied by five unmarried sisters. Loftus Wigram Arkwright builds new Parndon Hall for his wife and son Loftus Joseph. L.W. Arkwright is crippled in a riding accident.**
1870 Forster's Education Act. Free elementary education. 1872 Secret Ballot. 1873-1890s 'Great Depression' in British agriculture. 1878 Electric lighting invented. Edison and Swan.	1869 Church restored by Loftus Wigram Arkwright. 1871 Revd William Oliver. 1873 Tower of Latton church extensively repaired.	1876-1904 Race meetings on Latton Common from Rundells (Loftus Wigram Arkwright's home before Parndon Hall). **1879 Bush Fair closed by L.W. Arkwright.**
1888 Essex County Council established.	1886 Revd Spencer Nairns MA vicar and Diocesan Inspector of Schools 1901-04, Rural Dean 1907. 1888 Parish church chancel repaired. 1888-1895 St Mary Magdalene church, Potter Street enlarged.	1886-1912 Miss Charlotte Beadle teaches thirty pupils in school opposite the Clock House. **1889 Loftus Wigram Arkwright dies. Only son Loftus Joseph Arkwright inherits Mark Hall**

National events	Religious matters	Local events
		manor.
		1890 Elizabeth Arkwright dies.
		1891-3 Loftus Joseph Arkwright leases Mark Hall to Josiah Caldwell.
		1894 Loftus Joseph Arkwright leases Mark Hall to Newman Gilbey.
		1894 Loftus Joseph Arkwright marries Julia, eldest daughter of Josiah Caldwell.
1894 Local Government Act. Epping Rural District Council established. Vestries cease to have power.		1898 Latton mill ceases trading.
1898 Spanish American War	Mark Hall becomes a Centre for Catholic Mass – the Apostolate of the Sacred Heart.	
1899-1902 Boer War		
1901 Death of Victoria. **EDWARD VII**		1901 Population of Latton 226.
	1905 Revd Austin Oliver MA – vicar, son of William Oliver. Protestant church life declines.	
1903 First aeroplane flight. Orville Wilbur Wright.	St Mary-at-Latton church falls into disrepair.	
1906 Liberal landslide.		
1909 First old age pensions. Ford's model T. Cheap cars.		
1910 Death of Edward VII. **GEORGE V** Labour Exchanges. National Insurance.		
		1912 School opposite Clock House closes.
1914 Archduke Franz Ferdinand assassinated at Sarajevo.		1916 Fire at Latton Mill.
1914-1918 First World War.		
1918 Votes for women over 30.		
1918-20 Spanish flu pandemic.		
1924 First Labour ministry under Ramsay Macdonald lasts nine months.		
1926 General Strike.		1926 Latton Mill is pulled down.
1928 All men and women over twenty-one allowed to vote.	1927 Miller Christy & Canon Fisher excavate trench on summit of Stanegrove Hill. Romano-British temple identified.	
1929 Fleming's discovery of penicillin.	1932 Further excavations by Hill and Coterill reveal southern courtyard of the Temple.	**1930 All Arkwright property is transferred to Mark Hall Estates Ltd.**
1933 Hitler becomes German Chancellor. Reichstag fire.		
1934 Hitler becomes Dictator of Germany.		
1936 Spanish Civil War.		
1936 **EDWARD VIII** Abdication.		
GEORGE VI		
1938 Austria annexed by Germany. Munich agreement.		
1939 Conscription begins in		

National events	Religious matters	Local events

Britain.
1939 Germany invades Poland.
1939 Allies declare war on the
  Axis powers.
1939-45 Second World War.
1939/40 Evacuation of children
  and some adults from large
  towns. 1,200,000 people
  moved.
1940 British troops evacuated
  from Dunkirk.
1940 Food rationing.
1941 America declares war on
  Japan and Germany.
1942 The Beveridge Report is
  published.
 	
1945 VE Day. End of war in
  Europe. Two atomic bombs
  are dropped on Japan.
  VJ Day. End of war with
  Japan.
 	
1946 First meeting of United
  Nations Assembly.
1946 First New Towns Act.
1948 The National Health
  Service begins to operate.
	1942 Revd Brian Fairclough – vicar.
	
	1945 Rocket bomb damages St Mary-
	  at-Latton church.
		1942 Newman Gilbey dies.
		  Commander John Arkwright is
		  killed at sea.
		
		**1943 The Gilbeys leave Mark
		  Hall.**
		**Women's Land Army at Mark
		  Hall.**
		
		1947 March. Harlow is selected as
		  a New Town. Designated area
		  covers five parishes including
		  Latton.
		Proposal to use Mark Hall as
		  central office. New Town
		  Development Corporation begins
		  to buy Arkwright's land.
		**1947 Nov. Fire at Mark Hall.
		  Land Army leave but some
		  girls return when the Victorian
		  wing is adapted for them.**

	1949 No services in St Mary-at-
	  Latton church. Toc H branch formed
	  to restore the church.
	1950 Church reconsecrated by the
	  Bishop of Barking. Services in
	  church resumed after bomb damage.
	1951-4 Revd Oliver White – vicar,
	  also vicar of Harlow Common.
		**1950 Loftus Joseph Arkwright
		  dies at Parndon Hall. His only
		  remaining son Godfrey
		  Arkwright inherits.**
		First Avenue is constructed. **Mark
		  Hall garden wall curved to
		  accommodate Muskham Road.**
		  Neighbourhoods: Mark Hall
		  North and South, Mark Hall
		  Moors and the Lawns tower
		  block built in Mark Hall park.

1952 Elizabeth II
 	
1953 Crick and Watson discover
  structure of DNA double helix.
	1952 The old vicarage becomes Moot
	  House Community Centre.
	The new vicarage is built adjoining
	  Latton Church.
	
	1954 Revd Peter O'Beirne – vicar.
	Godfrey Arkwright's son John inherits
		1952 Duke of Edinburgh opens
		  Edinburgh Way.
		**1951-60 East wing of Mark Hall
		  used by first New Town
		  children, then by Tany's Dell
		  school.**
		
		1954 Godfrey Arkwright dies.

National events	Religious matters	Local events
1957 Treaty of Rome (EEC)	the patronage of Latton and Little Parndon churches. 1960 A church hall is built on the edge of the old site of Mark Hall. Extensive cellars are revealed.	1955 Parish boundaries are changed. Latton loses southern and northern parts. 1957 Elizabeth Way is named to commemorate the visit of Elizabeth II and Duke of Edinburgh. **1960 Exploration of Mark Hall cellars.**
1961 Yuri Gagarin makes first space flight. 1961 Berlin Wall built. 1962 Cuban crisis.	1962-71 West Essex Archaeological Group carry out excavations of the Temple site. Factory building alters the altitude of Stanegrove Hill.	**1960 The last remnant of the Mark Hall mansion is demolished. Only the stables survive. The walled gardens are used as a plant nursery 'Muskham Road Depot'.**
1963 Britain's first application to join EEC vetoed. 1967 France vetoes Britain's second application to join EEC. 1969 First moon landing. 1969 British troops sent to Northern Ireland. 1971 Decimal coinage introduced in Britain. 1972 Britain joins the EEC. 1979 First woman Prime Minister. Margaret Thatcher.	1963 Revd Ian Stuchberry – vicar. 1964 Fire in church. 1965 Complete restoration of church. 1969 Silver gilt alms dish etc. stolen from church. (See 1602) 1969 Revd Barry Rose – vicar. 1971 Church vestry built. 1977 The church tower is restored. 1979 Revd John Pratt – vicar.	1970 Population of Latton 10,000. 1973 Harlow Museum opens in Passmores House. 1980 Harlow Development Corporation is wound up. **1982 The Cycle Museum opens in the adapted stables of Mark Hall.**
1989 Berlin Wall demolished. 1991 Civil war in Yugoslavia 1991-93 Gulf War. The Internet and mobile phones revolutionise communication. 2001 Attack on World Trade Centre and Pentagon. 'War on Terror' (al-Qaeda) begins in Afghanistan. 2003-9 Iraq war. 2005 Terrorist attack on London Underground.	1985-6 Further excavations on the Temple site reveal evidence of a Belgic round house. 1989 Revd Peter Beech – priest in charge then vicar. 1994 First women ordained as priests in Church of England. 2000 Revd Shaun Conlon – vicar Split in Church of England over women bishops. 2008 Revd Lynn Hurry – vicar. 2009 Pope Benedict XVI invites disaffected Anglo-Catholics to join the Roman church.	**1984 Mark Hall gardens are opened to the public.** 1996 Church Langley is built east of the old London road 2001 Passmores Museum is closed. **2002 The Cycle Museum becomes the Museum of Harlow.** 2002 New Hall housing area is begun around New Hall farm. **2006 The Museum car park is enlarged and a new east entrance through the old wall is constructed.** 2008 'North Harlow' is planned beyond the Stort in Hertfordshire.

Index

The Altham, Arkwright, Gilbey, Lushington and Parker families are listed chronologically.